D1520104

LUCK'S MISCHIEF

LUCK'S MISCHIEF

Obligation and Blameworthiness
on a Thread

Ishtiyaque Haji

OXFORD
UNIVERSITY PRESS

OXFORD
UNIVERSITY PRESS

Oxford University Press is a department of the University of
Oxford. It furthers the University's objective of excellence in research,
scholarship, and education by publishing worldwide.

Oxford   New York
Auckland   Cape Town   Dar es Salaam   Hong Kong   Karachi
Kuala Lumpur   Madrid   Melbourne   Mexico City   Nairobi
New Delhi   Shanghai   Taipei   Toronto

With offices in
Argentina   Austria   Brazil   Chile   Czech Republic   France   Greece
Guatemala   Hungary   Italy   Japan   Poland   Portugal   Singapore
South Korea   Switzerland   Thailand   Turkey   Ukraine   Vietnam

Oxford is a registered trade mark of Oxford University Press
in the UK and certain other countries.

Published in the United States of America by
Oxford University Press
198 Madison Avenue, New York, NY 10016

© Oxford University Press 2016

Library of Congress Cataloging-in-Publication Data
Haji, Ishtiyaque.
Luck's mischief : obligation and blameworthiness on a thread / Ishtiyaque Haji.
pages cm
Includes bibliographical references and index.
ISBN 978-0-19-026077-4 (hardcover : alk. paper) — ISBN 978-0-19-026078-1
(ebook) — ISBN 978-0-19-026079-8 (online content)
1. Fortune—Moral and ethical aspects.   2. Free will and determinism.
3. Responsibility.   I. Title.
BJ1461.H259 2016
170—dc23
2015021201

1 3 5 7 9 8 6 4 2
Printed in the United States of America
on acid-free paper

For my wife, Shaheen.

CONTENTS

ACKNOWLEDGMENTS

I'm extremely pleased to acknowledge the help I received from others in writing this book.

I am deeply grateful to David Copp, Ryan Hebert, Michael McKenna, David Palmer, Carlos Patarroyo, Derk Pereboom, and Michael J. Zimmerman for comments or discussion on various chapters, sections, or topics.

I'm especially indebted to Joseph Campbell and Alfred Mele. Each read complete drafts of the manuscript and provided highly useful and much appreciated criticism and guidance.

I give many thanks to Anne Sanow for proofreading the manuscript, and to Suvesh Subramanian (Project Manager with Newgen KnowledgeWorks), Jamie Chu (editorial assistant, OUP), and the rest of the production team at OUP for their invaluable assistance. Lucy Randall (philosophy editor, OUP) deserves special mention here. She was extremely helpful and supportive from the start to the finish.

Parts of this book derive from some of my previously published articles. With permission from Springer: "Blameworthiness and Alternate Possibilities," *The Journal of Value Inquiry*

48 (2014), 603–21. With permission from Taylor and Francis: "Luck, the Range of Obligations, and Frankfurt Examples," *Philosophical Papers* 43 (2014), 317–44. With permission from Cambridge University Press: "Education's Ultimate Aims and Freedom to do Otherwise," *Social Philosophy and Policy* 31 (2014), 81–108. Published with the permission of Cambridge Scholars Publishing: "Semicompatibilism's Scope." In Ish Haji and Justin Caouette, eds., *Free Will and Moral Responsibility*. Newcastle upon Tyne: Cambridge Scholars Publishing, 2013, 142–64. I am grateful to these publishers for their permission to draw upon these essays.

During the writing of this book I received support, for which I am also very grateful, from the Calgary Institute for the Humanities at the University of Calgary.

LUCK'S MISCHIEF

Chapter 1

Luck's Hijacking of Obligation and Responsibility

1.1 LUCK'S THREAT TO OBLIGATION AND RESPONSIBILITY

There is an age-old and captivating argument for skepticism regarding moral responsibility. In the form of a dilemma, the argument features determinism in one horn and the falsity of determinism—"indeterminism"—in the other. Determinism is the thesis that for any given time, a complete statement of the nonrelational facts about that time, together with a complete statement of the laws of nature, entails all truths. A world is deterministic if and only if the proposition expressing the thesis of determinism is true at that world. In any such world, at any instant, there is exactly one physically possible future (Van Inwagen 1983, 3).

Incompatibilism regarding moral responsibility is the view that determinism is incompatible with our being morally responsible—our being morally blameworthy or praiseworthy—for any of our conduct. The concept of *being to blame* of central concern in this book essentially appeals to desert. When blameworthy, one is deserving of a certain type of judgment. It is important not to confuse blameworthiness with outward treatment or behavior that purports to express an apt private judgment (Zimmerman 1988, 4; Haji 1998). Analogously, praiseworthiness has to do with the deservingness of an appropriate sort of inner judgment.[1]

Addressing the deterministic horn, one esteemed argument for incompatibilism regarding responsibility proceeds from the premise that free will is a precondition of responsibility (Van Inwagen 1983; Ginet 1990; O'Connor 2000; Ekstrom 2000). Our having free will with respect to doing something, for instance, making a decision or performing some overt action—an action that essentially involves peripheral bodily movement—entails our having the power both to do and to refrain from doing what we did (Van Inwagen 2008, 329). "Refrain" is to be understood as preserving an ambiguity. You can refrain from performing some action, A, if you bring about its negation, or if you bring about something else, B, that precludes your bringing about A.

Versions of the consequence argument (among other arguments) seek to establish that determinism and free will are incompatible because determinism precludes our ever being able to do otherwise.[2] In Peter van Inwagen's famous summary of this sort of argument: "If determinism is true, then our acts are the consequences of the laws of nature and events in the remote past. But it is not up to us what went on before we were born, and neither is it up to us what the laws of nature are. Therefore, the consequences of these things (including our present acts) are not up to us" (1983, 16). Assuming that if an act is "not up to" one, one could not have refrained from performing it, if sound the argument upholds the conclusion that determinism expunges free will.

This conclusion, in turn, is an essential plank in the esteemed argument for the incompatibility of determinism and moral responsibility: If determinism is true, one lacks the freedom to do otherwise. But one is morally responsible for having done something only if one could have done otherwise (the principle of alternate possibilities—PAP). Hence, determinism rules out moral responsibility (Van Inwagen 1983; Ginet 1990; O'Connor 2000; Ekstrom 2000).

Another acclaimed argument for incompatibilism concerning responsibility exploits the principle that ultimate origination is a precondition of responsibility (Strawson 1986; 1994; Kane 1996; Pereboom 2001; Hodgson 2005). The underlying thought here is that if one is morally responsible for say, a decision, the decision must be "up to one" in the sense that one must be its "ultimate source." If one makes a decision on the basis of surreptitiously implanted causal springs of action, such as proximal desires and beliefs, then it seems that the decision is not "up to" one. Furthermore, plausibly, because the decision ultimately derives from a source over which one lacks control, one is not responsible for this decision. Determinism, relevantly like covert manipulation, appears to preclude "ultimate origination" of our behavior: If our world is deterministic, our choices were already in the cards. The complete state of the world at a time prior to which there were any human beings, in conjunction with the laws of nature, entails, for instance, the true proposition that Obama chooses to run for the presidency of the United States in 2008.

Turning now to the horn featuring indeterminism, it has been widely thought that regarding responsibility, things fail to get any better if appropriate events in the etiology of our choices or actions are not deterministically caused by prior events. One event deterministically causes a second if and only if the first causes the second, and given the laws of nature and the past, there is no chance that the first occurs without causing the second. An event nondeterministically causes another if and only if the former causes the latter, and it is consistent with the laws of nature and the past that the former occurs and not have caused the latter. It may be proposed that responsibility for our choices requires that apt reason states of the agent nondeviantly and *nondeterministically* cause these choices. This sort of causation appears to make room for alternative possibilities (arguably, barring Frankfurt-style interveners or Frankfurt-style examples). It also seemingly gives us freedom from control by the past, thereby apparently ensuring that the reins of control are squarely in our hands: We are the ultimate originators of our choices. Unfortunately, as Hume (1739 [2000]) and others cautioned, indeterministic choice may not be the panacea for the concerns that determinism seemingly engenders for responsibility. For it has been argued that indeterminism entails luck or randomness, but these things are not compatible with the control that moral responsibility demands (Hobart 1934; Mele 1999a; 1999b; 2006; Van Inwagen 2000; Franklin 2011; Haji 2012b; Pereboom 2014).

In sum, the familiar and venerated age-old dilemma concerning responsibility may be put in this way. If determinism is true of some world, then in that world no one has "responsibility-grounding" control. But it is also the case that if determinism is not true of some world, then in that world no one has such control. Either determinism is true of some world or it is not true of that world. Therefore, in any world one lacks responsibility-grounding control. Without such control, no one is ever morally responsible for anything.

It merits emphasis that this traditional dilemma attempts to cast doubt on whether we are morally responsible for our conduct by questioning whether we have, broadly, the *control* that responsibility (or free action) requires; the putative threat to responsibility is lack of appropriate control.

Needless to say, there have been various responses to the dilemma. Some have questioned the first horn, others the second, and yet others, both. Although I have said some things about this debate in other works, my contribution to it in this book will be relatively limited.

There is an analogous, although generally far less discussed threat, to moral obligation. Moral obligation, just like moral responsibility, requires control (or freedom). Again, it may credibly be thought that obligation presupposes that we have alternative possibilities; no action is morally obligatory, permissible, or impermissible for one unless one could have done otherwise. In a chapter on free will in his *Ethics*, G. E. Moore concurs with this view. He writes:

> An action is only right, if it produces the best *possible* consequences; and by "the best *possible* consequences" was meant "consequences at least as good as would have followed from any action which the agent *could* have done instead." It does, therefore, hold that the question whether an action is right or wrong does always depend upon a comparison of its consequences with those of all the other actions which the agent *could* have done instead. It assumes, therefore, that wherever a voluntary action is right or wrong . . . it is true that the agent *could*, in a sense, have done something else instead. This is an absolutely essential part of the theory. (1912, 102–03)

Regarding impermissibility, for instance, if it is impermissible for one to do something, then one ought not to do it. One part of *Kant's Law* that "ought" implies "can" says that if one ought not to do something, one can refrain from doing it. Hence, if it is impermissible for one to do something, one can refrain from doing it. But determinism expunges alternatives (or so assume). So if impermissibility and, in general, obligation requires avoidability, and determinism precludes our being able to do otherwise, then determinism and impermissibility are not friendly mates. Furthermore, in the wake of various concerns with indeterministic choice, arguably, even if such choice opens the doors to our having alternative possibilities, it does not accommodate the *control* that obligation demands. So we are led to the conclusion that regardless of whether determinism is true or false, nothing is ever morally obligatory for anyone.

At the crux of these sister dilemmas concerning responsibility and obligation lies the common denominator that general metaphysical views—determinism or indeterminism—in conjunction with reasonable premises or theses about free action, responsibility, or obligation threaten obligation and responsibility.

I want to generate a new skeptical argument for less sweeping but nevertheless disturbing conclusions vis-à-vis responsibility and obligation that invokes luck. Provisionally, something is subject to luck if it is beyond our control. For example, you may refrain from reprimanding your boss only because you are too timid, your timidity having largely to do with your childhood upbringing over which you had little or no control. The novel skeptical argument exploits luck's effects first on obligation and then responsibility.

Apropos obligation, departing significantly from the previously sketched dilemma concerning obligation, the argument makes no appeal to determinism (or indeterminism), but instead exploits luck to show that we frequently lack alternatives. Since alternatives are required for obligation, luck undermines obligation. The argument then uses this result together with principles that link responsibility to obligation to derive the further skeptical result that the range of what we are morally responsible for is curtailed.

Attending to obligation first, the argument seeks to show that the range of obligation in our world is reduced in that frequently, what may be taken to be an obligation for a person at a time is really no obligation as of this time for this person at all. This argument shares with the previously sketched dilemma concerning obligation the premise that obligation requires alternatives. Furthermore, it attempts to show that we often lack alternatives. So it has relevant kinship with the previously outlined dilemma that attempts to convince us that if determinism is true we have no "obligation relevant control" owing to our not having alternatives. But it departs significantly from this dilemma in that it makes no appeal to determinism (or its falsity) to show that we lack alternatives. Rather, regardless of whether or not our world is deterministic, it is in the end *luck* that frequently precludes our being able to do otherwise.

A bit more carefully, I argue that factors influencing the way we are, together with a plausible principle that ties motivation to ability (principle *Motivation/Ability*), undermine the range of what it is obligatory for us to do. These factors need not have so affected us insofar as we could have been different sorts of creature. Furthermore, it is beyond our control, and thus it is a matter of luck that they influence us in the way they do. In virtue of its being a matter of luck that these factors influence us as they do, it is also a matter of luck—it is beyond our control—that frequently, what is seemingly obligatory for us is not obligatory for us.

The underlying core idea of principle *Motivation/Ability* is fairly straightforward. Construe "action" liberally to include choices, garden-variety overt actions, intentional omissions, and so forth. One cannot, at a time, intentionally perform an action at that time unless either one has, at that time, motivation—an appropriate pro-attitude—to perform that action, or in the absence of having such motivation, one can, at that time, acquire motivation to perform the action. Let "desire" be an umbrella term for the relevant pro-attitude. Then, put simply, the principle linking motivation to do something with ability to do it says that one cannot, at a time, intentionally perform an action at that time unless one has or can acquire, at that time, a desire to perform that action. But frequently we neither had the desire nor the ability to acquire the apt desire to perform a different action from the one we performed. A loving and devoted mother, typically, will not have the desire, nor will she be able to acquire the desire (during the appropriate temporal interval), to fail to protect her child from impending danger. So normally, she will have no alternative to protecting her child. The mother's not having an alternative will ultimately be a function of factors that are beyond her control independently of whether determinism effaces alternatives. She may be psychologically incapable of not being able to refrain from protecting her child because of the way she was raised, and she may have had little or no control over her early upbringing. In this fashion, her not being able to do otherwise has nothing to do with determinism per se but (as I will argue) much to do with luck. If it is true, however, that obligation requires that we have alternatives, then what is seemingly obligatory for the mother—protecting her child—is not, after all, obligatory for her. In short, if obligation presupposes that we could have done otherwise, but luck frequently prevents us from doing otherwise, then our range of obligation narrows considerably.

It would be to no avail to appeal to indeterministic choice to rescue obligation. If such choice requires that one could have done otherwise consistent with the past and the laws remaining "fixed" (at least in the absence of Frankfurt-style or functionally similar interveners), and luck regularly precludes us from doing otherwise, frequently one could not have done otherwise. So again, recurrently, what may seem to be an obligation for one would *not* be an obligation for one.

Turning now to luck and responsibility, in addition to a freedom (or control) requirement, responsibility also has what we may call a "deontic requirement" (or a "moral requirement"). At least in a preliminary characterization (to be sharpened up in a subsequent chapter), this requirement concerns suitable connections between praiseworthiness and obligation or permissibility, on the one hand, and blameworthiness and impermissibility, on the other. Confining attention to blameworthiness, many have championed the principle that blameworthiness requires impermissibility. One is morally blameworthy for an action only if it is morally impermissible for one to perform that action. Luck narrows the range of what it is impermissible for us to do in virtue of frequently precluding us from being able to do otherwise. But then if the proposed deontic principle is true—if blameworthiness does indeed require impermissibility—the range of blameworthiness narrows as well; people may not be blameworthy for much of what many may have credibly thought they were deserving of blame.

The principle that blameworthiness requires impermissibility has rivals. A notable one severs the link between blameworthiness and impermissibility, and instead ties blameworthiness to belief in impermissibility. Roughly, one is blameworthy for an action only if one performs it while nonculpably believing that it is impermissible for one to perform it.[3] If this alternative principle is true, then a person may erroneously but nonculpably believe that many actions she cannot refrain from doing (because of the sort of person she is, for instance) are impermissible for her to do, and so may be blameworthy for doing them. However, if rational and enlightened about her error concerning the moral statuses of her actions, her enlightenment would absolve her from blameworthiness; she would not be blameworthy for pertinent seeming wrongdoings. Blameworthiness would hang on a thread; it would be sustained by "deontic irrationality"—being mistaken about the primary moral statuses (being obligatory, permissible, or impermissible) of one's actions.[4]

Again, it is worth remarking that this threat to the scope of blameworthiness—to things we are blameworthy for—has nothing to do per se with determinism or indeterminism. The threat comes from a different direction: Luck often precludes our being able to do otherwise, impermissibility requires avoidability, and (provisionally) blameworthiness is nontrivially associated either with impermissibility or nonculpable belief in impermissibility.

This argument—or, more appropriately, sequence of arguments—will be complemented with a second set of arguments from luck that also supports a narrowing of the range of things for which we are blameworthy. Unlike the first string of arguments, these supplemental arguments do not appeal to the view that we often find ourselves with no alternatives other than the one we perform. Rather, they exploit what is presumably the widespread phenomenon that owing to factors not in our control, obligation can change with the passage of time. Suppose as of a certain time that you, the lifeguard, ought to rescue the child who is drowning, and you ought to do so quickly. But as you hurriedly prepare to enter the ocean, unbeknownst to you a great white shark, formerly not around, positions itself between you and the child, and will eat you before you can reach the child. It is now no longer true that at this somewhat later time, you ought to rescue the child because you cannot, as of this later time, do so. Or suppose that on Monday, it is impermissible for you, the doctor, to give medicine B to a patient on Wednesday because unlike B, medicine A, which is also available, will cure the patient with no unpleasant side effects. However, suppose you deliberately plan on doing wrong by giving B, and you do give B on Wednesday. But now imagine the following twist in the case. Unbeknownst to you, the supply of A is exhausted on Tuesday, and because of this, as of Tuesday it is no longer impermissible for you to give B on Wednesday. Indeed, suppose you ought, as of the time A is unavailable, to give B on Wednesday. It seems that life is full of such scenarios in which because of luck—owing to factors beyond one's control—the rights and wrongs of the scenario change with the passage of time. If one is blameworthy for doing something only if it is impermissible for one to do it, as of Tuesday, you are not to blame for giving B to your patient. If one is blameworthy for doing something only if one does it while nonculpably believing that it is impermissible for one to do it, then if you are aware of the moral status of your pertinent action—as of Tuesday, it is no longer impermissible for you to give B—again you won't be blameworthy for giving B (assuming you now give B in the nonculpable belief that it is obligatory for you to give B). The general point is that frequently, what we believe is obligatory or impermissible for us turns out not to be obligatory or impermissible (whatever the case may be) because of the changeability of obligations with passing time, and this should, in turn, render plausible the view that the range of things for which we are blameworthy is more limited than what we may have thought.

Luck's detrimentally affecting obligation and responsibility has significant implications two of which are addressed in some detail. First, one's character influences the types of action one can or cannot perform. The extent of this influence is, of course, controversial. Imagine a George Washington endowed with sundry virtues—civility, loyalty, temperance, and so forth—and that the influence of these virtues on his conduct precluded him from doing various things on many occasions. He could not tell a lie nor betray a friend (unless forced to choose between exemplifying one or another of these virtues, for instance, lying to remain loyal). Then the range of obligations for Washington narrows considerably. Departing from what one might reasonably expect, as one becomes more virtuous insofar as one is committed to doing what is seemingly obligatory for one, what one may take to be obligatory for one will not in fact be obligatory for one. And as one hardens one's heart to morality because of the sort of person one is or has made oneself, pertinent actions that may seemingly be impermissible for one will not be impermissible for one.

Imagine a villain who performs vile deeds that she cannot avoid performing. One may initially think she is blameworthy for at least some of these deeds if one is willing to entertain the admittedly contentious view that avoidability itself is no bar to blameworthiness. But if blameworthiness requires impermissibility, and impermissibility requires avoidability, then the villain would not be blameworthy for the deeds she cannot but perform. If blameworthiness requires nonculpable belief in what it is impermissible for one to do, then if not deluded about the moral statuses of her vile deeds—they are not morally impermissible for her because she cannot avoid performing them—then yet again she would not be blameworthy for them.

Second, it appears uncontroversial that one primary goal of moral education is to do whatever we can to help our children develop into morally conscientious agents who are disposed to fulfill their obligations, to do things for which they are praiseworthy, and to avoid wrongdoing and conduct for which they are blameworthy. But if the scope of obligation and blameworthiness is narrow—perhaps far narrower than what we may have hitherto assumed—then it seems that we would have to rethink these goals. Education should not aim for what is largely beyond our reach.

1.2 SYNOPSIS

The plan of the book is as follows. In chapter 2, first I briefly address the notion of luck. I then rehearse arguments for the thesis that moral obligation, permissibility, and impermissibility require alternative possibilities. Toward the end of the chapter I revisit Frankfurt examples to set the stage for chapter 3. In this third chapter I respond to objections, some deploying Frankfurt examples, to arguments in the previous chapter that obligation requires alternatives. In many of these examples factors beyond one's control preclude one from doing anything *other* than what one does without playing any role in bringing about what one does. If obligation requires free will, and so requires that one could have done otherwise, whatever one does that it is unavoidable for one to do in a "Frankfurt situation" is something it is *not* obligatory for one to do.

In chapter 4, I start by explaining why Frankfurt examples pave the way to exposing how obligation is subject to luck in an interesting way. I then refine and defend principle *Motivation/Ability*. This principle is an essential plank in an argument for the claim that there appear to be many circumstances in life that resemble Frankfurt situations insofar as although an agent does something—for instance, she refrains from betraying confidences, or she recoils from robbing the poor box, or she rescues her child from imminent harm—factors not in her control prevent her from doing otherwise. In such cases, as in the Frankfurt examples of interest, each of these acts or intentional omissions that one would normally and plausibly take to be obligatory for the agent is not in fact obligatory for her. In other words, I show that principle *Motivation/Ability*, together with considerations of luck, sustains the conclusion that our range of obligations is narrow.

In chapter 5 I forge crucial associations among luck, diminishing obligation (or impermissibility), and diminishing blameworthiness. I introduce three different candidates for the deontic requirement of responsibility. I defend my preference for one of them. I go on to argue that no matter which of these candidates is true, if we are not deontically irrational in that we are aware of the moral statuses of our actions, omissions, and so forth, the scope of blameworthiness narrows—we are (presumably) blameworthy for far less than what we may have credibly thought. I then introduce a second set of arguments for diminished blameworthiness that appeals to luck's rendering our obligations susceptible to change over time. I end this chapter with the proposal that luck also detrimentally influences nonmoral varieties of both obligation and blameworthiness.

In chapter 6, I first examine the relationship among obligation, responsibility, and character. Virtue seems to threaten obligation. The stronger one's commitment to doing what is seemingly obligatory for one, whatever is supposedly obligatory for one will not in fact be obligatory for one. Furthermore, and just as paradoxically, vice seems to exclude impermissibility. As one steels oneself against doing what it is morally obligatory or permissible for one to do because of the sort of person one is or has made oneself, pertinent actions that may seemingly be impermissible for one will not be impermissible for one. I then attend to some ways in which free will and luck are considered in discussions about education's purposes. Although philosophers of education have disputed what the ultimate goals of education should be, as I previously alluded to, there seems to be a fair measure of consensus that education should aim at helping children to become morally upright adults (people who comply with their moral obligations), and virtuous and praiseworthy adults, acting from laudable character traits and being disposed to do what is or what they believe to be obligatory or permissible. But considerations from the previous chapters expose the concern that general skeptical challenges owing ultimately to luck undermine the claim that most persons are able, for example, to act uprightly. If the skeptical challenges are compelling, they cast doubt on the proposal that among education's ultimate moral aims is uprightness. So what should these aims be?

Finally, in chapter 7 I reflect on lessons that the sort of constrained skepticism about responsibility for which I argue has for the traditional dilemma concerning determinism and responsibility.

NOTES

1. In later parts of the book I will briefly address nondesert-involving accounts of blameworthiness advanced or discussed, for example, by Schlick (1939), Sher (2006), Persson (2013), and Pereboom (2014).
2. Carl Ginet introduced the Consequence Argument in 1966. He refines this argument in 1990 and 2003. Wiggins advances a version of the Consequence Argument as well in 1973. In personal correspondence, Joseph Campbell suggested that Galen Strawson's "impossibility argument" may be regarded as a perturbation of the Consequence Argument.
3. Strictly, the principles are not rivals because each specifies an alleged necessary condition of blameworthiness. However, frequently, proponents of the one reject the other.
4. As I will clarify in subsequent chapters, my thesis about the diminished scope of blameworthiness does not rest on broadly skeptical concerns that we do not, for example, know which normative ethical theory—one that specifies necessary and sufficient conditions for obligation—is true. There is some discussion of this sort of broad concern in Rosen 2004.

Chapter 2

Obligation and Alternative Possibilities

I begin by expanding on the notion of luck. I then summarize considerations for the view that having alternative possibilities is a precondition of obligation. Finally, I revisit Frankfurt-style examples in preparation for ensuing discussion.

2.1 LUCK

Something is subject to luck, roughly, if it is beyond our control. Moral obligation is so subject in some familiar ways. For example, an important kind of luck is luck with respect to the results of our behavior or resultant luck. If the bullet of the gun you have fired fails to hit Jack, your intended victim, because its pathway is blocked by a speeding truck, it is a matter of luck that you do no wrong in not killing Jack, although some of your other behavior, such as deciding or attempting to kill Jack, may be wrong. For another example, a second important kind of luck is luck with respect to the situation in which one finds oneself or situational luck.[1] Suppose, as a result of a series of events with which you had little to do, you are forced to make an agonizing choice: If you refuse to kill an aged person, a thousand other innocent people, including yourself, will die. Not implausibly, you ought to kill the one to spare the others.[2] The sort of situational luck here having to do with one's "external situation"—"circumstantial luck"—is, of course, bad or ill luck. Obligation is also susceptible to another species of situational luck—"constitutive luck"—that has to do with one's lacking control over being the kind of person one is.[3] Ralph may have refrained from chasing the child only because of his poor eyesight, this deficiency wrought by the onset of a disease over which he had no control. In the next two chapters I show how circumstantial luck, sometimes in conjunction with constitutive luck, detrimentally affects obligation. Subject to combinations of these varieties of luck, many acts that are plausibly taken to be obligatory at times for persons will not be obligatory for these persons at all.[4] Some spadework is needed before tackling luck's threat to obligation.

One concern with the preliminary characterization of luck—something is a matter of luck if it is beyond our control—has to do with its insensitivity to the chance or probability that certain events that are beyond one's control will occur (or fail to occur). It is not in any person's control that the earth spins on its axis. Even so, owing to this being the case, it would be untenable to conclude that its spinning is a matter of luck for anyone, and this is presumably because the probability of its continuing to do so is very high (see, e.g., Zimmerman 2011, 122). This defect is mentioned only to set it aside. Another concern is that while we may accept the initial characterization of luck with which we commenced, there are different distinctions regarding how something may be within or beyond one's control, and this affects our understanding of luck. For instance, there is the common distinction between partial and complete control. One has complete control over something only if its occurrence does not depend on anything that is beyond one's control. No one has such control over anything; at best, any control that anyone has over something is partial. There is, in addition, the well-known distinction between direct and indirect control. One has indirect control over something provided one has control over it by way of having control over something else; one has direct control over something provided one has control over it that is not indirect. There are yet other distinctions such as the distinction between regulative (or two-way) control and guidance (or one-way) control. One has regulative control with respect to an action when one has an alternative and no matter which alternative one performs, one has control in doing it. With guidance control one does have control in doing what one does but one has no other alternatives (or no other robust alternatives).[5] So when it is claimed that luck is a matter of something's not being in one's control, "control" is multiply ambiguous, and our rough and ready introductory characterization of luck inherits this ambiguity.

A way to proceed is to chip away at the initial account partly by attending to the various distinctions concerning control. However, this will not be done here. Instead, examples will be advanced that, hopefully, will suffice to illustrate the sort of luck to which what is frequently seemingly obligatory is subject.

Reflect on this intriguing sequence of cases that Michael Zimmerman advances:

> Suppose that George shot Henry and killed him. Suppose that Georg shot Henrik in circumstances which were, to the extent possible, exactly like those of George (. . . [including] what went on "inside" the protagonists' heads as well as what happened in the "outside" world), except for the fact that Georg's bullet was intercepted by a passing bird, . . . and Henrik escaped injury. Inasmuch as the bird's flight was not in Georg's control, the thesis that luck is irrelevant to moral responsibility implies that George and Georg are equally morally responsible. (2002, 560)

Having suggested that George may well be responsible for *more things* than Georg, but denying that George is *any more* responsible than Georg, Zimmerman sketches another case:

> Suppose, as before, that George shot at Henry and killed him. Suppose also . . . that Georg did not kill Henrik; suppose now, however, that this was not because he took a shot that was intercepted by some unfortunate bird, but rather because he took no shot at all. And suppose that this was because of something quite fortuitous: Georg sneezed just as he was about to shoot . . . or a truck pulled up in front of Henrik, blocking Georg's line of fire . . . Whereas in the case involving the bird, luck intervened after the shot took place, thereby preventing Henrik's death, in this sort of case the intervention occurs earlier, before Georg has a chance to act at all. But the cases are united in that, in all of them, Georg would have freely killed Henrik but for some feature of the case over which he had no control. This being so, it seems that we must conclude here, as before, that Georg is as culpable as George. The circumstances that conspired to save Henrik afford Georg no excuse. (2002, 563)

Maybe some will take exception to Zimmerman's conclusion that Georg is as culpable as George (assuming that George is culpable). Nevertheless, one would be hard-pressed to deny that in the second and third cases it was a matter of luck that Georg did not kill Henrik. It is this sense of luck that is central to the interests of this book.

Lest one still have concerns that the relevant sense of luck is too amorphous, it may help to reinterpret my main thesis to be that owing to factors beyond our control, the range of what we take to be obligatory for us is far narrower that what we may initially have supposed.[6]

2.2 OBLIGATION AND ALTERNATIVES

Next, drawing partially from previous work, I turn to motivating the view that obligation requires dual control. As I said in the opening section of the book, one has free will regarding an action, mental or otherwise, just in case one can both perform—one can bring about—and one can refrain from performing it. One can refrain from doing something, A, if one brings about *not-A* or one brings about something else, B, whose bringing about is incompatible with bringing about A. The sense of "can" of interest is the personal one in claims such as "One is morally responsible for doing, or it is morally obligatory for one to do, something only if one can do it." Take the canonical form of obligation statements to be agent- and time-relativized in this way: as of time, $t1$, agent, S, ought to do A at time $t2$, where $t1$ may be $t2$ or a time earlier than $t2$. The first temporal index indicates the time at which the obligation is incurred, the second the time at which the obligation is to be discharged.[7]

I sketch three (perhaps not unrelated) routes to the conclusion that obligation requires free will. The relatively simplest route draws on the principle that the moral "ought" implies "can" or *Kant's Law*:

> *Kant's Law*: If S morally ought, as of time, $t1$, to do A at $t2$, then at $t1$ S can do A at $t2$; and if S morally ought, at $t1$, not to do A at $t2$, then at $t1$ S can refrain from doing A at $t2$.

In this law, "ought" expresses overall moral obligation as opposed to prima facie obligation, and the "can" at issue is at least the "can" of specific ability and opportunity. If you ought, as of a certain time, $t1$, to donate to a charity at a later time, $t2$, then, at $t1$, you have the opportunity to donate to this charity at $t2$. Furthermore, you have the specific, in contrast to merely a general ability, at $t1$, to donate to this charity at $t2$. You can have a general ability to donate to a charity even in circumstances in which there are no charities to which you can donate, but you cannot have a specific ability to donate in such circumstances. In addition, needless to say, "can" in *Kant's Law* does not refer to the "can" of broadly logical possibility nor physical possibility. Finally, the "can" under scrutiny does not imply that one has the dual ability both to do and to refrain from doing what one does, although having the dual ability would suffice for having the sort of personal control at issue (Haji 2002, ch. 2; 2012a, 22–23).

One more qualification is important. One is indirectly obligated regarding something just in case one is obligated regarding it by way of being obligated regarding something else; one is directly obligated regarding something just in case one is obligated regarding it but not indirectly so. As Zimmerman (2006, 595, 602; 2008, 90–91, 149–50) cautions, direct obligations are restricted to intentional actions one can perform; not so with indirect obligations. Suppose Ted has a direct obligation to turn on the furnace. He cannot, however, turn it on without activating the relevant mechanisms within of which he knows nothing whatsoever; so he ought to activate these mechanisms. In his circumstances he can perform this indirect obligation but not intentionally.

Kant's Law captures the compelling thought that moral obligation requires freedom or control. Unfortunately, few have reflected on the control requirements of moral permissibility and impermissibility. Surely, it is just as credible that permissibility and impermissibility require control as it is that obligation requires control. I cannot see what would sustain the view that it can be impermissible (or permissible), as of some time, for one to do something at that time, if one cannot, at that time, do it then. Wouldn't deontic judgments regarding moral impermissibility and permissibility be empty or trivial if it could be the case that it can be impermissible (or permissible) for one to do something that one cannot do?

To support this point, in previous work I drew attention to an analogy: Praiseworthiness requires control (or freedom) whatever that control or freedom is. We cannot be morally responsible for what is not in our control, or as Zimmerman proposes, the degree to which we are morally responsible cannot be affected by what is not in our control (2002, 559). But if praiseworthiness requires control, without cogent argument to the contrary, blameworthiness requires control too.

Take it, then, that in the absence of any good reasons to believe otherwise, impermissibility and permissibility require control. The next issue concerns the nature of the control they require. I have proposed that, minimally, just as the moral "ought" entails the "can" of ability and opportunity—the sense of "can" here is the personal sense of "can"—so do impermissibility and permissibility, again, unless there are cogent reasons to believe differently. One consideration in support of this view, to which I will briefly revert below, is that just like obligation, permissibility is tied to reasons of a certain sort ("objective" or "external reasons"): Necessarily, if it is morally obligatory or permissible for one to do something, then one has a (defeasible) reason to do it. But one cannot have an objective reason to do something unless one can do it. Thus, both "ought" and "permissibility" entail "can." If they do, then barring reasons to think differently, "impermissibility" entails "can" as well. It will become clear that in favor of the principle that each of "permissibility" and "impermissibility" implies "can," I appeal both to the symmetry of deontic judgments and the interdefinability of deontic operators.

A second consideration derives from a powerful analysis (or sort of analysis) of the concept of obligation:

(MO): A person, S, ought, as of t, to see to the occurrence of a state of affairs, p, if and only if p occurs in some world, w, accessible to S at t, and it is not the case that p's negation (not-p) occurs in any accessible world deontically as good as or deontically better than *w*. (See, e.g., Feldman 1986, 37; Zimmerman 1996, 26–27)

Think of deontic value as the "goodness value" of worlds. More generally, deontic value is that value in virtue of which acts (omissions, states of affairs), or more generally, whatever can have one or more of the primary normative statuses of *being obligatory, permissible,* or *impermissible,* have one or more of these statuses. *MO* has it that the obligatory is the deontically best. The axiological issue of just what is deontically best is of no significance for us. Some may identify what is so best, for example, with what is intrinsically best, others with maximal compliance with God's commands, yet others with choice behind a Rawlsian veil of ignorance, and so forth. If worlds are accessible to you in which you do something, and no better worlds are accessible to you in which you fail to do this thing, then according to *MO*, you ought to do this thing.

More intuitively, and simplifying somewhat as I customarily will, if *MO* is true, as of some time, you morally ought to perform an act—an act is *morally obligatory* for you—if and only if you can do it, and it occurs in all the best worlds accessible to you at this time. In all your best life histories, you perform this act at the relevant time. As of some time, it is morally permissible for you to perform an act if and only if you can do it and it occurs in some of the best worlds accessible to you at this time. And as of some time, it is impermissible for you to perform an act if and only if you can do it and it does not occur in any of the best worlds accessible to you at this time. According to *MO*, on each occasion, one ought to do the best one can. *MO* validates both "ought" implies "can" and "permissibility" implies "can"; if *MO* is true, these principles are true too. Once again, if "ought" and "permissibility" imply "can," with no good reason to believe otherwise, "wrong" implies "can" too.

While I basically agree with *MO*, I offer two refinements. The first, to which I turn next, revises *MO* to make it perspicuous that (direct) obligation presupposes agency; if one is directly obligated to do something, then one can *intentionally bring it about*. The second, described toward the end of this section, highlights the fact that (direct) obligation requires dual intentional control; if one is obligated to do something, both one can intentionally do and one can intentionally refrain from doing it.

Regarding the first adjustment compare:

(i) *P* occurs in some world, *w*, accessible to *S* at *t*,

and

(ii) There is a world, *w*, accessible to *S* at *t* in which *S* brings it about that *p*.

(i) may be satisfied even if you aren't the agent of the occurrence of *p*, whereas (ii) requires that you are the agent of its occurrence. It seems that *MO* includes (i). However, as I have proposed obligation presupposes agency and, hence, (ii) is more apt.

Similarly, compare: (iii) *Not-p* occurs in some world, *w**, accessible to *S* at *t*,

and

(iv) There is a world, *w**, accessible to *S* at *t* in which *S* refrains from bringing about *p*.

(iii) requires that *not-p* occurs. So, if *p* stands for the state of affairs *Ryan's right hand is raised*, then (iii) requires that Ryan's right hand isn't raised. (iii) doesn't preserve the desirable "ability to do otherwise" ambiguity (inherent in "refraining") previously noted. In addition, (iii) may be satisfied even if you aren't the agent of *not-p*. So, regardless of anything about Ryan, if someone else holds Ryan's arm down, clause (iii) is satisfied. In contrast, (iv) can be used to preserve the desirable "ability to do otherwise" ambiguity because it simply requires that the agent isn't the agent of *p*'s occurrence, and you can fail to be the agent of *p*'s occurrence regardless of whether *p* in fact occurs. Also, (iv) includes an agency requirement that (iii) lacks.[8] We may now reformulate *MO* in this way:

> *MO-1*: A person, *S*, morally ought, as of *t*, to see to the occurrence of a state of affairs, *p*, if and only if there is a world, *w*, accessible to *S* at *t* in which *S* brings about *p*, and it is not the case that *S* refrains from bringing about *p* in any accessible world as good as or better than *w*.

A third consideration in favor specifically of "impermissibility" implies "can" appeals to the following principles.

> *Impermissible/Permissible Possibility*: If, at *t*, it is impermissible for *S* to do *A* at *t*, then, at *t S* can do something else, such as refraining from doing *A*, which it is permissible for *S* to do at *t*.

I find this principle plausible. Indeed, I think a logically stronger principle is true too:

> *Impermissible/Obligation Possibility*: If, at *t*, it is impermissible for *S* to do *A* at *t*, then, at *t S* can do something else, such as refraining from doing *A*, which it is obligatory for *S* to do at *t*.

Suppose you've made a promise, and it's impermissible for you not to keep it, that is, it is impermissible for you to break it. Then it seems plausible that you ought to keep it. Keeping the promise precludes you from breaking it, and breaking it precludes you from keeping it. We can generalize: If, at some time, t, it is impermissible for you to do something, A, at t, then, at t, you ought to do something, C (such as refraining from doing A), that is incompatible with your doing A—C precludes you from doing A—and doing, A, in turn, precludes you from doing C. But then it follows immediately that if it is impermissible for you to do something, then there is something else that it is obligatory (and, hence, permissible) for you to do.

Assume, now (for *reductio*), that one denies that "impermissible" implies "can." However, one endorses the view that "ought" and "permissible" each implies "can" perhaps because one finds *MO-1*—the principle that one ought to do the best one can—endearing. In addition, include among these "starting assumptions" the assumption that there are no genuine conflicts of obligation. Imagine a situation in which, as of t, you cannot do some heinous deed, A, at t. Given the starting assumptions, at t, it is neither obligatory nor permissible for you to do A at t, although it may be that at t, it is impermissible for you to do A at t. But then both principles *Impermissible/Permissible Possibility* and *Impermissible/Obligation Possibility* are violated. Although (let's suppose), at t, it is impermissible for you to do A at t, it is false that, at t, you can do something else it is obligatory or permissible for you to do then.

In a nutshell, if obligation requires control, so do permissibility and impermissibility; and if obligation requires a certain sort of basic control—that we can do what we are obligated to do—impermissibility and permissibility require this sort of basic control as well.[9]

To show that obligation requires free will, we may now argue as follows: If it is impermissible for one to do something, one ought not to do it. If one ought not to do something, one can refrain from doing it. Hence if it is impermissible for one to do something, one can refrain from doing it. But it is also true that if it is impermissible for one to do something, one can do it. So there is an alternative possibilities requirement for impermissibility. Regarding obligation, if one ought to refrain from doing something, then it is impermissible for one to do it. Furthermore, if it is impermissible for one to do something, one can do it (from "impermissible" implies "can.") Therefore, if one ought to refrain from doing something, one can do it. But it is also true that if one ought to refrain from doing something, one can refrain from doing it. In other words, just as there is a requirement of alternative possibilities for impermissibility, so there is such a requirement for obligation.

Finally, there is no similar way to derive the proposition that permissibility, likewise, requires alternative possibilities. For even if it is agreed that "permissible" implies "can," there is no principle like the principle that moral "ought not" is equivalent to "impermissible" that will allow us to infer that "permissible" implies "can refrain." Nevertheless, it is very plausible that "permissible" does imply "can refrain." For, first, as I have underscored, unless we have sound reason to believe otherwise, the control requirements of permissibility should not differ from those of obligation and impermissibility. Second, if we deny that "permissible" implies "can refrain," inasmuch as obligatoriness and impermissibility do require alternative possibilities, we are in danger of being encumbered with the dubious view that it is morally permissible for one to do whatever acts, heinous or otherwise, that one cannot avoid doing. To elaborate briefly, suppose one cannot refrain from performing some odious deed. Then since obligation and impermissibility require that one be able to do otherwise, this deed is neither obligatory nor impermissible for one. The only options, it seems, is that the deed is amoral for one—that is, it is not obligatory, permissible, or impermissible for one—or it is permissible for one. Since the latter is, presumably, unacceptable, we should opt for the former instead. Finally, as Ryan Hebert explains, *MO-1*, together with the result I derived for the principle that "ought" implies "can refrain," may be used to show that "permissibility" implies "can refrain" by focusing on information about best worlds accessible to one when something is permissible for one.[10] If *A* is permissible for you, you do *A* in some of your best accessible worlds. What are you doing in your other best accessible worlds? If it is permissible for you to do *A*, then either it is obligatory for you to do *A*, or it is optional for you to do *A*. If the former, then "permissible" implies "can refrain" as "obligation" implies "can refrain." If the latter, then neither *A* nor its negation is obligatory; both *A* and *not-A* are permissible for you. If *not-A* is permissible for you, you bring about *not-A* in some of your best accessible worlds. Hence, if *A* is optional for you, you can refrain from doing *A*. It follows that if *A* is permissible for you, you can refrain from doing *A*.

In sum, this line of argument for the view that obligation requires alternatives essentially relies on three principles: *Kant's Law*, "ought not" is equivalent to "impermissible" (*Equivalence*) and "impermissible implies "can" (*Impermissible/Can*). The first two are highly plausible (although, needless to say, not uncontested). Denying the third, it would seem, requires either denying that impermissibility, unlike obligation, requires control, something unsustainable, or that impermissibility requires a different species of basic control than obligation, something highly suspect (see Haji 2012a).

The marginally more complicated route to the same conclusion that obligation requires free will invokes the essential connection between obligation and reason. Starting with some preparatory work, first, let's distinguish between normative (as opposed to merely explanatory) reasons one has to do various things, and normative reasons one takes oneself to have to do various things, or abbreviating, between objective and subjective normative reasons. Objective reasons are facts dissociated from the agent's desires or attitudes that are intrinsically motivating. More carefully, use "motivating desire" to refer to attitudinal states of mind (or their neural realizers) that are, constitute, or include motivation. If R is an objective reason for an agent, S, to do something, R is not a motivating desire of S, does not have a motivating desire of S as a constituent, and is not even in part a fact, truth, proposition, or the like about any actual motivating desire of S (Mele 2003a, 77). *Pro tanto* objective reasons can be outweighed by other reasons, as opposed to all-things considered reasons, which cannot be outweighed. Each *pro tanto* reason has a certain weight. If your *pro tanto* reasons to act in some way are stronger than those to act in any other way, then you reasons-wise ought to act in this way. If you have sufficient *pro tanto* reason to act in two or more ways, and no better reason to act in any other way, then it is reasons-wise permissible for you to act in either of these ways. Finally, if you have most *pro tanto* reason not to act in a certain way, then acting in this way is reasons-wise forbidden for you. (Hereafter, unless the context makes clear, it will be *pro tanto* reasons that are at issue although the qualifier "*pro tanto*" will frequently be omitted.)

Objective reasons contrast with one's subjective reasons which amount to what one *takes* to be one's objective reasons. One has a subjective reason to do something if and only if one believes that one has an objective reason to do it. For example, House desires to cure his ailing patient, and believes, on the evidence available to him, that giving medicine M to this patient will cure him. He believes, too, that he morally ought to give M to this patient. However, if giving M will in fact kill the patient, then although House takes himself to have sufficient (objective) reason to give M to this patient, he has decisive objective reason not to do so. As "subjective reason" is construed in this book, he has a subjective reason to give M.

The distinction between objective and subjective reasons roughly parallels the distinction between doing what it is morally obligatory for one to do (one's absolute or objective moral obligation), and doing what one takes to be morally obligatory for one to do (one's subjective moral obligation).

Obligation is associated with objective reasons:

Obligation/Objective Reasons (OR): Necessarily, if an agent, S, has a moral obligation to do something, A, then the agent has an objective (*pro tanto*) reason to do A.

I don't know what sort of argument may be advanced to support this principle because it seems so basic; not less basic, in any event, than the principle that obligation or responsibility require control. It may simply be that obligations of any kind are conceptually linked to reasons of the given kind, moral obligations to moral reasons, for instance (see, e.g., Vranas 2007, 172–73).

Why believe, though, that obligations are tied to *objective pro tanto* reasons and not either to subjective reasons or to reasons essentially associated with intrinsically motivating attitudes such as desires? The crux of the matter is that the view (roughly) that some things are morally impermissible or morally obligatory for an agent irrespective of what desires or beliefs that agent has is compelling.[11] You may believe, on the evidence available to you, that giving medicine M to a sick patient will cure the patient. But if giving M will in fact kill the patient, you do wrong in giving M. You do wrong despite your subjective reason: You believe (let's assume) that you have a *pro tanto* reason to give M, whereas in fact you have no such reason. Indeed, you have decisive *pro tanto* reason *not* to give M. Similarly, you do wrong despite your pertinent Davidsonian reasons: You desire to cure the patient, believe you can cure the patient, and also believe you morally ought to cure by administering M; your having of this desire and these beliefs (in conjunction with other pertinent antecedents of action) causally (and nondeviantly) issues in your giving M. None of this, though, need tell against your act not being wrong for you.[12]

Henceforth, I will use "it is O-reasons-wise obligatory, impermissible, or permissible for one to do something" to signal that such reason-wise appraisals are appraisals from the point of view of objective reasons. It is relatively easy to establish that if it is O-reasons-wise impermissible for one to do something, then one can refrain from doing it. Start with the truism that if one has most moral reason to do something, A, and thus if morality *requires* that one do A, then one can do A. In other words, the moral "ought" implies "can." Suppose, now, that of one's objective reasons to do one of various things on some occasion, one has *most (objective) reason* to do A. Then it seems that one *can* do A. One cannot have an "obligation"—it cannot be necessary—from the point of view of reason, for one to do something if one cannot do that thing. Just as there is an association between the "ought" of morality and "can," there is a similar association between the "ought" of reason and "can." Indeed, the moral "ought" implies "can" principle appears just to be a more restricted version of the following general principle:

O-Reasons-Wise "Ought" Implies "Can": If one has most objective reason to do something, A, and, thus, if one O-reasons-wise ought to do A, then one can do A.

Again, *precluding compelling reasons to think otherwise,* if O-reasons-wise "ought" requires a species of control, O-reasons-wise "permissibility" and O-reasons-wise "impermissibility" require this very species of control as well: If it is O-reasons-wise permissible or O-reasons-wise forbidden for you to do something, then you can do it. Invoking an argument analogous to the argument previously advanced for moral obligation's and moral impermissibility's requiring free will, we can show that O-reasons-wise obligation and O-reasons-wise impermissibility also require free will. If O-reasons-wise obligation and O-reasons-wise impermissibility require that one can do otherwise, I see little reason to deny that O-reasons-wise permissibility, too, requires that one have alternatives. We may conclude, with one proviso in mind, that there is an alternative possibilities requirement for the truth of judgments of objective *pro tanto* reasons.

Here is the proviso: It may be that it is not morally obligatory, permissible, or impermissible for a person, as of a time, to perform a certain action at that time; as of this time, it is amoral for the person to perform the action (at this time). Analogously, it may be O-reasons-wise "arational" for a person to perform an action in that it is not O-reasons-wise obligatory, permissible, or impermissible for this person to perform the action. Suppose it is not O-reasons-wise arational for a person to perform some act (in the interests of simplicity, ignore relevant temporal indices). Then it is O-reasons-wise obligatory, permissible, or impermissible for the person to perform this act. Furthermore, it strikes me that, necessarily, if it is morally obligatory, permissible, or impermissible for one to perform an act, then it is not O-reasons-wise arational for one to perform that act; rather it is O-reasons-wise obligatory, or permissible, or impermissible for one to perform it. But there is a requirement of alternative possibilities for O-reasons-wise obligation, permissibility, and impermissibility. Hence, we may conclude that if it is morally obligatory, permissible, or impermissible for one to do something, then one could have done otherwise. Streamlining the argument: If one morally ought to do something, or if it is morally permissible or impermissible for one to do something, then it is O-reasons-wise obligatory, permissible, or impermissible for one to do it. If it is O-reasons-wise obligatory, permissible or impermissible for one to do something, then both one can do it and one can refrain from doing it. Therefore, if one morally ought to do something, or if it morally permissible or impermissible for one to do something, then both one can do and one can refrain from doing it. In other words, obligation, permissibility, and impermissibility presuppose our having free will.

There is a third route to the conclusion that having alternatives is a precondition for obligation. Assume that whenever one performs an action, mental or otherwise, one could not have done otherwise; one never has alternatives. Then as of any time, there is a single world accessible to one: the world in which one chooses, or acts, or intentionally fails to act, as one does. Suppose, in such a world, as of time, t, Joe A-s at t. But the obligatory is the deontically best: roughly, as of t, one ought to do A at t if and only if one brings about A at t in all the deontically best worlds accessible to one at t. Regarding the primary moral status of A, there are three options. On the first option, on each occasion of choice or action, the world in which Joe chooses or acts as he does is the deontically best world. But then, as of any time, if Joe does something—no matter what—at that time, it is obligatory for Joe to do it then. This latitudinarian view is surely implausible. There is no good reason to endorse the view that if any action of an agent is such that it is unavoidable for that agent, then it is obligatory for the agent to perform it. On the second option, on each occasion of choice or action, the world in which Joe chooses or acts as he does is a deontically nonbest world. But then, as of any time, if Joe does something—no matter what—at that time it is impermissible for Joe to do it then. This view is just as unreasonable as the first. There is no good justification for the view that it is impermissible for an agent to perform any action that she cannot refrain from performing. On the third option, on each occasion of choice or action, whatever Joe chooses or does on this occasion is amoral for Joe: It is, as of the relevant time, not obligatory, permissible, or impermissible for Joe; it lacks any of these primary moral statuses. This option is preferable to the other two. Given this consideration, one may venture that obligation, permissibility, and impermissibility require alternatives. (Here, I take no stance on whether the alternatives are "weak" alternatives that one can have even if determinism is true or "strong" alternatives that determinism supposedly rules out. I will revert to this issue in the last chapter.) Briefly put, obligation requires dual control, the ability to perform and to refrain from performing an action.

We may finally introduce the second refinement of *MO* to capture the requirement of alternative possibilities for moral obligation:

> *MO-2*: A person, *S*, morally ought, as of *t*, to see to the occurrence of a state of affairs, *p*, if and only if there is a world, *w*, accessible to *S* at *t* in which *S* brings about *p*, there is a world, *w**, accessible to *S* at *t* in which *S* refrains from bringing about *p*, and it is not the case that *S* refrains from bringing about *p* in any accessible world as good as or better than *w*.

(We may easily derive from *MO-2* "wrong" implies "can": If, as of *t*, it is morally wrong for a person, *S*, to see to the occurrence of a state of affairs, *p*, at *t**, then, as of *t*, S can refrain from bringing it about that p at *t**.)

I close this section on this note: Maybe some won't accept the principle that "impermissible" implies "can." If one fails to accept this principle, then one won't accept the principle that "ought" entails "can refrain from." Presumably, however, one will still accept the principle that "impermissible" entails "can refrain from." I will argue that this principle, together with other considerations, sustains the view that the range of what it is morally impermissible for us to do is narrow.

2.3 STAGE-SETTING FOR OBJECTIONS: FRANKFURT EXAMPLES

In the next chapter, I entertain objections to the view that obligation requires alternative possibilities. A number of these objections appeal to Frankfurt examples. I review these examples in the remainder of this chapter.

In a template of such an example, in its initial stage (Stage 1), Augustine is morally responsible for stealing some pears. Next, this stage is modified so that something precludes Augustine from doing anything incompatible with stealing but *without* in any way interfering in Augustine's actually stealing as it turns out. A mind reader, Ernie, who can tell what Augustine is about to do, will do nothing if he detects some reliable and involuntary sign Augustine displays that he, Augustine, is about to steal, but will force Augustine to steal if he discerns the reliable and involuntary sign that Augustine is about to refrain from stealing. The "insurance policy" is never invoked because Augustine proceeds exactly as before, so Ernie has no need to intercede. Since Augustine in the absence of Ernie is morally responsible for stealing, and since in the modified stage (Stage 2) Augustine does not behave any differently, he is morally blameworthy for stealing here too, even though he could not have done otherwise (Frankfurt 1969; Kane 1996; 2013; Fischer and Ravizza 1998; Pereboom 2003; 2014; Fischer 2006; 2010; 2013; Mele 2006; Haji 2009a). Hence, this Frankfurt example—*Theft*—appears to show that the principle of alternate possibilities is false.

However, these examples face serious objections. One concerns the rationale for the claim that in Stage 2, when all alternatives save the one performed are presumably eliminated, Augustine is still responsible for stealing the pears. The gloss of the rationale previously advanced is that as Augustine acts no differently in this stage than he does in the first (because the intervener does not show his hand), since he is responsible in the first stage, he must be responsible in the second as well. It seems that implicit in this sort of rationale is this principle:

(R1): If something (e.g., the failsafe mechanism's elimination of a person's alternative possibilities) does not in any way influence how a person's decision is caused, then it cannot bear on the issue of the person's moral responsibility.

However, R1, as David Palmer (n.d.) and others (e.g., Widerker 2009) have argued, is false. Here is a slight variation of Palmer's counterexample against R1: Augustine decides to steal the pears in spite of believing it is morally impermissible for him to do so. His decision to steal is caused by his desire to do the self-interested thing, and his belief that so deciding would satisfy this desire. Augustine's belief that it is impermissible for him to decide to steal in *no way* influences how his decision is caused by his desire to do the self-interested thing and his belief that so deciding would satisfy this desire. According to R1, the fact that Augustine believes it is morally impermissible for him to decide to steal *cannot* bear on the issue of his moral responsibility for his decision. But this is false because this fact *is* relevant to his moral responsibility. He is *more* blameworthy, it would seem, if he decided to steal while believing that it is morally wrong for him to do so than if he had made the decision to steal *without* believing it to be morally wrong (Palmer n.d.; also see Widerker 2009, 97–98).

However, one need not invoke R1 to defend the proposal that Augustine is blameworthy for stealing (in Stage 2). The primary contention to be supported is that since the failsafe mechanism—the counterfactual intervener and his mind-reading gismo—does not affect the way in which Augustine acts, if Augustine is responsible in the initial scenario with no fail-safe mechanism, he should be responsible in the second, too. Alternatively, assume that (A1) Augustine is indeed responsible in Stage 1. Then he is responsible in Stage 2 as well. Why so? Incompatibilists generally have advanced two broad considerations in favor of the view that determinism is incompatible with responsibility: (i) Responsibility requires freedom to do otherwise—the ability and the opportunity to do otherwise—but determinism precludes such freedom. (ii) Responsibility requires that we be the ultimate originators of our action, but determinism precludes ultimate origination; it precludes freedom from control by the past. It is the first consideration that Frankfurt examples are designed to challenge. Given (A1)—the assumption that Augustine is responsible for stealing in Stage 1, we can argue for (A2)—he is responsible for stealing in Stage 2 as well—in this way: Presumably, if Augustine is responsible in Stage 1, he is so because he satisfies what is deemed to be a set of necessary and sufficient conditions for moral responsibility. If this set, as some incompatibilists might insist, includes the condition that the agent is free to do otherwise, suspend judgment on this condition because it is the very one under scrutiny, and pay attention to the others. This same set of conditions is satisfied in the second scenario, and the failsafe mechanism has no influence on its members. So, there is good reason to believe that Augustine is responsible in this scenario as well.

Perhaps the most potent objection to Frankfurt examples is the dilemma objection initially elegantly formulated by Robert Kane (1985, 51; 1996, 142–44, 191–92) and then developed independently by Carl Ginet (1996) and David Widerker (1995, 247–61). I sketch this objection in connection with "prior-sign" Frankfurt examples although a similar objection can be deployed against certain Frankfurt examples that do not feature any such sign. The objection is in the form of a dilemma. If the involuntary sign, the cue for intervention, is reliable in the sense of being infallible, it can only be so because states of Augustine prior to the occurrence of the supposedly free action (or choice) are causally sufficient for this action (and the sign indicates this). But if that is the case, then a *deterministic* relation obtains between the prior sign and Augustine's subsequent action, and this begs the question against incompatibilists who believe that determinism is incompatible with freedom or responsibility. On this first horn of the dilemma, the incompatibilist will insist that Augustine is not responsible for her action because it was causally determined. If, on the other hand, the involuntary sign is not infallible and is only reliable in some weaker sense, then an agent (such as Augustine) who acts freely in a Frankfurt example retains the ability to do otherwise when he acts on his own. On this second horn, the connection between the prior sign and subsequent action (or choice) is not deterministic. The presence (or absence) of the prior sign is, thus, consistent with the agent acting or choosing in a manner other than the manner in which he does. So on this second horn, Augustine could well be responsible for his action. But the incompatibilist will claim that the principle of alternate possibilities remains unscathed, as he could have done otherwise.

In reply to the Dilemma Objection, Frankfurt defenders have responded in many different ways. For example, some have attempted to reject the second horn by developing Frankfurt examples that include indeterminism: Even though the pertinent action, such as Augustine's stealing the pears, is nondeterministically caused, the agent could not have done otherwise but is, seemingly, morally responsible for what he does or chooses (Mele and Robb 1998; 2003; Hunt 2000; 2005; Pereboom 2001; 2014; Mele 2006). Others, attending to the first horn, have attempted to argue that it is not damaging to include determinism in Frankfurt examples

(Haji 2009a; Fischer 2010). Here is an example that incorporates determinism:

Pemba decides on his own to squeeze the trigger at time, $t1$, and squeezes the trigger at $t1$, thereby bringing it about that Rubens is killed by $t2$. Assume that his decision to squeeze the trigger is non-deterministically caused. In this case, *Murder-1*, a libertarian would presumably agree that, provided all other conditions of moral responsibility are met, Pemba would be morally responsible for his decision and for the state of affairs *Rubens being killed by $t2$*.[13]

Modifying *Murder-1*, imagine that Black implants a mechanism in Pemba that initiates a certain deterministic process—process p—in Pemba's brain. Process p causes Pemba to arrive at the very decision that he does to squeeze the trigger at the precise time $t1$ when he indeterministically decides on his own to squeeze the trigger. So there are two independent causal routes, one indeterministic (Pemba's ordinary practical reasoning) and the other deterministic (the sequence of events triggered by the fancy mechanism), neither influencing the other, but each causally producing the very same event—Pemba's deciding at $t1$ to squeeze the trigger—in *Murder-2*.[14] The mechanism works in lockstep with Pemba's indeterministic deliberative process—process d—between the time at which Pemba starts to deliberate about killing Rubens and time $t1$ at which he arrives at his deadly decision. As p unfolds, it "neutralizes" neural pathways whose activation is required to allow Pemba to deliberate, at each stage in his deliberations, in ways different from the way in which he does and that would culminate in a decision not to kill Rubens, without affecting what goes on in d. For instance, imagine that having reflected on his reasons, at time, t, Pemba forms the all-things-considered best judgment that he ought to murder Rubens. By t, p has neutralized neural pathways that would allow Pemba to form a best judgment contrary to the one he forms at t without affecting d. Borrowing a card from Alfred Mele and David Robb's Frankfurt case (1998, 104–05), by $t1$, p has neu-tralized all "nodes" in Pemba for decisions contrary to a decision at $t1$ to kill Rubens but without influencing what goes on in process d. If this still allows for "divergences" in the two processes in that Pemba's reasoning favors the decision not to kill Rubens, process p prevails; p trumps indeterministic process d.[15] Now we may argue in this way:

(1) Determinism's (or process p's) elimination of Pemba's alternative possibilities does not in any way influence how Pemba's decision is caused by the indeterministic causal pathway.

(2) If determinism's elimination of Pemba's alternative possibilities does not in any way influence how Pemba's decision is caused by the indeterministic causal pathway, then determinism's elimination of Pemba's alternative possibilities cannot bear on the issue of Pemba's moral responsibility.

(3) If (1) and (2), then determinism's elimination of Pemba's alternative possibilities cannot bear on the issue of Pemba's moral responsibility.

Therefore, (4) determinism's elimination of Pemba's alternative possibilities cannot bear on the issue of Pemba's moral responsibility.

Some may object to this "dual pathway" Frankfurt case in this way: If we agree that libertarians who endorse the principle of alternative possibilities—"PAP defenders"—cannot require that Pemba's deadly decision not be causally determined on the grounds that they would be unduly insisting that it is decided at the outset that PAP is true, then it seems that PAP *rejecters* should be sub-ject to an equivalent dialectical requirement. That is, just as PAP defenders cannot employ any claims (such as the question-begging nature of determinism) that would entail unduly insisting at the outset that PAP is true, neither must PAP *rejecters* employ any claims that entail unduly insisting at the outset that PAP is *false*. So if PAP rejecters want to use the dual pathway case to refute PAP, they cannot simply present the case and then just *assume* or *assert* (without any supporting argument) that Pemba is responsible even though he could not have done otherwise. For if they were to do this, they would be employing a claim (the claim that Pemba can be responsible even though he could not have done otherwise) that entails unduly insisting at the outset that PAP is false.[16]

In reply, I recommend (as intimated previously) that when thinking about Frankfurt examples, the relevant parties initially suspend judgment on whether PAP is true. Maybe characterizing the relevant stance as involving *suspension* of judgment might be misleading. What I have in mind is this. Genuinely curious about PAP, one approaches it without any prior commitment to its truth or falsity. After all, PAP is prima facie plausible. But there are also prima facie reasons to question it. Some of these reasons are historical. For example, many have thought that divine foreknowledge rules out alternative possibilities without compromising responsibility (e.g., Hunt 1999), and there is John Locke's famous locked-door thought experiment (1975 [1690], Bk. II, ch. ii, sec. 10). But there are other reasons, too. So, for instance, we have Frankfurt's set of cases in which although someone threatens an agent to do something, it is not the threat that moves the agent to action but the agent's prior deliberations (Frankfurt 1969). The curious parties may be compatibilists, libertarians, or persons who have not made up their minds on whether or not determinism is compatible with responsibility. So imagine a group of investigators who more or less agree on the broad contours of what is required for responsibility; they concur more or less on a wide set of conditions. But they are genuinely perplexed about PAP, or at least they are unsure about whether PAP is one of these conditions. To make headway, it would be pointless for either party to assume, right at the outset, that PAP is true or false. What would be learned by so doing? Indeed, this sort of stance would be in tension with their original concern regarding PAP. In the interests of progress, they examine a proposed Frankfurt example; imagine it is the dual pathway example that features Pemba.

They then inquire into the following: If one thinks that Pemba is not responsible in the Frankfurt scenario, why is it so? Didn't Pemba act in just the way in which he did in the first scenario? Didn't he satisfy the conditions (with the exception of the condition that he could have done otherwise) regarding which there was consensus? Let's remind ourselves that many (though not all) varieties of libertarianism do not differ from their best compatibilist rival in any substantial respect save requiring nondeterministic causation at appropriate junctures in a decision's etiology.

A libertarian (or a PAP defender) might insist that Pemba could have done otherwise in the scenario without the fail safe mechanism. That's the relevant difference. But then isn't this just tantamount to insisting on the truth of PAP, and isn't this, once again, at odds with the original uncertainty over PAP?

What of the suggestion that the PAP rejecter is in the same sort of predicament as the PAP defender. *Is* she? We can also imagine PAP rejecters and defenders agreeing on a list of intuitively responsibility-subverting factors. For example, they might agree that Pemba is not morally inapt, not relevantly deceived, and not prey to mind-altering psychosurgery. Furthermore, as I stressed earlier, both PAP rejecters and defenders—or, all who are genuinely ambivalent about PAP's credentials—can agree on other requirements of responsibility, such as one's action's or decision's being nondeviantly caused by apt reason states (something several libertarians and compatibilists share), being an ultimate originator, or

OBLIGATION AND ALTERNATIVE POSSIBILITIES

performing an action while nonculpably believing that it is impermissible for one to perform it. The curious investigators now have good prima facie reasons to believe first, that Pemba in Murder-2 *is* seemingly morally responsible: No responsibility-undermining factors appear in the actual sequence leading to his decision, and the more or less uncontroversial conditions previously agreed-upon for responsibility are apparently all satisfied. Furthermore, they seem to have good reason to believe that if Pemba is not responsible, it isn't because he lacks alternatives.

Finally, the investigators might inquire into what might be gained by including the condition that one could have done otherwise into the mix of agreed-upon conditions that, for dialectical purposes, excluded this condition. For example, does this added condition somehow enhance one's responsibility-level control or does it have bearing on some epistemic condition? If it isn't clear, or there are doubts about, whether being able to do otherwise contributes positively, then this result, together with the prior ones of having at least prima facie reasons to believe that Pemba is responsible even though he could not have done otherwise, further supports the view that PAP is suspect.

There is much more to be written on whether or not Frankfurt examples are cogent. I will address these examples further in subsequent chapters. Suffice it to say that these examples give us good, preliminary reason to believe that the principle of alternate possibilities is questionable.

NOTES

1. The terms "resultant luck" and "situational luck" were introduced in Zimmerman 1987.
2. See, e.g., Bernard Williams's case of Jim and the Indians in 1973, 99.
3. I borrow the terms "circumstantial luck" and "constitutive luck" from Nagel 1976.

4. See Zimmerman (2006) for a highly insightful discussion on obligation and luck.
5. These and other pairs of distinctions can be found in, e.g., Zimmerman 2006, 591–94. Fischer and Ravizza (e.g., 1998) coin the terms "guidance control" and "regulative control."
6. Not that I think this is a great improvement; as I've cautioned, "control" itself is ambiguous.
7. For simplicity, hereafter mention of these indices in obligation statements will be assumed but frequently omitted.
8. The exact nature of the requirement depends on how narrowly you want to interpret the "refraining."
9. An extensive defense of "wrong" implies "can" is to be found in Haji 2012a.
10. Personal correspondence with Ryan Herbert. Many thanks to Ryan for this point.
11. I realize that this claim would be rejected by those people—Bernard Williams (1981), for example, and more recently Mark Schroeder (2007)—who think that *pro tanto* reasons in some way depend on desires.
12. Some may, of course, say that if a doctor gives a medicine to a patient that the doctor sincerely and responsibly believes will cure the patient, what the doctor does is not wrong even if it turns out that the medicine unexpectedly kills the patient. Intuitions about these sorts of case can conflict. I'm inclined to claim that the doctor does objective wrong (but is not blameworthy); and that the doctor fulfills his subjective obligation: she does what she believes she has an objective obligation to do. See Zimmerman (2008; 2014) for a sustained defense of the view that one (morally) ought overall to choose that option that is prospectively best. The prospectively best option is the one that it is most reasonable to choose given one's relevant evidence.
13. Here, I set aside concerns of luck. See sec. 7.4.
14. Compare this case with Mele and Robb's (1998; 2003). In Mele and Robb's case, process *p* will cause the relevant agent to make the germane decision unless the agent makes this decision on her own.
15. Fischer (2010) has also developed Frankfurt examples that feature determinism.
16. I thank David Palmer for this objection.

Chapter 3

Obligation Presupposes Alternatives

A Defense

In this chapter I defend the view that a precondition of obligation is the having of alternatives by responding to objections to this view.

3.1 NELKIN ON A NOVEL INTERPRETATION OF OIC

I have advanced considerations for the following principle (Dana Nelkin calls it OICDW).

> OICDW: (i) If S ought to have performed action A, then S could have refrained from performing action A, and (ii) if S ought not to have performed action A, then S could have performed action A. (Nelkin 2011, 102)

Nelkin rejects this principle. She writes:

> Unlike OIC ["ought" implies "can"], OICDW is not generally taken to be axiomatic, and is not often discussed. Nevertheless, one might defend it on grounds of symmetry, as Haji does . . .

Haji takes OICDW to be just as plausible as OIC itself. But he also argues for it on the basis of a kind of presumption of symmetry. If you do something wrong, you have to be able to do otherwise (per OIC), and if you do something obligatory, it must be the case that you should be able to do otherwise in such a case, too. Obligation and wrongness are members of the same deontic family, and actions falling into each category ought to meet this same requirement. As a supporting analogy, he points to praise and blame, which, he argues, should also be treated symmetrically when it comes to the ability to do otherwise ... I do not find this reasoning convincing, however. The rational abilities view [to be outlined below] is itself a view according to which praiseworthy and blameworthy actions do not *both* require the ability to do otherwise. The asymmetry between praiseworthy and blameworthy actions ... *simply falls out of* a unified and natural account of responsible action. The initial presumption of symmetry seems overridden by this fact. And being members of the same deontic family, as wrongness and obligatoriness are, does not in itself seem to constitute good reason to believe they must *both* satisfy the particular condition of being able to do otherwise. Thus, I conclude that OICDW is insufficiently motivated. (2011, 102–03)

Consider, first, Nelkin's proposal that I argue for OICDW on the basis of a kind of presumption of symmetry. "If you do something wrong, you have to be able to do otherwise (per OIC), and if you do something obligatory, it must be the case that you should be able to do otherwise in such a case, too. Obligation and wrongness are members of the same deontic family, and actions falling into each category ought to meet this same requirement" (Nelkin 2011, 103). A crucial premise in my argument for the view that it is morally obligatory for one to do something only if one could have done otherwise appeals to the "impermissibility" implies "can" principle (*Impermissible/Can*). Remember the crux of the argument: If one ought not to do something, it is impermissible for one to do it. If it is impermissible for one to do something, one can do it (*Impermissible/ Can*). So if one ought not to do something, then one can do it. As the previous discussion should make evident, I argue for *Impermissible/ Can* by calling on an analysis of the concept of obligation, the nature of reasons, and principle *Impermissibility/Permissible Possibility*. Elsewhere (2012a), I have defended *Impermissibility/Can* against objections. I concede that obligation, permissibility, and impermissibility are symmetric in this fashion: Each presupposes that we have ("deontic-relevant") control or freedom. I presume this is *not* controversial. I have further conceded that one may propose that the control impermissibility requires differs significantly from the control obligation requires. Specifically, the challenge would be that whereas "ought" implies "can," "impermissibility" does not, although both obligation and impermissibility do require control. Presumably, a partisan of this asymmetric view would support it with reasons. I will be happy to attempt to evaluate these reasons when I see them.

Worth emphasis, too, is the following. Nelkin accepts OIC. She concurs that obligation requires control, and the basic control it requires is the ability (and opportunity) to do whatever one is obligated to do or refrain from doing. But if one is entitled to presume that obligation requires this sort of control (in the absence of good reason to believe otherwise), why is one not also entitled to presume that impermissibility requires this sort of control (again, in the absence of sound reason to believe otherwise)?

Consider, next, Nelkin's assertion that as "a supporting analogy . . . [Haji] points to praise and blame, which, he argues, should also be treated symmetrically when it comes to the ability to do otherwise . . . I do not find this reasoning convincing, however.

The rational abilities view is itself a view according to which praise-worthy and blameworthy actions do not *both* require the ability to do otherwise. The asymmetry between praiseworthy and blame-worthy actions . . . *simply falls out of* a unified and natural account of responsible action. The initial presumption of symmetry [that both obligation and impermissibility entail avoidability] seems overridden by this fact" (2011, 103). Three comments are in order. First, Nelkin ventures that the asymmetry between praiseworthy and blameworthy actions simply "falls out" of a unified and natu-ral account of responsible action. Similarly, my position is that the symmetry between obligation and permissibility—each entails "can"—is validated by a powerful analysis of moral obligation. Furthermore, there is no reason to believe that impermissibility differs from obligation and permissibility in this respect. Indeed, I have endorsed the following analysis of obligation. A person, S, morally ought, as of t, to see to the occurrence of a state of affairs, p, if and only if there is a world, w, accessible to S at t in which S brings about p, there is a world, w^*, accessible to S at t in which S refrains from bringing about p, and it is not the case that S refrains from bringing about p in any accessible world as good as or better than w.[1] The analyses of permissibility and impermissibility share the first two clauses of this analysis. On my view, then, there is a real sense in which the symmetry in control requirements for obliga-tion, permissibility, and impermissibility "falls out" of a formidable account of moral obligation. Second, it is worth stressing yet again that when I argue for the relevant symmetry—each of "obligation," "permissibility," and "impermissibility" entail "can"—I am careful to insist on the following: I propose that *unless there is good reason to believe otherwise*, if "obligation" and "permissibility" entail "can," "impermissibility" implies "can" as well. Should one have such reasons, these reasons should have their day in the court of ratio-nal scrutiny. Third, regarding the "supporting analogy" to which

I appeal—the control that praiseworthiness demands is of the same sort that blameworthiness does barring convincing rationales to believe otherwise—I have reservations about the reasons Nelkin advances to support her position that praiseworthiness and blameworthiness have different control requirements. I want to address this third point in some detail. To do so, a summary of Nelkin's rational abilities view of responsibility will be helpful.

The rational abilities view entails that whereas blameworthiness requires that one could have done otherwise, praiseworthiness does not. This asymmetry thesis stands opposed to what appropriate Frankfurt examples seemingly show: Blameworthiness and praiseworthiness are symmetric insofar as neither requires one's having alternative possibilities. As a prelude to introducing the rational abilities view, consider this pair of cases that John Fischer and Mark Ravizza develop. In *Hero* Martha is walking along a beach when she sees a child struggling in the water. Quickly, she deliberates about the matter and rescues the child. Had she even begun to think about not saving the child, she would have been overwhelmed by literally irresistible guilt feelings that would have caused her to jump into the water and save the child anyway (1992a, 76). Intuitively, Martha is morally responsible for saving the child even though she could not have done otherwise. In *Villain*, Joe pushes a child off a pier as a result of his own deliberations. Had Joe displayed the relevant, involuntary neurophysiological sign for not carrying out his original plan of drowning the child, some counterfactual intervener, Max, would have ensured that Joe would not have refrained from pushing the child. But Joe acts on his own, in the absence of any intervention from Max. Intuitively, he is blameworthy although he could not have done otherwise (1992a, 77). Fischer and Ravizza conclude that praiseworthiness and blameworthiness are symmetric with respect to not requiring alternative possibilities. Dub this conclusion *Symmetry*.

David Widerker (1991), Derk Pereboom (2014, 142), David Copp (1997; 2003), and most recently, Nelkin (2011) have given an interesting argument against *Symmetry*. Here is Nelkin's version of the argument regarding the blameworthiness component of *Symmetry*:

(1) If S is blameworthy for having performed action, *a*, then S ought not to have performed action *a*.

But putting that together with OIC [the "ought" implies "can" principle]—or, strictly, the second part of it:

(2) If S ought not to have performed an action *a*, then S could have refrained from performing action *a* yields PAP-Blame:

(3) PAP-Blame: A person is morally blameworthy for what he has done only if he could have done otherwise.

For if S is blameworthy for having performed action *a*, then S could have refrained from doing what she in fact did; or, in other words, she could have done otherwise. (I will call this piece of reasoning from (1) and (2) to Pap-Blame "the Derivation"). (2011, 100–01)[2]

Indeed, Nelkin offers two defenses of the principle that blameworthiness requires alternatives. One, the *Derivation*, is predicated on the principle that blameworthiness requires impermissibility:

Blameworthiness/Impermissibility: (Necessarily) one is blameworthy for doing something only if it is impermissible for one to do this thing.

The other consists in arguing, contrary to Fischer and Ravizza, that although Joe in *Villain* is blameworthy for pushing the child to her death, he could have done otherwise. This second defense invokes a novel interpretation of *Kant's Law*.

Nelkin's disagreement with *Symmetry* ultimately derives from her rational abilities view of moral responsibility: "People are responsible when they act with the ability to do the right thing for the right reasons, or a good thing for good reasons" (2008, 497). Nelkin speaks of praiseworthiness for doing "*the* right thing" for *the* right reasons. "*The* right thing" usually means the *obligatory* thing. (If there is a unique permissible thing, it is obligatory.) However, it is possible that no options are obligatory but some are permissible and others impermissible. So maybe we should think about the rational abilities view in this way: First, in some situations, if there is a unique permissible option, then it is obligatory for the relevant agent. In such situations, if the agent does not have the ability to perform this option for the right reasons, then she would not be responsible for performing any of the options. The stress on "the right reasons" seems significant; one can do something obligatory for good ("the right") or bad reasons. If OIC is true, a situation in which one cannot do the obligatory thing for the right reasons is not the impossible one in which one cannot do the thing it is obligatory for one to do; rather, it's one in which, for some reason, one can do the obligatory thing but not *for the right reasons* whatever these turn out to be. Second, in other situations no options are obligatory, but some are permissible. In such situations, if the agent does not have the ability to perform any of the permissible options for right reasons (again, whatever these are), then she would not be responsible for performing any one of the options.

Regarding the first sort of situation in which there is an option that is obligatory, suppose you do something that it is impermissible for you to do. The rational abilities view implies that you are morally responsible—blameworthy—for performing this impermissible option only if you could have done the obligatory thing (for the right reasons). Regarding the second sort of situation in which no option is obligatory but some are permissible, again suppose you do something that it is impermissible for you to do. The rational abilities view has it that you are blameworthy for doing this thing only if you could have done something it was permissible for you to do (for the right reasons). So the rational abilities view underwrites the following striking asymmetry.

> *Asymmetry*: Whereas one can be praiseworthy for doing something despite not having alternatives, one cannot be blameworthy without having alternatives.[3]

As Nelkin comments, the "asymmetry between praiseworthy and blameworthy actions, while perhaps initially unexpected, *simply falls out of* a unified and natural account of responsible action" (the rational abilities account) (2011, 103).

Examples such as the following initially motivate and illustrate the asymmetry thesis:

> Suppose that you have promised to help a friend during a difficult time, and that following through is the right thing to do. If you follow through on your promise because you made the promise and value helping your friend, then you have the ability to do the right thing for the right reasons, and thereby meet the relevant condition for responsibility. If, on the other hand, you fail to keep your promise, then whether you are responsible for your actions depends on whether you have the ability to do what you fail to do. So in the case in which you do the right thing for the right reasons, no ability to do otherwise is required; in the case in which you do not do the right thing for the right reasons, such an ability is required. (2008, 499)
>
> Consider a woman [Rosa] who jumps into the waves in order to save a drowning child, keenly focused on the need of

the child and the great good of her life that is at stake. Now even if she couldn't have done otherwise, she is responsible and praiseworthy. . . . On the other hand, if someone does not respond to relevant reasons, for example, by not jumping in to save the child) then whether she is responsible or not will depend on whether she could have done otherwise. If she could not have done otherwise, she lacks the relevant ability, and so is not responsible. In short, the ability to do otherwise functions in an asymmetric way—you need it if you act badly, but not if you act well. (2008, 501–02)

These pairs of examples suggest two different versions of the asymmetry thesis.

Asymmetry-1: To be morally responsible—blameworthy— for overall bad actions, one must be able to do otherwise, but this ability is not required to be responsible—praiseworthy—for overall good actions.

Asymmetry-2: To be morally responsible—blameworthy— for impermissible actions, one must be able to do otherwise, but this ability is not required to be responsible—praiseworthy—for permissible actions.

Fischer and Ravizza's *Hero* and *Villain* attempt to discredit *Asymmetry-1*. I confine discussion primarily to the blameworthiness part of more general *Asymmetry*, the thesis that blameworthiness for an action requires that one could have refrained from doing it, or blameworthiness for an intentional omission requires that one could have done what one omitted to do. Nelkin gives two primary rationales for the view that unlike praiseworthiness, blameworthiness does require alternative possibilities, her positive defense that calls upon the blameworthiness requires impermissibility principle (*Blameworthiness/Impermissibility*), and her negative defense that invokes a novel conception of *Kant's Law* (alternatively, OIC). I discuss the latter now and give reasons to reject *Blameworthiness/Impermissibility* later.

Nelkin concedes that what Joe does in *Villain* is "inevitable," so there is a sense in which Joe (just like Martha in *Hero*) does not have the ability to do otherwise. She explains that in "this sense, having an ability to do X is precluded when it is inevitable that the agent will not do X (call this the 'inevitability-undermining' sense)" (2011, 66). However, she proposes that there is another sense, the interference-free capacity sense, in which both Joe and Martha have the ability to do otherwise. According to this view of ability, an agent has an ability to X if (i) the agent possesses the capacities, skills, talents, knowledge, and so on which are necessary for X-ing, and (ii) nothing interferes with or prevents the exercise of the relevant capacities, skills, talents, and so on (2011, 66). Regarding Fischer and Ravizza's challenge from Frankfurt examples to the rational abilities view, Nelkin comments:

> Fischer and Ravizza recognize that the success of their argument hinges on what notion of "ability" is at stake. Yet, they argue, even on Wolf's understanding of "ability", Joe lacks the ability to do otherwise "for were he to try to [do the right thing for the right reason], Max's device would prevent his exercising the relevant capacities, skills, etc., required to refrain from pushing the child into the water" (1992a, p. 378, n. 9). I believe that this is a misreading of Wolf's characterization. What is needed to remove one's ability to do something in the relevant sense (call it the "interference-free capacity") is either the removal of the capacities, talents, skills, and so on (the presence of which is not in dispute) or the actual interference with or prevention of the exercise of those capacities.

The fact that Max's device *would* interfere or prevent such an exercise in counterfactual circumstances does not entail *actual* interference or prevention. For this reason, Fischer and Ravizza's Frankfurt-style case does not constitute a decisive objection to the asymmetry of the rational abilities view. (2011, 66–67)

Nelkin seems to concede that with an ever vigilant, properly responsive counterfactual intervener on the scene (Max does not, for instance, fall asleep on the job, he does not lose his resolve to ensure that Joe kills the child, and so forth), barring, for example, sudden death, Joe cannot do otherwise, in the sense of being able to *bring about* something other than what he does, in his circumstances. With Max poised to interfere were Joe to display the apt involuntary sign, if Joe could have brought about something else instead, it would not be true that what Joe does is "inevitable." But Nelkin also insists that in the interference-free ability sense of "can," Joe *can* do otherwise. Furthermore, she suggests that Joe has this ability in his circumstances because what is needed to remove this ability is "either the removal of the capacities, talents, skills, and so on," things a mere counterfactual intervener does *not* remove, or "the [actual] interference with or prevention of the exercise of those capacities" (2011, 66); again, something absent in a Frankfurt case. At the end of the last quoted passage, Nelkin emphasizes that the "fact that Max's device *would* interfere or prevent such an exercise in counterfactual circumstances does not entail *actual* interference or prevention" (2011, 66).

Think of Joe's predicament in this way: Assume that were the counterfactual intervener, Max, not around, Joe's two salient alternatives would be the following:

a1: Push the child off the pier.
a2: Comfort the child.

Nelkin is of the mind that in the interference-free sense of "ability," Joe can do otherwise: He has the capacities, skills, knowledge, and so forth to do a2, and nothing actually prevents him from doing something else in his Frankfurt situation (2011, 67). She affirms that the interference-free capacity is not a general capacity, such as having the general capacity to type on a desert island when one has no keyboard, for such a capacity is "insufficient for the kind of ability that is needed in order to be responsible" (2011, 67). She writes:

> Even in the Frankfurt-style cases, it seems that the protagonists have more than this; they have the skills, talents, and knowledge, but they also have unimpeded use of their bodies and uncluttered piers in their sights. The circumstances provide all that they might need to act, but for a *counterfactual* intervener. That is, the circumstances are conducive for their acting, except that something *would* intervene in some way, on some sign or other. The idea of being interference-free that I prefer, then, is that nothing is actually preventing you from acting otherwise (though it *would* under different circumstances). (2011, 67)

Furthermore, she suggests that Joe does have an alternative "in a sense precluded by Frankfurt-style cases" (2011, 70, 115). Joe has what we may call a "weak" alternative. Nelkin needs this to sustain her view that blameworthiness requires alternatives:

> One might worry that in the interference-free sense of ability, one can have the ability to do otherwise while lacking any genuine alternatives; thus, the intuitively appealing idea that alternatives are necessary for blameworthiness would fail to be captured if the interference-free sense of ability is used ... One way to reply to this challenge is to suggest a corresponding

sense of "alternative" such that if one has an interference-free capacity, one does have an alternative. (2011, 69–70)

Indeed, Nelkin proposes that "can" (or its cognates) in OIC and in PAP-Blame (the principle that persons are blameworthy for what they have done only if they could have done otherwise) be interpreted in the interference-free sense (2011, 115).

One may concur that an agent in a Frankfurt situation may well have the sort of ability that Nelkin identifies, an ability that is not a mere general ability but something more nuanced and full-bodied.[4] It is, however, significant that there is no scenario in which Joe is able to exercise such an ability *as long as an ever vigilant counterfactual intervener remains in the scenario.*

Reflecting on Nelkin's strategy, I am reminded about one aspect of the dispute between some compatibilists and incompatibilists regarding determinism and free action. Incompatibilists of the relevant sort insist that free action requires that, given exactly the same past and the laws, the agent be able to do otherwise, something they claim determinism precludes.[5] They may insist, furthermore, that determinism does not in any way affect the agent's properties—perhaps intrinsic properties—whatever these are, that "ground" the agent's capacities to do otherwise. Nonetheless, agents cannot do otherwise, in the specified sense, if determinism is true. The notion of "can" (or "cannot") in this incompatibilist claim may be thought of as being relatively "strong." These incompatibilists would agree with compatibilists who believe that free action requires that agents be able to do otherwise that, for instance, if determinism is true, it may well be that an agent would do otherwise if the past or the laws were different. The notion of "can" these compatibilists employ is comparatively "weak." When Nelkin proposes that Joe has an alternative "in a sense precluded by Frankfurt-style cases (2011, 70, 115)," one may hark back to the incompatibilist's

strong "can": Like determinism (according to these incompatibilists), the Frankfurt setup precludes Joe from bringing about something other than what he does bring about, although we may concur
that in some weaker sense of "can" or (its cognates), Joe could have
done otherwise.

To assess this interesting strategy to undermine Frankfurt
examples, I focus primarily on Nelkin's recommendation that "can"
in OIC be interpreted in the interference-free sense (2011, 115).
Assuming that OIC is not in question, at the heart of one battle
concerning obligation is this issue. Does obligation (or impermissibility) require Nelkin's weak alternatives or yet more robust alternatives? Let "S IF-can do A" express the proposition that S can do
A in the interference-free sense of "can." Remember, S IF-can do
A does *not* entail S can bring about A. (In *Villain*, Joe IF-can comfort the child even though he cannot bring it about that he comforts
the child.) If we let "S O-can do A" stand for the proposition that
S can do A in the ordinary ability and opportunity sense of "can"
that entails that S can bring about A, then S IF-can do A does not
entail S O-can do A. Construing "can" as "IF-can," OIC now says:

New-OIC: If S morally ought to do A, then S IF-can do A; and if
S morally ought not to do A, then S IF-can refrain from doing A.
(Temporal indices have been omitted.)

For ease of exposition, let "Nelkin's Theory" stand for some
normative theory concerning obligation that, in conjunction with
relevant facts, implies that Joe ought to comfort the child (he ought
to do a2) in his Frankfurt situation even though he cannot bring
about a2. We may suppose that advocates of Nelkin's Theory accept
New-OIC because it is entailed by this theory. Again, I proceed in
this way merely for convenience; I do not mean to saddle Nelkin
with what may be challenged to be an implausible normative theory.

To evaluate whether obligation requires only weak or more robust alternatives, I advance four considerations. First, Nelkin's Theory has counterintuitive results. Consider a variation of the following case introduced in the first chapter. Ted has come down with a disease. Doc's best course of treatment is to give two consecutive doses of medicine A. The next best course of treatment is to give two consecutive doses of medicine B. Anything else leads to death (Feldman 1986, 11–12). Suppose treatment is to begin on Monday. Intuitively, Doc ought to give A on Monday and then again on Tuesday. Augment the case with a counterfactual intervener who is hell-bent on Doc's giving two consecutive doses of B. Even if he wanted to, Doc couldn't give A on Monday followed by A on Tuesday. Assume that, being morally imperfect, Doc freely gives B on Monday (in the sense of "free"—whatever it precisely is—in which it is true that Joe in *Villain* freely pushes the child off the pier). If Nelkin's Theory is true, as of Sunday Doc *ought* to give two consecutive doses of A (even though he O-can't give A—he can't give A in the ordinary ability and opportunity sense of "can"—on Monday or on Tuesday). This is (partly) because on Sunday Doc has the (weak) alternative of giving A on Monday and what we may call the "strong" alternative of giving B on Monday. This alternative is strong because Doc can *bring about* his giving B on Monday. Briefly, if Nelkin's Theory is true, as of Sunday, it is obligatory for Doc to give A on Monday because Doc has both the weak alternative to give A on Monday (he IF-can give A on Monday) and the strong alternative to give B on Monday, and the former alternative is overall better than the latter in the sense that if it were performed—if Doc could bring about his giving A on Monday—the world would be overall better. But if Doc ought to give A on Monday, then it is *impermissible* for him to do anything else. So on Monday, it is impermissible for him to give B on Monday even though he O-can give B on Monday. I suspect many would find this result hard to swallow.

Given that Doc cannot bring it about that he gives A on Monday (or on Tuesday), as of Monday in all the best worlds accessible to him—worlds he can make actual—he gives two consecutive doses of B. In short, Doc can *cure* the patient only by first giving B on Monday; so how can any plausible moral theory yield the result that as of Monday, it is *morally forbidden* for Doc to give B on Monday *when he O-cannot give any other medicine on Monday*?

Elaborating, suppose skeptics of one bent of the result that it is morally impermissible for Doc to give B on Monday accept OIC but resist the view that one's having an obligation to do something entails one's being able both to bring *and* to refrain from bringing it about; they resist the view that obligation requires "two-way" control. Envision these skeptics as accepting *MO-1*:

> *MO-1*: A person, *S*, morally ought, as of *t*, to see to the occurrence of a state of affairs, *p*, if and only if there is a world, *w*, accessible to *S* at *t* in which *S* brings about *p*, and it is not the case that *S* refrains from bringing about *p* in any accessible world as good as or better than *w*. (Roughly, if there's a world accessible to you in which you do something, and there is no as good or better world accessible to you in which you refrain from doing this thing, then you ought to do this thing.)

MO-1 entails OIC. Opposed to Nelkin, such skeptics will claim that since Doc (in his Frankfurt situation) O-cannot bring about his giving A to Ted either on Monday or Tuesday, his giving A is simply not an option in his alternative set as of the time treatment begins. But as of this time, in all the best worlds accessible to him, Doc gives B on Monday; hence he *ought* to give B on Monday. If Nelkin's Theory, however, is true, he ought *not* to give B on Monday. Driving what these skeptics see as this problematic result is *New-OIC*.

Next, suppose skeptics of another bent accept the view that one cannot have an obligation to do something unless both one can do and one can refrain from doing it. Think of these skeptics as accepting *MO-2*:

> *MO-2*: A person, *S*, morally ought, as of *t*, to see to the occurrence of a state of affairs, *p*, if and only if there is a world, *w*, accessible to *S* at *t* in which *S* brings about *p*, there is a world, w^*, accessible to *S* at *t* in which *S* refrains from bringing about *p*, and it is not the case that *S* refrains from bringing about *p* in any accessible world as good as or better than *w*.

In addition to accepting *MO-2* they also accept OIC (as *MO-2* entails OIC), and they reject the view that the alternatives obligation requires are Nelkin's weak alternatives. Then, once again, these others will claim that it's false that as of the time treatment begins, it is *impermissible* for Doc to give B. Of course, they would also claim that, as of this time, it is false that it is obligatory or permissible, for Doc to give B; rather, in their estimation, it is amoral for Doc to give B on Monday; *Doc's giving B* lacks any of the primary morally deontic statuses of *being permissible, being impermissible,* or *being obligatory.*

How do we adjudicate among these three conflicting results or intuitions: As of Monday, it is impermissible for Doc to give B (on Monday), or it is obligatory for Doc to give B, or it is amoral for Doc to give B? The answer is not obvious.[6] I share with the position of the skeptics who believe that Doc ought to give B on Monday, the view that, as of a time, if one O-cannot perform an action (even if, at that time, one IF-can perform it), that action is not in one's alternative set. Given her commitment to *New-OIC*, Nelkin may simply rejoin that, in the dialectical context, accepting this view is question-begging. So maybe there is no winner here. Still, the example highlights the crucial point that Nelkin's position that as of Monday, Doc ought to give A on Monday is highly contentious.

Second, moving beyond intuition, if Nelkin's Theory is true, then Joe ought (in his Frankfurt situation) to comfort the child—to bring about a2—even though he cannot bring about a2 (or so assume). Suppose MO-2 is true. Then it is false that Joe ought to bring about a2. If we accept MO-2 we should (rationally) reject Nelkin's Theory, and vice versa. There are strong reasons to accept MO-2 and, thus, OIC as MO-2 validates OIC: MO-2 is a powerful analysis of the concept of moral obligation. For example, it very neatly solves many deontic puzzles, and with (a fairly rich set of) amendments, it can accommodate categories such as the supererogatory and the suberogatory (see, e.g., Feldman 1990; Zimmerman 1996; McNamara 1996a; 2011b; Hebert n.d.). What reasons are there to accept New-OIC, an implicate of Nelkin's Theory? As far as I can discern, Nelkin's primary rationale seems to be that, given the derivation, blameworthiness requires alternatives, and in his Frankfurt predicament, Joe is blameworthy for pushing the child to her death. However, with Max on the watch Joe cannot bring about anything other than pushing the child. So, he must have alternatives of a different sort, weak alternatives. I believe the reasons that favor OIC—OIC's being entailed by MO-2—are more compelling than those that favor Nelkin's rationale for New-OIC.

Third, I previously said that direct obligations are restricted to intentional actions one can perform; not so with indirect obligations (Zimmerman 2006, 595, 602; 2008, 90–91, 149–50). Again, suppose Ted has a direct obligation to turn on the furnace. He cannot, however, turn it on without activating the relevant mechanisms within of which he has no knowledge; so he (indirectly) ought to activate these mechanisms. This indirect obligation is one that, in his circumstances, he O-can perform but not intentionally.

Now, OIC partisans might argue as follows: (1) Necessarily, if one has a direct obligation to do A, then one O-can intentionally do A. (2) Necessarily, if one O-can intentionally do A, then one can bring about A. (3) Therefore, necessarily, if one has a direct obligation to do A, then one can bring about A. But if Nelkin's Theory is true, it may be that one cannot bring about A (for example, Joe cannot bring about his comforting the child) even though one may have a direct obligation to do A. So Nelkin's Theory is incompatible with (1).

Nelkin might take issue with (1), insisting that all she requires is (1*): Necessarily, if one has a direct obligation to do A, then one IF-can intentionally do A. (2) should then be replaced with (2*): Necessarily, if one IF-can intentionally do A, then one IF-can do A. If one grants, as one should, that in *Villain,* Joe IF-can comfort the child, then one should also grant that Joe IF-can *intentionally* comfort the child. As long as nothing removes Joe's relevant capacities, and nothing actually prevents Joe from exercising these capacities, he IF-can intentionally comfort the child. Here, however, the following should be borne in mind. There is no relevant scenario that includes a diligent counterfactual intervener in which Joe brings about his comforting the child. OIC partisans might rejoin that *one's being able intentionally to do A* entails *one's being able to bring about A*, and not merely *one's being IF-able to do A*. They may invoke these sorts of examples to marshal support for their view: In *Scene-1*, a child is drowning. You O-can easily rescue her. Assume that you have a direct obligation to do so. *Scene-2* is just like the former except that, unbeknown to you, there is a diver in the water between you and the child who will kill you if you enter the water. Proponents of OIC will say that as of the time you have not entered the water and the diver is keeping watch, you have no obligation to save the child (although you may think you have such an obligation). In contrast, presumably, proponents of *New-OIC* will claim that as of this time, you do have a direct obligation to save the child: although as of this time you O-cannot intentionally save the child, you IF-can intentionally save the child. Again, Nelkin may simply dig in her heels and deny that having a direct obligation to do something entails being able to bring it about. So there may be no clear winner here either.

Fourth, and finally, suppose Sally ought to take the garbage to the dump (she ought to do D). She can't do so unless she first loads the truck with the garbage. The prerequisites principle (*Prerequisites*) says that if you ought to do something, A, and you can't do A without doing B because B is a necessary prerequisite to doing A, then you ought to do B too (see, e.g., Feldman 1986, 41–42; Zimmerman 1996, 73; 2014, 52–56).[7] *Prerequisites* entails (together with the pertinent facts) that Sally ought to load the truck—she ought to do L—first. Suppose, at this earlier time, she doesn't want to do L; she much rather mix paint, and she does so. Yet again, a pesky counterfactual intervener ensures that she cannot but mix paint. Still, she IF-can (but not O-can) do L. So, we may suppose that if Nelkin's Theory is true, then Sally ought to do L even though she cannot bring about L—she O-cannot do L. Do we have violation of the prerequisites principle?

Assume that as of 9:00 Sally ought to do D (go to the dump) at 11:00, and given *Prerequisites*, as of 9:00 she ought to do L (load the truck) at 10:00. It follows that as of 9:00, Sally can do D at 11:00, and as of 9:00 Sally can do L at 10:00. Since "can" is ambiguous between "O-can" and "IF-can," distinguish four versions of *Prerequisites* (VP1, VP2, VP3, and VP4). Each differs from the others by whether it entails one of P1, P2, P3, or P4 respectively:

P1: As of 9:00, S O-can do D at 11:00; and as of 9:00 S IF-can do L at 10:00.

P2: As of 9:00, S O-can do D at 11:00; and as of 9:00 S O-can do L at 10:00.

P3: As of 9:00, S IF-can do D at 11:00; and as of 9:00 S O-can do L at 10:00.

P4: As of 9:00, S IF-can do D at 11:00; and as of 9:00 S IF-can do L at 10:00.

Which version of *Prerequisites* does the example presuppose? Not P1 because it is false that Sally O-can do D at 11:00. We may suppose that because of the counterfactual intervener, as of 9:00, it's false that she O-can do L at 10:00. If Sally cannot bring about L earlier, and L is a necessary prerequisite to doing D, then it's false that she O-can do D. Since VP1 entails P1, and P1 is false, VP1 is false too. Not P2 because it's false that as of 9:00 Sally O-can do L at 10:00. She IF-can do L at 10:00, but it's not true that she O-can do L at 10:00.

Not P3 because it's false that as of 9:00 Sally O-can do L at 10:00. Not P4 because it's false that as of 9:00, Sally IF-can do D at 11:00. Why? As long as the counterfactual intervener is on the watch, there is no time between 9:00 and 11:00 at which Sally brings about the truck's being loaded. But if this is so, then at any time between 9:00 and 11:00, at this time, there *is* something that actually prevents her from exercising her capacity to take the loaded truck to the dump—the truck's not being loaded. We should, consequently, conclude that Nelkin's Theory is incompatible with *Prerequisites*.

Some might take these consequences of *New-OIC* to be acceptable, or if they see them as "costs," may conclude that the advantages of *New-OIC* outweigh these costs. Others might judge that these consequences should give us reason to reject *New-OIC*. Minimally, we are entitled to conclude that Nelkin's strategy to undermine Frankfurt examples is highly controversial.

Prior to leaving this section on Nelkin, let's revisit the *Derivation*:

(1) If S is blameworthy for doing A, then S ought not to do A.

(2) If S ought not to do A, then S can refrain from doing A.

(3) Therefore, if S is blameworthy for doing A, then S can refrain from doing A.

(2) is ambiguous between:

(2a) If S ought not to do A, then S can bring it about that S not do A,

and

(2b) If S ought not to do A, then S IF-can refrain from doing A, that is, S can in the interference-free sense of "can," refrain from doing A. Keep in mind that in this sense of "can," *S can refrain from doing A* does not entail *S can bring it about that S not do A*.

Presumably, in Nelkin's view "can" in both (2) and (3) are to be interpreted in the interference-free sense of "can." The conclusion, (3), does not entail that blameworthiness requires alternatives in that the agent has the ability to *bring about* something other than what she does.

This result has some interesting consequences. First, contrary to appearances, there is no real disagreement between Nelkin and myself or others like Fischer and Ravizza who argue that blameworthiness does not require that one could have done otherwise in the sense that one could have brought about an alternative. (That isn't to deny that there may be other disagreements.) Second, again against initial impressions, there *is* a substantive difference between Nelkin and myself over whether impermissibility, for example, requires that one could have brought about something other than what one brought about. I affirm this principle whereas, it appears, Nelkin is not committed to it. She is bound only by the condition that if it is impermissible for one to do something, then one IF-can refrain from doing it; but *one IF-can refrain from doing something* does not entail *one has the ability to bring about some alternative instead.*

Finally, the two-path Frankfurt example I advanced in the previous chapter appears to be one in which Pemba is morally responsible for deciding to kill Rubens by a certain time even though, it seems, he IF-cannot refrain from so deciding.

3.2 AN ARGUMENT FROM FRANKFURT EXAMPLES

Frankfurt examples nicely serve to expose a tension between popular accounts of two requirements of blameworthiness, its control requirement and its moral requirement if it is true, as partisans of these examples would have us believe, that whatever its other features, the account of the control that blameworthiness presupposes is a one-way account; having alternatives is not a precondition of blameworthiness. We have already introduced the relevant account of the moral requirement:

> *Blameworthiness/Impermissibility*: Necessarily, one is morally blameworthy for something (for example, an overt action) only if it is impermissible for one to do it.

Reverting to our Frankfurt example, *Theft*, we may assume that in Stage 1, although Augustine steals the pears, he could have refrained from stealing them. We may also reasonably assume that in this stage it is impermissible for him to steal the pears. In Stage 2, however, Augustine cannot but steal the pears. Since impermissibility requires avoidability, it is false that in Stage 2 it is impermissible for Augustine to steal the pears. Suppose, now, that blameworthiness requires impermissibility. Then we can infer that in Stage 2 it is false that Augustine is blameworthy for stealing the pears. So, it may be proposed, it cannot both be the case that the principle of alternate possibilities concerning blameworthiness (PAP-Blame)—persons are morally blameworthy for what they have done only if they could have done otherwise—is false, and the principle that blameworthiness requires impermissibility is true. A one-way account of control for moral responsibility suggested by Frankfurt examples, whatever it precisely amounts to, appears to conflict with the moral requirement of blameworthiness if this requirement entails that a precondition of blameworthiness is impermissibility.

3.2.1 *Frankfurt Examples and* Kant's Law

One may, however, be convinced both that Frankfurt examples impugn PAP-Blame and *Blameworthiness/Impermissibility* is true. So how could one reasonably renounce the former without giving up the latter? One strategy is to jettison *Kant's Law*. It is the principle that "ought not" is equivalent to "impermissible" (*Equivalence*) together with *Kant's Law* that generates the result that impermissibility requires avoidability (if it is impermissible for one to do something, one ought not to do it [from *Equivalence*)]; if one ought not to do something, one can refrain from doing it [from *Kant's Law*]; so, if it is impermissible for one to do something, one can refrain from doing it). Renounce *Kant's Law* and this result is blocked. Indeed, some might propose that if Frankfurt examples undermine PAP-Blame, they should undermine *Kant's Law* as well. At least intuitively, even in Stage 2, it is impermissible for Augustine to steal the pears. As this is so, and the conjunction of *Equivalence* and *Kant's Law* entails that impermissibility requires avoidability, assuming *Equivalence* is unassailable, the culprit is *Kant's Law*.

However, it is not clear that this way of rejecting the principle that impermissibility (or obligation) requires avoidability is cogent. Notice that *Kant's Law* (if one ought to do something, one can do it), a power or control principle, is pertinently like the following highly credible control principle.

Blameworthiness/Control: One is blameworthy (or, more generally morally responsible) for performing an action only if one can perform it.

This principle simply affirms the connection between control and blameworthiness (or moral responsibility). It expresses the widely held and plausible view that one is morally responsible for an action only if one has control regarding it. Notably, Frankfurt examples do not undermine this principle. The principle of alternate possibilities regarding blameworthiness:

PAP-Blame: One is morally blameworthy for having done something only if one could have done otherwise,

is a conjunction of *Blameworthiness/Control* and

Action: One can perform an action only if one can refrain from performing it (Zimmerman 1996, 86).

It is *Action* that provides the alleged link between blameworthiness and alternative possibilities. However, Frankfurt examples undermine *Action*.

If Frankfurt examples leave unscathed the principle that blameworthiness requires control (*Blameworthiness/Control*), they should leave unscathed the principle that obligation requires control (*Kant's Law*) or that impermissibility requires control:

Impermissibility/Control: It is impermissible for one to do something only if one can do it.

The link between obligation and alternative possibilities is provided not by *Action* but by *Impermissibility/Control* and *Equivalence*. Bear in mind the apt argument: If one ought not to do something, it is impermissible for one to do it; if it is impermissible for one to do something, one can do it; therefore, if one ought not to do something, one can do it. Together with the principle that if one ought not to do something, one can refrain from doing it, we derive the principle that obligation requires alternatives. Just as Frankfurt examples do not impugn the principle that impermissibility (or obligation) requires control, so they do not impugn *Equivalence*.

There is, then, this significant difference between *PAP-Blame* and the principle that obligation requires alternatives: Regarding the former, essential to the link between blameworthiness and alternative possibilities is principle *Action*, but *Action* is false as Frankfurt examples confirm. Regarding the latter, essential to the link between obligation and alternative possibilities are *Impermissibility/Control* and *Equivalence* (and not *Action*). Frankfurt examples threaten neither of these principles. Or, minimally, if one grants that these examples leave untouched the principle that blameworthiness requires control, one should also grant that they leave untouched the principle that impermissibility (or obligation) requires control. Moreover, it is implausible to suppose that Frankfurt examples undermine *Equivalence*.

3.2.2 *Frankfurt Examples and Action*

Helen Steward, however, has recently questioned whether Frankfurt examples do indeed impugn *Action*, the principle that says that (necessarily) if something is an action for one, then one can refrain from performing it. To appreciate why she rejects this principle, an outline of some of her views on agency and action will be helpful.

In her engaging book (2012), Steward proposes that one cannot be morally responsible for anything (and we may add, nothing can be morally obligatory for one) unless one is an agent, but in the view that Steward dubs "Agency Incompatibilism," agency and action (and, hence, free action) presuppose the falsity of determinism.

Steward maintains that an agent has the power to make its body or parts of its body move. An action is a causing by the agent of some movement or part of its body. When one makes a decision, for example, one causes some movement in one's brain (33). In Steward's view, the "existence of actions is simply *logically* related to the existence of agents, so there cannot be an action that does not have an agent" (82). She theorizes that the causation by an agent whenever the agent performs an action is irreducible substance causation. Steward further proposes that we have the movements of agency only when some matters are "up to" an agent; some matter is up to an agent when she acts at a time only if the agent *settles* some matter at that time. In her view, actions are settlings of things by agents (e.g., 38–39, 43, 82). What one always settles when one acts is how one's body will move or change in some respect (44). In addition, one can settle some matter at a time only if that matter isn't already settled (26, 39, and 40), as it would be if determinism were true. So it is settling that presupposes indeterminism:

> The alternate possibilities that truly make trouble for determinism relate not to such high-level powers as the capacity to make either of the choices presented by any arbitrary moral or practical dilemma . . . but rather to the far more basic powers that animals must possess over the movements of their bodies through space and time if they are truly to count as the sources and controllers of those movements. For each segment of activity undertaken by a given animal . . . it must be the case that the animal in question had the power, at the time of executing that activity, to refrain from doing so, either by doing something else at the time in question or by doing nothing. Putative activities of which this is not true I claim, cannot count as settlings by the animal at the time of action of what is to happen to its own body, and so cannot be actions or activities of the animal at all. And these powers . . . cannot be understood in such a way as to be compatible with determinism; these are two-way powers that really do require that certain possibilities be left open by the world, for unless they are, room cannot be made for these activities to be happenings that settle certain matters that are genuinely up to the agent, as opposed to being merely the inevitable outcome of events occurring inside her body. It is this . . . that is the true source of the most powerful and plausible version of the principle of Alternative Possibilities; and moreover . . . it makes possible . . . a convincing response to the Challenge from Chance. (126–27)

Elsewhere in the book, Steward says that an action occurs only if its agent possesses a relevant refrainment power (an RRP) in respect of that action (184, 186, 188). One cannot have this power in a world at which determinism is true. So her view seems to be that nothing can be an action unless, holding "fixed" the past and the laws of nature, its agent could have done otherwise. This is pretty close to what *Action* entails about action.

The notion of settling that Steward invokes is a technical one. She says, "we can think of each matter that is subject to settling as expressible by means of a question [of] the form $[p \vee \neg p]$, whose answer is (metaphorically) decided at a certain point in time, when it becomes impossible either that p should obtain or that $\neg p$ should" (39). It appears that she takes settling to be something of this sort: An action performed at time t settles at t whether p just in case that action either suffices for its being the case that p or suffices for its being the case that not-p, and nothing prior to t suffices for either of these.[8] This notion of settling differs from some other familiar ones that do not presuppose indeterminism. So for instance, when one makes up one's mind about what to order for the main course at one's favorite bistro, there is a perfectly respectable sense in which one settles what one will have for the main course; the notion of settling here does not assume the falsity of determinism.

Steward rejects any compatibilist rendering of settling, such as the view that a certain agent could have decided otherwise, and so could have settled something differently from the way in which she did, if no one forced the agent to decide as she did, or she "possessed a general decision-making capacity at the time that was in perfect working order and which [she] could then have exercised so as to have made the opposite decision, if [she] had seen good reason to do so" (140). Steward argues that the causal theory of action, prominent among many compatibilists, that has it that an action is an event that is nondeviantly caused by one's apt reason states (or their neural realizers), faces difficult problems including the problem of causal deviance and the problem of the disappearing agent. According to the former, causal theorists ("causalists") have no means to distinguish causal chains associated with overt action from deviant motion-producing chains.[9] According to the latter, the causal theory is inconsistent with there being any actions because if an action is an event that is produced by agent-involving events or states (or their neural realizers), there is no room for agents anymore; the theory makes agents "vanish."[10] Steward is critical of various proposed attempts to meet or evade these problems. It would, however, be premature to conclude that these problems are insuperable. Let us simply grant that these are costs of endorsing a causal theory of action; these are problems that causalists must address.

However, as Steward is well aware, her proposal that no activity of an agent qualifies as an action unless it is an (indeterministic) settling also faces costs, one of the most prominent of which is that a world at which determinism is true has neither any agents nor any actions. Imagine such a world much like ours in which humanoids and other creatures engage in behavior much of which includes bringing about various events that appear to be intentional actions. Call these events "*actions." It isn't pellucid what *actions would be in Steward's view. Maybe they would be intentional doings, performances, or processes (unlike, for example, events that merely occur or happen in these humanoids, such as the beating of their hearts). Furthermore, we may suppose that there is a conventional sense of "settling" in which human (and perhaps some other) agents in this world settle various matters: On numerous occasions, when deliberating about what to do, they have not made up their minds regarding which *action (including *actions that are mental events, *decisions) to bring about. In this sense of "settles," they settle what *action to perform when they make *decisions. Philosophers in this world may want to give an account of *actions. How are such events to be differentiated from events that are not *actions (mental or otherwise)? In thinking about this topic, some of the philosophers may well opt for a causal theory of *actions. A lively debate may rage about various other topics concerning *actions, including how to differentiate intentional *actions from those that are nonintentionally performed, developing a view of akratic *actions, defending causal theories from the problem of deviance, addressing the disappearing *agent objection (where *agents are entities that perform *actions), distinguishing between *actions that are free and those that are not, and so forth. My suspicion is that almost everything we have to say about *action* in the actual world would be duplicated by philosophers and others in this imaginary world with the understanding that they would be addressing *action*. Some in the imaginary world may continue to deny that *agents are agents proper or that *actions are *bona fide* actions because *actions* require the settling of matters (where the notion of settling here is Steward's technical notion) that have not already been settled owing to determinism, and, given the putative logical connection between actions and agents, there cannot be actions without agents. But this would not in any way diminish interest among relevant parties in the pertinent dialogue regarding *actions.

Interestingly, Steward writes:

> We have conceded only that it is *conceivable* that physicists might one day discover something that entails determinism. And at that point, no doubt, if I did not want to give up the claim that there are agents [and so, actions, as in Steward's view, there is a logical association between the notions of *being an agent* and *being an action*], I would have to look anew at my arguments for the incompatibility of agency and determinism to see whether they might be less strong than I had thought at first. (124, note omitted)

So perhaps Steward herself may not be averse to reconsidering the view that *actions in our imaginary world are not just plain actions.

A second cost with Steward's account of action, as Clarke (2014) argues, is that the modal notion of settling at a time is open to a variety of interpretations, some not inconsistent with determinism, and that Steward seems not to have given cogent reasons to prefer her interpretation to some rival that does not require indeterminism in her analysis of what it is for an action to settle some matter. A third cost I will address later (in chapter 7) is that Agency Incompatibilism seems to run afoul of the so-called luck objection that appears to plague some other libertarian contenders. In brief, just as she regards the account of action that causalists endorse—some variation of the causal theory of action—not to be cost-free, Steward's own settling account is not cost-free either.

The primary point of this brief excursus involving putative costs is simply this: Both the causalist's and Steward's relevant views on action have costs; it isn't that one is cost-free. So the mere fact that each of these views has costs should not provide proponents of either with any prima facie advantage in assessing Frankfurt cases.

Mindful of this point, consider this sort of challenge from Frankfurt examples to Steward's view that one performs an action only if one could have done otherwise. In Stage 1, S does A. We imagine that S could have moved her body in different ways, or she could have halted the progression of events along the pathway that leads to her doing of A, or she could have altered the speed of some of her relevant bodily movements involved in her A-ing. In other words, we may suppose that S has the general capacity to move her body in different ways and she can exercise this capacity in Stage 1. In Stage 2, S proceeds just as she does in Stage 1. She retains the *general* capacity to move her body in different ways. But she cannot move her body any differently from the way in which she moves it in Stage 1 because of the failsafe mechanism. My intuition is that S is an agent in Stage 2, and that A is an action of hers. Steward disagrees. Regarding a compulsive hand-washer, she says:

What seems to be utterly crucial, what cannot be entirely imagined away without imagining away agency itself, are the powers of organization and ordering one possesses in the service
of one's ends (however unfree one may be with respect to the
question how those ends themselves come to be established),
of the movements and changes in one's body, the production
of which constitutes one's activity. It seems that the possession and exercise of at least *some* such power is necessary for
the occurrence of an action. Suppose, for example, that qua
compulsive washer, I could do absolutely none of the following: *stop* washing if the situation suddenly demanded it . . .
change the direction in which my hands rotate, *slow down or
speed up* the motions in question, move my hands from under
the hot tap when it becomes too hot, turn the tap in the appropriate direction if the water is coming out too forcefully or
not forcefully enough, etc. if I simply possessed none of these
powers, to settle the particular details of the action I execute
I simply could not be said to be its agent at all. My "action"
would thereby be revealed to be no production of mine, but
rather of some sort of complex automotive mechanism, not
something in which I exert my powers to settle how things
will be with respect to a certain part of the world in the service
of my ends. The alternative possibilities one needs for action
are ones deriving from the necessity, if one is to be an agent,
of having power over one's own body: of having the power,
in respect of at least some of the particular movings of limbs,
digits, or other changes in one's bodily state that constitute
one's . . . [A-ing], not to have made those very movements or
changes. (184)

Ponder Steward's claim that "My 'action' would thereby be
revealed to be no production of mine, but rather of some sort

of complex automotive mechanism, not something in which I exert my powers to settle how things will be with respect to a certain part of the world in the service of my ends" if I did not have the sorts of alternative possibilities associated with moving my body that she describes in the passage. This is puzzling. We find no changes in S's intrinsic properties in Stage 2 (because, among other things, the fail safe mechanism never kicks in). In this stage S also retains the general ability to move her body in certain ways. We may additionally suppose that there are appropriate causal connections between her reason states and her A-ing (the sorts of connection that causalists or even "teleological" theorists favor). Why should S's lacking the pertinent alternatives (during the relevant temporal period when the fail safe mechanism is "operative") render it true that S's A-ing "would thereby be . . . no production of . . . [S's], but rather of some sort of complex automotive mechanism"? Even in the world I invited readers to consider in which *agents make *decisions, such decisions are things that *agents intentionally bring about and, thus, it is false that such decisions are not productions of those who bring them about.

In another passage, relevantly like the previous one quoted, still addressing the compulsive who cannot refrain from pressing a button Steward says:

> We must imagine, if we are to imagine away all RRPs [relevant refrainment powers], that she cannot stop the motion once it has begun, even if (for example) threatened with a gun. In addition, she has no means whatever by which to guide and control her finger once its motion is initiated, any more than I can guide and control what happens to my leg when it is hit by a hammer just below the knee and I experience a reflex

jerk. In what sense, then, is this agent the agent of an action? Everything that happens is dictated by the occurrence of processes that she is entirely unable to veto, suspend, or otherwise control or alter. That, according to the Agency Incompatibilist, is as much as to say that she does not act, for there is nothing whatever that she truly settles; neither, whether, nor when nor where, nor how she will press the button. And if she settles none of these things, her pressing of the button cannot have been an action. (186)

First, a word of caution: The scenario Steward invites us to imagine when thinking about agency and action in a Frankfurt case should not mislead one. In such a case, in Stage 2, S is neither threatened with a gun nor coerced in any other way. Stage 2 unfolds in just the way in which Stage 1 does. Second, and importantly, Steward urges that S "has no means whatever by which to guide and control her finger once its motion is initiated, any more than I can guide and control what happens to my leg when it is hit by a hammer just below the knee and I experience a reflex jerk." Causalists, however, will insist that S *does* guide and control her action if her action is nondeviantly and otherwise appropriately caused by her reason states (or their neural realizers); in their view control is essentially causal. Furthermore, causalists can readily distinguish between knee-jerk like events and actions (intentional or otherwise). We are left again with the thought that the absence of pertinent alternatives, even supposing no intrinsic changes in S, and so even supposing that S retains the general capacity to move her body in relevant ways but cannot, because of the failsafe mechanism, exercise these capacities in more than one direction in Stage 2, usurps agency. It remains unclear why a causalist should accept this thought.

3.2.3 Frankfurt Examples and Specific Versus General Abilities

Next, for another objection, reconsider the variation of the Frankfurt example in which Augustine fails to do what he seemingly ought to do: refrain from stealing the pears. The objection is that we can consistently preserve the view that even in Stage 2, Augustine has a moral obligation not to steal and insist that obligation requires avoidability. Rather than working with a highly restricted reading of "can" in *Kant's Law*, what some call the "can" of specific ability, the sense in which an agent *can* do what she ought to do is meant to be more general.[11] General abilities like this need not be limited to what one is able to do, given one's motivations or circumstances, just as they are. On this proposal, we preserve an "ought" implies "can" and "cannot" principle, but we are just more permissive about the reading of the ability claim in *Kant's Law*.

A proper assessment of this objection awaits candidate accounts of the general ability (or, more expansively, the broader ability) at issue. However, sidestepping details of any such account, there does seem to be a hard-to-pin-down although intuitive distinction between specific and general abilities, and we can work with this intuitive understanding to respond to the objection. Positioning the objection in context, intuitively, although Augustine does not have the *specific* ability to refrain from stealing in his Frankfurt predicament, he retains the *general* ability to refrain from stealing. Ernie, together with his mind-reading machinery, does not in any way affect this general ability because he never shows his hand. If the ability in question that "can" expresses in *Kant's Law* is this sort of general ability, one might propose that Augustine (in Stage 2) of the pertinent Frankfurt example has both the (general) ability to steal and to refrain from stealing (although in his actual circumstances he lacks the specific ability to refrain from stealing). Consequently, we can hold on to the view that if one ought to do or avoid doing something (if, for instance, Augustine ought to refrain from stealing), one can do and can avoid doing it (when it is understood that "can" expresses general ability) even if it turns out that one lacks the specific ability to do or to refrain from doing that thing.[12]

This way of understanding the "can" in *Kant's Law* has high costs. Indeed, the prior discussion on Nelkin's unorthodox interpretation of "can" should bear this out. To clarify, let "*S* General-can do *A*" express the proposition that *S* can do *A* when "can" expresses general ability. Then, to introduce further terminology, *S General-can do A* does not entail *S can bring about A*. (Augustine General-can refrain from stealing even though in his circumstances he cannot bring it about that he refrains from stealing; remember, with Ernie on the scene it is unalterable for Augustine that he steals.) If we let "*S Specific-can do A*" stand for the proposition that *S* can do *A* in the specific ability and opportunity sense of "can" that entails that *S* can bring about *A*, then *S General-can do A* does not entail *S Specific-can do A*. Roughly, if one has the general ability to do *A*, it does not follow that in one's situation, one can bring about *A*. Construing "can" as "General-can," *Kant's Law* now says:

General-Kant's Law: If *S* morally ought to do *A*, then *S* General-can do *A* (*S* has the general ability to do *A*); and if *S* morally ought not to do *A*, then *S* General-can refrain from doing *A*.

It should now be clear that *General-Kant's Law* is relevantly just like Nelkin's *New-OIC*: If *S* morally ought to do *A*, then *S* IF-can do *A*; and if *S* morally ought not to do *A*, then *S* IF-can refrain from doing *A*. The very sorts of problem that plague *New-OIC* also plague *General-Kant's Law*. To illustrate with just one example we have employed, In *Scene-1*, you Specific-can easily rescue the child who is drowning. Assume that you have an obligation to save her. *Scene-2* is just like the former with the exception that you are unaware that there is a diver in the water between you and the child who will kill you if you even attempt to enter the water. If *Kant's Law* is true, then as of the time you have not entered the water and the diver is keeping watch, you have *no* obligation to save the child because as of this time you can't *bring it about* that you save the child. But if *General-Kant's Law* is true, you *do* have an obligation to save the child. You have the general ability to save the child because the diver has not intervened and your germane general abilities remain unscathed. Again, this appeal to general abilities seems irrelevant. For all rhyme and reason, with the diver poised to kill you, you are just as relevantly "incapacitated" as you would have been if you were tethered to your seat and, thus, were unable to get to the child.

3.2.4 Does Blameworthiness Require Impermissibility?

Rather than abandon *Kant's Law*, and hence, abandon the principle that impermissibility requires avoidability, a "Frankfurt defender" may opt for another strategy: abandon the principle that blameworthiness requires impermissibility. The Frankfurt defender may insist both that blameworthiness does not require alternatives (as Frankfurt examples seemingly show), and Augustine is indeed blameworthy for stealing the pears in Stage 2 even though it is not true that it is impermissible for him to steal the pears (in this stage).

I have argued that various considerations call into question the principle that blameworthiness requires impermissibility (e.g., Haji 1998; 2002; 2012a). Here, I merely summarize one of them because this consideration provides valuable groundwork for later discussion.

One can be blameworthy for "ranked" *permissible* options. The normative statuses of the (morally) permissible, the impermissible, the obligatory, the omissible, and the optional are common coinage. Again, let deontic value be that value in virtue of which whatever can have one or more of these normative statuses have one or more of them. Then we may assume that the obligatory option is the deontically best option, and we leave it open in what deontic value consists.

The notion of "nonranked" (or equally ranked) permissible options is familiar: There are situations in which nothing is obligatory—no option is maximally deontically best—but in which two or more options have equal deontic value, and the deontic value of each such (permissible) option exceeds that of all other options. But as Paul McNamara, among others, has proposed, our ordinary moral conceptual scheme allows for the notions of permissibly doing the least one can do, and permissibly doing more than one has to do (see McNamara 1996a; 1996b; 2008; 2011a; 2011b). If this is so, it is possible to have a range of "ranked permissible options," some such options being deontically better than others. Elaborating, McNamara proposes that a range of acceptable alternatives yields ranked permissible options, with two extreme poles—the best of the permissible alternatives and the least of those—with the prospect of doing more than the least of those or permissibly less than the best of those. Here is an instructive example:

[Contact:] Suppose that in virtue of promising to get in touch with you, I become obligated to do so. Suppose . . . I can fulfill this obligation in two ways: by writing you a letter or by stopping by . . . My other obligations make me too busy permissibly to do both. Finally, suppose that, morally speaking, I put in a better performance if I pay you a visit rather than write you, even though either one is permissible. Then if I *do the minimum morality demands*, I will write rather than visit . . . The important thing to note is that what is necessitated by

meeting morality's demands in a minimally acceptable way is not
to be confused with doing what I am obligated to do . . . Some
such notion is vital to the concept of supererogation. For if it is
possible for me to discharge my obligations in a supererogatory
way (in a better than minimal way), then it ought to be possible
for me merely to discharge them in a minimal way—and vice
versa. (1996a, 424–26)

To reemphasize, with *ranked* permissible options one can do
something permissible that is precluded by doing the permissibly least one can do. An act is beyond the call if and only if it is
permissible and precluded by doing the minimum (McNamara
2011a, 228). With ranked alternatives, one can also do something
permissible that is precluded by doing permissibly more than one
has to do. An act is permissibly suboptimal if and only if it is permissible and precluded by the maximum (McNamara 2011a, 229).

It is relatively uncontroversial that one can be praiseworthy for
going beyond the call. For instance, one can be praiseworthy for
doing what it is supererogatory for one to do. McNamara proposes
this analysis of the supererogatory: An act is supererogatory for an
agent, *S*, if and only if it is optional for *S* to do, it is praiseworthy for
S to do, it is not blameworthy for *S* to omit, and it is precluded by
doing the least *S* can do (see, e.g., McNamara 2011a, 223).[13] Because
any supererogatory act is precluded by doing the least that one has
to, or, in short, precluded by doing the (permissibly) minimum,
and one is praiseworthy for such an act, one can be praiseworthy for
going beyond the call.

What, however, of being blameworthy for doing something that
is precluded by doing the minimum? Ponder this case:

MailPerson-1: Heavily indebted to a ruthless loan shark, Mia is
in desperate need of cash to avoid broken bones. On her mail

route one morning, she passes by the billionaires' home which is ablaze. Seeing the neighbors restraining the frantic parents, she quickly sizes up the situation and discerns her chance. "If I pull this off," she mutters to herself, "I'll be handsomely rewarded, and if I fail—well, it will still probably be far better than pulverized ribs!" So off she dashes into the inferno and the baby is saved. It is important to stipulate that Mia fails to act "from" or "out of" duty or any sense that she is doing anything permissible; she intends to rescue the baby solely for the purpose of saving her own skin.

It is not implausible to suppose that Mia does something that doing the minimum precludes—she saves the child—but she is not deserving of praise, it appears, for this deed. To cement this point, assume that if Mia does the minimum morality requires, she pulls the fire alarm, which is a block away, and directs the fire personnel to the blaze, and doing the minimum (in her circumstances) is incompatible with rescuing the child. With this sort of case in mind, it is not difficult to think of others in which one is blameworthy for doing something that goes beyond the minimum. In *MailPerson-2*, a second mailperson, Marion, rescues the child solely for the purpose of handing him over, for selfish gain, to traffickers in vital organs. She goes beyond the call but (given innocuous assumptions) is blameworthy for doing so.[14]

Partisans of *Blameworthiness/Impermissibility* may object that Marion is *not* blameworthy for saving the child because it *not* impermissible for Marion to save the child. However, she *is* blameworthy for handing over the child but her handing over the child is impermissible for her. This objection can be resisted. Marion might not end up handing over the child because in the nick of time she is prevented from doing so. Still, she might save only because she wants to hand over the child, and may realize that in so saving, she is doing something it is morally improper or amiss for her to do. I see no reason to deny that with the case so described, Marion is blameworthy for saving the child.

A second objection against Marion's case turns on distinguishing sharply between Marion's act of saving the child and her selfish motive—the desire for personal gain. If we keep this distinction squarely in mind, then it is not obvious that she is not praiseworthy for the act even if it is true that she is not praiseworthy for the motive.

Why, however, think that Marion is praiseworthy for her act? Some may propose that she is so because she does something it is permissible for her to do by risking harm to herself. This will, though, obviously not suffice for praiseworthiness. Suppose Marion bungee jumps, or enters a Formula 1 race. We may assume that it is permissible for her to do either of these things even if she runs the risk of suffering significant harm by jumping or racing. But she need not be praiseworthy for either.

Another suggestion is that plausible candidates for accounts of praiseworthiness support the view that Marion is praiseworthy for saving the child. It would take us too far afield to canvass all the rival candidates. I will draw simply on some of the central ones. On a Strawsonian view, a requirement of praiseworthiness is that one express good will in one's action. Adopting a Strawsonian view, regarding blameworthiness, Michael McKenna proposes that one is to blame for something only if one expresses a deficient (or a morally objectionable) quality of will in doing it. He explains that the quality of will one expresses in an action is a measure of the worth (or value) of the moral regard one has toward others (or oneself), and toward the relevance of moral considerations (2012, 59). Marion, however, apparently expresses ill will and not good will in saving the child, or at least she fails to express good will. On one formulation of a ledger view of moral responsibility, when one is praiseworthy for an action, one's moral worth is enhanced in performing it, and when blameworthy, one's moral worth is diminished. It is hard to see how saving the child enhances Marion's moral worth. To explain, Michael J. Zimmerman, who endorses a ledger view, proposes that to deserve praise for an action, one must be motivated by the thought (though perhaps not solely by the thought) that one will thereby be doing right (1988, 51); praiseworthiness requires that one does right, even if partly, for right's sake. One's motivation "to do right must . . . be in and of itself not just a *sufficient* but also a dominant or *primary* (or at least nonsecondary) motivation for bringing about" one's decision (52). In saving the child, it is clear that Mia does not satisfy this condition of doing right for right's sake, and, hence, it is implausible to suppose that her moral worth is *enhanced* in saving the child. Angela Smith recommends that to say that "a person is morally responsible for some thing is to say that it can be attributed to her in the way that is required in order for it to be a basis for moral appraisal," where nothing is implied about what that appraisal, if any, should be (2007, 467–68). Smith ventures that being responsible is primarily about actions, choices, or attitudes being properly attributable to, and so reflective, of one's "rational agency or activity in a way that would make them an appropriate basis for moral" appraisal (2008, 381). When negative, the appraisal expresses a demand to its target, calling upon her to be answerable for her rational activity. To be answerable for such activity, at least in principle she must be able to explain or justify this activity in terms of her reasons, and "to acknowledge fault if such a justification cannot be provided" (381). This justificatory demand implies that appraisals of being responsible (or answerable) are "appropriately directed only at features of a person that can be said to reflect her practical agency." These features include any that express "her judgments or evaluative assessments, regardless of whether . . .

those features reflect or have resulted from a voluntary choice on her part" (382). If Marion were to explain or justify saving the child in terms of her reasons, presumably her reasons would call for a *negative* appraisal (or appraisals) of her. Thus, praiseworthiness would not be one of these appraisals.

Turning to scenarios in which one does less than the maximum, one can be blameworthy for doing something it is permissibly suboptimal for one to do (or for "permissibly suboptimizing"). Consider

> *Delivery*: Suppose I can fulfill the obligation to see to it that you receive a parcel by noon today in these ways: (a1) deliver it personally; (a2) have someone drop it to your home; (a3) call you to collect it. Suppose, again, that my other obligations make me too busy permissibly to do any two of these things; doing one of them precludes me permissibly from doing any of the others. Finally, imagine that (a1) is better than (a2) and (a2) is better than (a3). I put in a better performance if I personally deliver the parcel than if I have it sent to you or call you to collect it. We may assume that if I call you, I do the permissibly minimum; I do something it is permissibly suboptimal for me to do. As I consider these options, I remember this incident: A month ago, you did me a small favor. You dropped off a present to a friend of mine in Buenos Aires while you were visiting that city. You made it clear at the time that what you did you did with no strings attached. I could now reciprocate. Although it is optional to return the favor I could provide you with a comparable benefit with little cost to myself.

Despite being aware of the relevant rankings, and recalling the owed favor, I deliberately call you.[15] I realize it would hardly have taken much for me to do significantly better—I could have dropped off the parcel on my way to work. It seems I am blameworthy for calling: I act in light of the nonculpable belief that I did something, as we may put it, I nonculpably took to be morally deontically amiss.

Suberogatory acts are roughly the symmetric flip sides of supererogatory ones. McNamara proposes that an act is suberogatory for S if and only if it is optional for S to do, it is blameworthy for S to do, it is not praiseworthy for S to omit, and it is precluded by the maximum S can do (see, for instance, McNamara 2011a, 231).[16] Since any suberogatory act is precluded by doing the most one can do, and one is blameworthy for such an act, again, one can be blameworthy for doing something that it is permissibly suboptimal for one to do.

Some may object that if (in *Delivery*) I am blameworthy for something, it is not for calling, but, for example, for not having a better moral character or for not being more thoughtful. However, as the tale is spun, nothing precludes me from being blameworthy for all three: calling (or failing to deliver the parcel personally), not having a better character, and not being more thoughtful. In addition, reflect on the proposal that I am blameworthy for failing to be more thoughtful. Perhaps what is being proposed is that I am blameworthy for being *disposed* to not being as thoughtful as I reasonably could have been. Perhaps this is so, but as already noted, this is consistent with my being blameworthy for calling. Maybe, though, an alternative is that I am blameworthy for not being thoughtful on the particular occasion. Spelling out the content of this claim, my not being thoughtful (in this "occurrent" sense of "not being thoughtful") *consists* in my calling you (and not delivering the parcel personally). But then we have no counterexample to the claim that I am blameworthy for calling, something it is permissibly suboptimal for me to do. Similar remarks apply to the claim that I am blameworthy for not having a better character. It may be true that I am blameworthy for having a certain, fairly stable long-term trait (or collection of such traits). This is consistent with my being blameworthy for calling. Or one might contend, instead, that I am blameworthy for expressing or manifesting some trait on the pertinent occasion, my calling being the manifestation on this occasion. Then again, we would have no counterexample to the view that I am blameworthy for calling.

As for praiseworthiness for doing something it is permissibly suboptimal for one to do, imagine that in yet another contact case, *Risky Contact*, you ought to contact Rick because it is only in this way that he can receive vital information he requires to save many innocent lives. Furthermore, each option to contact Rick involves real, unavoidable danger to yourself. Delivering the coded information personally is permissibly best although highly risky for you. Emailing the information is less risky but still permissible. You opt for the latter. Not unreasonably, you are praiseworthy for suboptimizing.[17]

It is possible to be morally blameworthy for going beyond the call and morally praiseworthy for doing the minimum, primarily because appraisals of blameworthiness and praiseworthiness are "agent-focused" appraisals, whereas those of permissibility, optionality, going beyond the call, and doing the minimum (among other "deontic" evaluations) are "act-focused" appraisals. The former variety of appraisal involves primarily assessments that impute fault or credit to the *agent*, and have to do with how the agent perceives her situation and options, or, simplifying, with what moves the agent to act. In contrast, the latter sort of appraisal involves assessments of the act (omission, state of affairs, or what have you) that turn on relevant properties of the act itself (such as, for instance, whether the act *is* your highest deontically ranked option). You may mistakenly perceive an impermissible act to be permissible but do it out of the best of moral intentions, you may (like Marion) go beyond the call for base reasons, or you may (morally) permissibly suboptimize (like our brave contact person) from a sense of moral duty. The morally best of your intentions need not, for instance, always be aligned with what is obligatory, beyond the minimum, or even permissible, and the worst of your moral intentions need not always be aligned with what is impermissible or below the maximum. In this way act- and agent-focused appraisals can come apart.

I have dwelled on permissibly going beyond the call and permissibly suboptimizing at some length partly because one should not dismiss these categories without argument. In addition, and significantly, as one can be blameworthy for doing something it is permissibly suboptimal for one do to, proponents of the view that a precondition of blameworthiness is wrongdoing are committed to denying the possibility of, for example, suberogation.

It's interesting that Frankfurt examples go some way toward establishing the possibility of suberogation. The constitutive elements of a suberogatory act are (i) being permissible; (ii) being deontically worse than some of its permissible alternatives; and (iii) being such that one is blameworthy for performing it. Frankfurt examples impel us to detach impermissibility from blameworthiness. In Stage 2 (in *Theft*) it is not impermissible for Augustine to steal the pears because in this stage he cannot refrain from stealing the pears and impermissibility requires avoidability. But he is still blameworthy for stealing the pears. If it is possible for Augustine to be blameworthy for an amoral act (his stealing the pears in a Frankfurt situation), it seems that it should also be possible for him to be blameworthy for a permissible action that is deontically inferior to some permissible alternative and which is such that he would not be praiseworthy for not performing it.

In sum, cases such as *MailPerson-2* and *Delivery* show that the principle that moral blameworthiness requires moral impermissibility is false, or minimally, highly suspect.

3.3 TRUTH AND THE FUNCTION OF "OUGHT" JUDGMENTS

Although Bruce Waller acknowledges the widespread appeal of *Kant's Law*, in his 2011 book he rejects this law. *Kant's Law* is an essential ingredient in my argument that obligation requires alternative possibilities. Referring to some of my previous work, Waller writes:

> Ishtiyaque Haji regards . . . [*Kant's Law*] as a central truth of ethics that enjoys "widespread intuitive support" and serves as a basic theorem in and thus is validated by "some of our best theories about the concept of moral obligation" (2000a, 352). Whatever its status as "a basic theorem," there is no doubt that it enjoys wide acceptance both within and without the contemporary philosophical community. But is that support warranted? (2011, 181)

He thinks not. Toward the beginning of a section entitled "Does "Ought" Imply "Can?" (181–87), against *Kant's Law* Waller first alludes to an argument from genuine conflicts of obligation. Suppose, as of some time, one ought to do one thing, *A*, and another thing, *B*. Then it seems that one ought to do both *A* and *B*. But if one cannot do both since doing one precludes doing the other (as would be the case if there were genuine conflicts of obligation), then *Kant's Law* is false (181). However, Waller does not add to the copious discussion of this contentious argument. Rather, responding to the comment that such conflicts cannot occur, he says:

The ancient Greeks were much less confident that the world was morally well ordered. Their gods were spiteful, arbitrary, and cruel, and the best human efforts could be thwarted by cosmic caprice . . . There may be many things that we ought to do and that we may strive to accomplish, yet be unable to achieve. In the centuries that followed, Aristotle's God was integrated into Christianity, and the Aristotelian-Christian notion of a morally well-ordered cosmos triumphed. In such a system, obligations and capacities must coincide: a just God would give no obligations beyond our abilities to fulfill them. But in the natural world, devoid of divine order, there is no such assurance. Having evolved in this world, it is hardly surprising that it accommodates us reasonably well, but fitting our moral obligations to our powers is well beyond what natural selection is likely to provide. Whatever one believes to be the source of one's obligations, there is no reason to suppose that the natural world is designed to help us meet them. (182)

A few sentences later, Waller adds:

When we look at it closely, "ought implies can" has little to rec-ommend it other than the exalted stature of Kant, the antin-aturalist desire to transcend the natural world and set humans apart from other animals, and the belief that some divine force imposes a moral order on the world so that we will never face the misfortune of having a moral obligation we are incapable of meeting. (182–83)

My defense of *Kant's Law* does not appeal to the "exalted stature of Kant," or to some antinaturalist desire to transcend the natural world (I have no such desire), or to a belief about some divine force (I have no such belief). Rather, I start with the thought that moral obligation, just like moral responsibility, requires control. The principle, roughly, that one can't be responsible for something that one cannot do or bring about captures a crucial aspect of the control that responsibility demands. Similarly, the basic control that obligation presupposes is encapsulated in the principle that one can't have an obligation to do something unless one can do it. I've then pursued a two-pronged strategy to defend this thought. First, I've examined arguments against *Kant's Law*; I find these arguments far from knock down. Next, I've advanced considerations in favor of *Kant's Law*. The chief of these is that this principle is validated by a powerful analysis of the concept of obligation, the doing-the-best-you-can analysis.

Having summarized a number of cases in which agents, some victims of a deprived childhood (such as Robert Alton Harris), did horrible things that they supposedly could not have avoided doing, Waller writes:

> It makes perfect sense to recognize that Harris is severely morally disabled, and that given who he is at this mature stage of life, he could not have resisted committing the murders, and he is incorrigible: far beyond his own powers of reform, and probably beyond the powers of contemporary psychological science. This recognition is very different from saying, "That tornado ought not to have killed that family." Robert Harris is not a tornado, but a person with rational powers (not super rational) who makes choices (though not super "ultimate" choices) and who might be capable of reform (. . . we should be very reluctant to judge someone as beyond reform). It may be somewhat disturbing to recognize that in the real world there are things we ought to do that we cannot do, moral obligations we cannot fulfill. Recognizing that is better than spinning out a "morally ordered" world to suit our moral wishes. (183–84)

I have doubts about whether, generally, defenders of *Kant's Law* are "spinning out a "morally ordered world" [one in which *Kant's Law* is presupposed] to suit . . . [their] moral wishes."

In a passage following the one last quoted, Waller advances this argument against *Kant's Law*. Suppose our moral obligations are limited to what we can do. Narrowing "our ethics" in this manner

> would severely limit the ethical judgments we can make and weaken our system of moral thought, and ethics could not function as well—if at all—for some of the most impor-tant things that moral thought does. I ought to repay the money you so kindly loaned to me, but I have suffered severe financial reverses, and I cannot do so. It's absurd to suggest that somehow—through some miracle-working financial power?—I really can. We could (if we are resolved to save "ought implies can" at any costs) stipulate that I do not have such an obligation, as I cannot fulfill it, but doing so will place limits on our system of moral thought that will hamstring important moral judgments. I ought to exert an effort to feed my hungry children, but if I suffer from severe learned helplessness, then I cannot exert such an effort. It is sad to think that the world is such that we sometimes have genuine moral obligations that we have not the power or resources to fulfill; if I believed in a just God, or a divinely well-ordered moral world, then it would be difficult for me to accept that the world can be like that. As a naturalist, I am disappointed—but not surprised—that the world often falls short of my moral ideals. (184)

Precisely what argument against *Kant's Law* this passage har-bors is not pellucid. But there is a sort of underlying theme running through some of the considerations that Waller advances against

Kant's Law. It's the thought that if obligations were restricted to what one has the ability and opportunity to do, morality would be "limited," or "impoverished," or morality could not serve the useful functions that it does. Confining, first, attention to the passage immediately preceding this paragraph, we may extract the following argument.

3.3.1 *The Argument from Limitation*

(1) If Kant's Law is true, then several "ought" judgments (with temporal indexes omitted, morally deontic judgments of the form "some person morally ought to do something") that we may have initially thought to have been true would not be true.

(2) It's false that several "ought" judgments that we may have initially thought to have been true would not be true.

Therefore, (3) *Kant's Law* is not true.

Line (1) is presumably based on the sorts of example that Waller gives in which even though some person cannot do something, some like Waller still believe that this person has an obligation to do this thing. Even if I cannot feed my children, Waller proposes, I morally ought to do so.

I confess to not being able to reconstruct any cogent rationale for line (2). The examples that Waller gives to support line (1) (such as the putative obligation to feed your children when you cannot do so) are not going to move the debate. They may be suggestive, but I'm unsure why a proponent of *Kant's Law* would find unpalatable the thought that in these examples, agents who cannot do what they seemingly ought to do fail to have an obligation to do these things. Alternatively, if these agents ought to do these things, then it is open to defenders of *Kant's Law* to explore the suggestion that the "ought" in question does not express the morally deontic "ought"; maybe what is at issue is the ideal "ought." For instance, it may be proposed that it (ideally) ought to be that one feed one's hungry children.

Waller sketches a case in which if

> Rita fails (or succeeds) in meeting her moral obligation to visit her hospitalized friend, then—given the full history of Rita's conditioned character, the full panoply of situational forces acting on her, the full consideration of all the factors that come to bear on the situation—Rita could not have fulfilled her obligation and could not have acted differently. But there is nothing in that claim that precludes the judgment that Rita was morally wrong to forgo the obligatory hospital visit. The denial that Rita is morally responsible and the denial of "ought implies can" maintain a substantive system of moral judgments; the denial that Rita has amorally failed in her moral obligation (though she could not do otherwise) leaves an impoverished system. (185)

Suppose some argument for the view that no one can ever be morally responsible for anything were sound. Then there is a sense in which our "moral system" would be impoverished: No judgments of the form "so and so is blameworthy or praiseworthy for doing or failing to do something" would be true. But in the absence of cogent explanation to believe otherwise, surely such impoverishment itself would not undermine the skeptical argument. Similarly, it would seem that if "maintaining" *Kant's Law* has the effect of relevantly impoverishing our "moral system," such impoverishment itself would not show that *Kant's Law* is false.

Waller has some interesting things to say about the function of "ought" judgments.

Sam ought to stop being jealous. Suppose we learn that Sam (because of his conditioning or genetics or other similar reason) cannot presently stop being jealous. It may still make sense to say that Sam ought to stop being jealous: it makes sense, and it may serve several useful functions. First, even if Sam cannot presently stop being jealous, if he believes that he ought to do so (perhaps as the result of being admonished to that effect), he might take steps to make it possible to stop being jealous in the future (for example, he might seek the services of a good psychotherapist). Second, "You ought not be so jealous" may be useful, even if we believe that Sam cannot presently exercise control over his jealousy, and indeed even if there are no steps available to Sam that would lead to gaining such control; even if he cannot stop being jealous, he may come to see it as a character flaw and not something to be acted upon, rather than a virtue that is a good guide to action. Furthermore, he may work to prevent his children from following in his own flawed path. Finally, even if we think that Sam has no chance of reform and that he will never even be capable of seeing his jealousy as a flaw, it may be useful to say that Sam ought not be jealous; such an admonition may help shape others who are currently more malleable to avoid such a character flaw. Of course, if Sam has no resources for reform, then it may be useless to tell *Sam* that he ought not be jealous, but that fact certainly does not make the statement false or incoherent. (186)

According to Waller, "ought" judgments (such as "Sam ought not to be jealous"), when aptly expressed, have the function of modifying behavior or character, either the behavior or character of the agent in question, such as Sam in the example, or the behavior or character of others, such as Sam's children or pertinent third parties. Let's focus on the class of what we may call "nondischargeable ought judgments." These are morally deontic judgments of the form "S morally ought to do A (or ought to refrain from doing A)" when S cannot do A (or cannot refrain from doing A). I agree with Waller that nondischargeable ought judgments are not incoherent; they make sense. We may also suppose that such judgments serve the functions Waller attributes to them, although one wonders whether they would serve these functions if they were false and it were generally known that they were so. Still, the primary question is whether these judgments are true. What is the link between what Waller takes their function to be—roughly, behavior modification—and their truth? It seems implausible to suppose that in virtue of serving the functions they do, they are true, or if one fails to find this implausible, we are owed an explanation of just why this is not implausible. As far as I can tell, Waller gives no account of the alleged connection between truth and function. Consider an analogy. Imagine, again, that someone advances an argument for the conclusion that no one is ever morally responsible for anything. (Perhaps this is Waller's own argument that appeals to luck.) Responsibility judgments of the form "Rita is morally blameworthy for not visiting her friend in hospital," are coherent or would be coherent, they make sense or would make sense, even if it is assumed that the argument for nonresponsibility is sound. Furthermore, suppose that these false judgments served some useful purpose. Perhaps, if expressed under apt circumstances, they would be conducive to attaining some morally desirable ends. That they would be useful in this fashion would not show that something was wrong with the argument for nonresponsibility and, hence, that the pertinent responsibility judgments were, after all, not false.

Waller contrasts Sam's case with the case of a doomed jetliner.

Contrast the case of jealous Sam with the earlier case: as we watch a doomed 747 plunge toward destruction, you say to me, "You ought not let that plane crash." Here the "ought" statement really is false; indeed, I shall have trouble even making sense of your statement. I share with Sam an incapacity to perform the action in question: he cannot stop being jealous, and I cannot rescue the airliner. But that common incapacity does not lead to a common result: the "ought" statement addressed to me is false, or perhaps nonsensical; the "ought" statement addressed to jealous Sam is true, useful, and quite intelligible. Thus, when it is not true that one can, it does not automatically follow that one is not a proper object of "ought" language. The difference is that no amount of moral resolve or proper conditioning or ethical admonition will make me into someone capable of rescuing malfunctioning jetliners. But when you say that I ought to avoid jealousy, or I ought to work harder at teaching, or I ought to stop smoking, that is to admonish me to do things that are within the capacities of at least some humans. If my smoking habit is such that I cannot overcome my addiction—perhaps I lack the psychological resources to make a concerted effort to stop, or perhaps even my best efforts will fall short of conquering my powerful addiction—it will still be useful to point out that I should stop smoking: perhaps not useful to me, though still intelligible, but useful to children whom you are admonishing not to follow my health-hazard example. (186–87)

Suppose Sam cannot avoid being jealous and Waller cannot rescue the doomed 747 jetliner. Consider these two propositions:

W1: Sam ought to avoid being jealous.
W2: Waller ought to rescue the jetliner.

I concur with Waller that W1 is coherent. I disagree with Waller's proposal that W2 is "perhaps nonsensical." I believe W2 makes sense—it is coherent—even though it is false. Why think that W2 but not W1 is false? The only suggestion I find in Waller is that whereas "no amount of moral resolve or proper conditioning or ethical admonition will make . . . [any person] into someone capable of rescuing malfunctioning jetliners, moral resolve or proper conditioning or ethical admonition may make some people alter their behavior or their character (in some desirable way). We are led, yet again, to the unexplained connection between utility and truth.

3.4 GRAHAM ON *KANT'S LAW*

Like Waller, Peter Graham rejects *Kant's Law* (OIC). In this section, I explain why Graham's rejection is problematic.

Graham's challenge to OIC rests on the proposal that the best explanation for the moral permissibility of some agents' actions is that various other agents morally ought not to do certain things that they cannot refrain from doing. Let's work with Graham's central illustration.

> TRANSPLANT: A surgeon has ten patients, each of whom will die of organ failure if he does not receive an organ transplant. The surgeon wants to save her patients and is convinced by philosophical arguments to the effect that it would be morally permissible to kill two people in order to save them. She notices that in another room of the hospital there are two innocent and unconscious tonsillectomy patients who are perfect organ matches for her patients. The only means by which the hospital janitor, who is aware of the situation, can stop the

surgeon from chopping up the two and redistributing their organs among the ten is by shooting her with his pistol. He does so and thereby kills her. (2011, 345)

Graham advances "two moral data" (2011, 345) regarding TRANSPLANT:

(1D) It is morally permissible for the janitor to kill the surgeon.

(2D) If the janitor had not killed the surgeon, the surgeon would have morally impermissibly killed the two people.

Graham claims that the "best explanation of (1D)'s truth is that (2D) is true" (2011, 346). Regarding the consequent of (2D), Graham ventures that,

(2E): The surgeon ought not to kill the two innocent patients,

is crucial to explaining (1D). But now suppose that the surgeon cannot refrain from killing the two patients. This may be so because as the events in another case, TRANSPLANT (COMPULSION), unfold, she (the surgeon) is compelled to save ten others, and the only way she can do so is by harvesting organs from the two tonsillectomy patients:

TRANSPLANT (COMPULSION): Everything is as it is in TRANSPLANT except that the surgeon cannot refrain from killing the two because the ten are her grandchildren, and she is as compelled to save them as is the most severe kleptomaniac to steal. (2011, 346)

Or, perhaps, the surgeon is in a Frankfurt situation. If counterfactual intervener Max discerns that the surgeon is about to refrain from killing the two, he will force the surgeon to kill them. But if the surgeon decides on her own, as she does, to kill the two patients, Max will not interfere.

In TRANSPLANT (COMPULSION) or the Frankfurt situation, the surgeon cannot refrain from killing the two innocent patients. Still, according to Graham, the best explanation of (1D): it is morally permissible for the janitor to kill the surgeon, retains, as a vital component, (2E): the surgeon ought not to kill the two innocent patients, despite the surgeon's not being able to refrain from killing them. In summary, Graham's argument distils to the following.

(1G) It is morally permissible for the janitor to kill the surgeon (a "moral datum").

(2G) If (1G), then the surgeon morally ought not to kill the two innocent tonsillectomy patients even though she cannot refrain from killing them. (The rationale for (2G) is that (2E) is an essential element of the best explanation of (1G).)

(3G) If the surgeon morally ought not to kill the two innocent tonsillectomy patients even though she cannot refrain from killing them, then OIC is false.

Therefore, (4G) OIC is false.

Against (2G), the premise that rests on Graham's proposed best explanation for (1D), many may exploit what they take to be the insight that just as moral responsibility requires control, so does moral obligation—no one can have a moral obligation to perform an action unless one freely performs it. They will, then, not take (2E) to be the best explanation of (1D). Remember, libertarians concerning responsibility affirm that determinism is incompatible with responsibility, and at least some people, at times, perform free actions for which they are responsible. Many but not all libertarians have proposed that responsibility requires two-way (or dual) control: For example, blameworthiness for an action requires that, consistent with the past and the laws of nature remaining the same, one be able both to perform and to refrain from performing that action. Such libertarians may similarly hold that obligation also requires dual control (e.g., see Kane 2014, 85–86). They may submit, additionally, that if one performs an action but lacks dual control regarding it, that action is not obligatory (or permissible, or impermissible) for that agent. Rather, as I have suggested, it is amoral for the agent. Such libertarians would be committed to the view that in TRANSPLANT (COMPULSION), and in the relevant Frankfurt situation, it is *amoral* for the surgeon to kill the two innocent patients. Still, they may endorse (1D): It is permissible for the janitor to kill the surgeon. Thus they would claim that the explanation of (1D)'s truth cannot be (2E): The surgeon *ought* not to kill the two innocent patients, but some alternative.

Likewise, it is open to compatibilists, who believe that responsibility is compatible with determinism, to champion the view that responsibility and obligation both require dual control, although a species of dual control that determinism leaves unscathed; and, moreover, if one lacks such control regarding some action, that action is amoral for one. Such compatibilists, like libertarians who uphold the view that obligation requires dual control, will deny that (2E) is the best explanation of (1D), and opt for an alternative. What alternative?

Imagine a libertarian (or compatibilist) who insists that obligation requires two-way control and advances a principle of this sort:

Best: The obligatory is the deontically best.

The principle may be refined in various ways. Here is a version we have seen before:

> MO: A person, S, ought, as of t, to see to the occurrence of a state of affairs, p, if and only if p occurs in some world, w, accessible to S at t, and it is not the case that p's negation (not-p) occurs in any accessible world deontically as good as or deontically better than w (Feldman 1986, 37).

It will do for now to proceed with the unrefined version, *Best*.

One might think that the two tonsillectomy patients do not deserve the treatment they would receive by the surgeon; it is unjust to harvest their organs. One might also worry that each of the ten who requires some vital organ does not deserve to receive an organ from a patient who is unjustly killed for her organs. Given these considerations, assume, further, that our libertarian (or compatibilist) co-opts Feldman's desert-sensitive axiology. In this axiology, the deontic value—roughly, the "goodness" value—of, for instance, a state of affairs in which some person receives some primary good (or evil), such as attitudinal pleasure (or pain), is a function of the fit between the primary goods (or evils) the person receives and the primary goods (or evils) the person deserves to receive. Again, the details of this interesting axiology need not detain us (Feldman 1992, 182–90; 1997, ch. 8). Call the combination of *Best* and this axiology, "*Best-Theory*." *Best-Theory*, together with the germane facts in TRANSPLANT, may well yield the result that it is permissible for the janitor to kill the surgeon despite its being true, as our libertarian (or compatibilist) will insist, that it is amoral for the surgeon to kill the two innocent patients (because she cannot refrain from killing them). But then, it seems, we have a perfectly good explanation of (1D): *Best-Theory*, in conjunction with pertinent facts, underwrites its truth.

Needless to say, I have simply adumbrated an explanation other than the one Graham favors of (1D). The general moral is that the correct normative ethical theory (one that specifies necessary and sufficient conditions for obligation), or perhaps, an analysis of the concept of obligation, in consort with relevant facts, provides an explanation of (1D).

One may raise the following concern. Suppose *Best-Theory* validates OIC: necessarily, if *Best-Theory* is true, then OIC is true. This is so, for instance, with *MO* if *MO* is the nonaxiological part of *Best-Theory*. It is also so with a variation of MO I favor:

> *MO-2*: A person, *S*, morally ought, as of *t*, to see to the occurrence of a state of affairs, *p*, if and only if there is a world, *w*, accessible to *S* at *t* in which *S* brings about *p*, there is a world, *w**, accessible to *S* at *t* in which *S* refrains from bringing about *p*, and it is not the case that *S* refrains from bringing about *p* in any accessible world as good as or better than *w*.

It may be objected that Graham's argument against OIC tells against *MO* (or *MO-2*), again supposing that either one of these principles is the nonaxiological component of *Best-Theory*: If *Best-Theory* is true, then OIC is true. But OIC is not true (given Graham's argument). So, *Best-Theory* is not true (or at least, its nonaxiological part is not true).

However, this objection has problems. Reviewing briefly, Graham's quarrel with OIC turns on the presumption that a vital element of the best explanation of (1D): It is permissible for the janitor to kill the surgeon, is (2E): The surgeon ought not to kill the two innocent patients, and this is so even when it is false that the surgeon can refrain from killing them. Graham's thought is that proponents of OIC cannot help themselves to this explanation because in those cases in which the surgeon cannot but kill the two

OBLIGATION PRESUPPOSES ALTERNATIVES

tonsillectomy patients, they are committed to denying that the surgeon ought not to kill them.

But we have seen that an advocate of *Best-Theory* (that has *MO* or *MO-2*) as its nonaxiological part can consistently give a perfectly good explanation of (1D)'s truth and deny that the surgeon ought not to kill the two innocent patients.

Maybe some might be tempted to perceive the dialectic as a "clash" of reasons: A version of *Best-Theory* whose nonaxiological component validates OIC provides a reason *for* OIC. Graham's argument provides a reason *against* OIC. Which of these reasons is more compelling? If there are powerful, independent reasons that support a suitable version of *Best-Theory*, and this version (together with germane facts) yields the result that (1D) is true ((1D), remember, the "moral datum," says: It is permissible for the janitor to kill the surgeon), then it remains unclear why one should prefer Graham's argument to this version of *Best-Theory*.

Finally, if one denies that "ought" implies "can," then, again, it would seem that, as the discussion above on some of Nelkin's views appear to confirm, one would have to give up on the prerequisites principle, something many would deem unacceptable.

3.5 PEREBOOM'S OBJECTIONS

Derk Pereboom raises a number of concerns with my views on reason and obligation. One is whether it is plausible that whenever some agent has an objective *pro tanto* reason to do something, that reason will be associated with reasons-wise obligation:

> One might question whether objective reasons are in fact closely connected with obligation. Haji says: "If an agent has a moral obligation to do something, then she has a reason to

do it" [Haji 2012a, 235]. This is, however, just a one-way connection. It's plausible that "if one ought to do something from the perspective of objective reasons, then one can do it" [Haji 2012a, 19], and that therefore the "reasons-wise 'ought' " implies "can." But is it also credible that whenever S has an objective pro tanto reason to do A, there will be some tie of that reason to obligation? Haji points out that if S has an objective pro tanto reason to do A, and that reason is not outweighed by objective pro tanto reasons to refrain from A, then S ought to do A. Yet S can also have an objective pro tanto reason to do A that is outweighed. This provides support for the claim that it's possible to have such a reason that's not tied to obligation. (Pereboom 2013)

Presumably, Pereboom's concern is not merely with the principle that whenever one has an objective *pro tanto* reason to do something, there will be some tie of that reason to some variety of *obligation* but rather to some variety of deontic appraisal—a judgment concerning permissibility, impermissibility, or obligation—which is such that a precondition of the truth of such a judgment is that one have alternatives. With this in mind, assume that S has an objective *pro tanto* reason to do A. Why believe there will be some tie of that reason to (some variety of) obligation, permissibility, or impermissibility?[18] Suppose this reason is not outweighed by other reasons of S, and is stronger than any other alternative of S. Then it is reasons-wise obligatory for S to do A. Speaking, next, to Pereboom's worry, suppose this reason *is* outweighed by other reasons in that there are stronger reasons for S to do something else instead. Then it is reasons-wise impermissible for S to do A. Suppose it is not outweighed by other objective reasons but is equally strong as some of them, and each of these equally strong reasons is stronger than the other alternatives of S.

Then it is reasons-wise permissible for S to do A. But there is an alternative possibilities requirement for reasons-wise obligation, permissibility, and impermissibility.

Now, as I previously explained, it may be that it is amoral for one to perform some action in that it is not morally permissible, impermissible, or obligatory for one to do it; amoral acts lack any of these primary moral statuses. Such acts may lack these statuses because they do not satisfy some freedom requirement for having any of these statuses. Analogously, again as I previously emphasized, it may be that from the standpoint of objective reasons it is not the case that it is reasons-wise permissible, impermissible, or obligatory for one to perform some action; rather, it is reasons-wise arational for one to do it. We may conclude that if it is not reasons-wise arational for one to perform an action, and one has a *pro tanto* reason to perform it, then it is reasons wise obligatory, permissible, or impermissible for one to perform it.

Additionally, in support of the view that one can have an objective *pro tanto* reason that is not tied to obligation, Pereboom says, "one might have an objective pro tanto reason to do A in virtue of A's realizing some good, and that good be independent of any deontic notion" (2013). Maybe it is true that the good in question is "independent of any deontic notion" but what about the objective *pro tanto* reason itself that S has to do A in virtue of A's realizing this good? Assuming it is not reasons-wise arational for S to do A, it is reasons-wise permissible, impermissible, or obligatory for S to do A. If S has such a reason to do A, then S could have done other than A.

Turning, now, to the following claim of Pereboom which is of primary interest:

> I propose that while there is a core sense of "ought" that does imply "can" . . . there is another that doesn't, and in this other

sense "ought"—which is not a notion of obligation—is tied to a notion of objective *pro tanto* reason. (2013)

Starting with a preliminary comment, elsewhere (e.g., 2002; 2012a) I've been engaged in this sort of debate: What sorts of moral judgment, if any, are threatened by determinism or its falsity? Incompatibilists and compatibilists about responsibility have long agreed that there is no dispute between them concerning the compatibility of determinism with various concepts of *being responsible*. But there is a serious dispute when the concept of *being responsible* is what we may label "traditional desert-entailing responsibility": Is determinism compatible with being deserving of praise or deserving of blame? Similarly, incompatibilists and compatibilists concerning moral obligation may have no fight whatsoever over whether determinism is compatible with various sorts of "ought" judgments. However, an interesting dispute would arise regarding what we may label "traditional (morally) deontic obligation" or simply "moral obligation," typical judgments of which are judgments such as "As of now, Sid all in (and not merely prima facie) morally ought to keep his promise now," or "As of now, Sandy morally ought not to return the book on Friday." For instance, both incompatibilists and compatibilists concerning traditional deontic obligation can agree that determinism does not endanger the truth of judgments of the ideal moral "ought," such as the judgment that it ought to be that no child starves to death, but may part company on whether determinism undermines moral obligation.

Pereboom proposes that there is an "ought" of specific agent demand. It implies "can," and it seems to be pretty much like (or perhaps even identical to) the traditional deontic "ought."

It's standard to differentiate between "ought to do" and "ought to be" claims (e.g., Humberstone 1971, Harman 1977; Haji

2002: 15). For instance, Mark Schroeder's (2011) distinguishes the action-related *deliberative* sense of "ought", and the *evaluative* "ought", as in "Larry ought to win the lottery" where Larry has been subject to a series of undeserved misfortunes. Kate Manne (2011) argues—plausibly to my mind—that the evaluative "ought" also applies to actions. She proposes that an evaluative "ought" claim does not (at least directly) entail a "can" claim, even when it concerns an action, while an "ought to do," which expresses a demand of an agent in a particular circumstance, does entail that she can perform the indicated action. We might call this last type an "ought" of *specific agent demand*. (2013)[19]

Pereboom contrasts the "ought" of specific agent demand with the "ought" of axiological recommendation that is or is very much like the "ought" to be. He says that uses of this "ought" propose to an agent as morally valuable a state of affairs in which she performs an action of a certain sort and recommends that she perform this action. Assuming that determinism precludes anyone's being able to do otherwise, while determinism undermines the "ought" of agent demand, determinism does not undermine the axiological "ought." Pereboom writes:

> Given determinism and that determinism precludes alternatives, when one tells an agent that he ought to refrain from performing some action in the future, the "ought" of specific action demand isn't legitimately invoked, but the "ought" of axiological evaluation still can be ... [The "ought" of axiological recommendation] is not at odds with determinism. Imagine it turns out that the agent performs the action anyway. If there was good reason to believe in advance that the agent has or could develop the requisite motivation, and especially if

there was good reason to think that articulation of the "ought" judgment would contribute to producing it, this use of "ought" would still have been legitimate. The "ought" of axiological recommendation is tied to an epistemic sense of can, i.e., to the condition that it's open that the agent will act in accord with the "ought" recommendation . . . The following principle specifies the connection: if it is appropriate for an appropriately situated agent T to tell S that he ought, in the sense of axiological recommendation, not to perform actions of A's type, then it is open for T that S will, in the future, refrain from performing actions of A's type. (2013)

Next, Pereboom proposes that although the "ought" of axiological recommendation does not imply "can," it is essentially associated with objective reasons.

My sense is that there's a robust notion of objective reason linked to this sense of "ought" and to the condition that involves the epistemic sense of "can." Suppose that if I gave to Oxfam it would feed hungry people. It's epistemically open to me that I will give, even though because I believe determinism is true it's also epistemically open to me that I will be causally determined to refrain from doing so, whereupon it would be the case that I cannot (in a pertinent metaphysical sense) give. In this situation its being epistemically open to me that I will give to Oxfam is sufficient for me to rationally consider the good resulting from my giving to Oxfam as a reason for me to do so. This would seem to be an objective *pro tanto* reason—my giving would really make people better off. It's also tied to "ought" judgments, albeit not to those of obligation and specific action demand, but rather to those of axiological recommendation. Thus it's also a notion of objective *pro tanto* reason we can take into account in deliberation (2013).

I concur with Pereboom that different senses of the moral "ought" should be distinguished. For example, there is the deontic "ought"—the "ought" of traditional moral obligation—and the ideal "ought." While the former entails "can," the latter does not (Haji 1998; 2002). So far, so good. Indeed, one may reasonably reason that since, the ideal "ought," unlike the "ought" of traditional deontic obligation, does not imply "can," what we have here are two different sorts of "ought." Another of Pereboom's interesting claims is that even the ideal "ought" or other "oughts" that do not entail "can" are or maybe tied to a "robust notion of objective reason." Perhaps the lesson Pereboom wishes to draw from all this is that, assuming it is not reasons-wise arational for one to do something, it is false that if one has an objective *pro tanto* reason to do it, one could have done otherwise. Elaborating, roughly, the strategy I use to attempt to show that reasons-wise "ought" implies "can" is this: Assume that the moral "ought" implies "can." If one morally ought to do *A*, one has an objective *pro tanto* reason to do *A*. If this reason is stronger than all the alternatives one has, one reason-wise ought to do *A*. But granting that the (morally) deontic "ought" implies "can," wouldn't it be implausible to suppose that reasons-wise "ought" does *not* imply "can"? One way to interpret Pereboom's relevant thought here is that it would not be implausible. It would not be because some moral "oughts" like the ideal "ought" or the axiological "ought" do not imply "can," and these "oughts" are also tied to objective reasons. In all cases involving these sorts of moral "ought," one can have an objective *pro tanto* reason to do something even though one cannot do this thing.

Suppose I don't know whether it is determined that I will give to Oxfam or it is determined that I will not give to Oxfam. (I don't know whether the past plus the laws entail the one or the other.) Given Pereboom's epistemic sense of "can"—roughly, you can do something consistently with what for all you know is the case because it is "open" that you develop the requisite motivation to do this thing even if determinism is presupposed, and even if determinism precludes you from being able to do this thing at the time you fail to do it—you still can give to Oxfam (see, e.g., Pereboom 2014, 141). Pereboom proposes that if I am rational, and I realize it is epistemically open to me that I give to Oxfam, I should "consider the good resulting from my giving to Oxfam as a reason for me to do so." Does nothing indeed count against this being an objective *pro tanto* reason?

Consider, first, this bit of reasoning: "It might be determined that I give to Oxfam or it might be determined that I refrain from giving to Oxfam. For all I know, then, I can bring it about that I give to Oxfam. So, I ought to give to Oxfam (where "ought" expresses all in traditional morally deontic obligation). This reasoning is obviously specious because it simply overlooks *Kant's Law*. From the fact that, for all you know, you can bring it about that you give to Oxfam, it does not follow that you *can* bring it about that you give to Oxfam. Hence, you cannot legitimately infer that you ought to give to Oxfam. Furthermore, you do not have an objective reason to give to Oxfam if, plausibly, no one can have an objective reason to do something that one cannot do.

Now consider this argument:

1. If it ought to be that you bring about A, then there is an objective reason for you to bring about A.

The rationale for line (1) is that just as the fact that you morally ought to do A is or provides you with an objective reason to do A, the fact that it ought to be that you bring about A is or provides you with an objective reason to bring about A

2. If there is an objective reason for you to bring about A, then you can bring about A.

This line is based on the assumption that objective reasons-wise "ought" implies "can."

3. Therefore, if it ought to be that you bring about A, then you can bring about A.
4. It's false that if it ought to be that you bring about A, you can bring about A.

Line (4) rests on the truism that unlike the moral "ought," the axiological "ought" does not imply "can."

As the first two premises generate a contradiction, at least one of them is false. It is clear that Pereboom rejects (2). He says:

> Like the "ought" of specific agent demand, the "ought" of axiological recommendation necessarily concerns agents and actions they might perform. But as for all claims about what ought to be, this use of "ought" should not be understood as presupposing a route accessible to an agent, via reasons for action, to her acting in some relevant way. One might be unsure about whether such a route is accessible, while the use of "ought" is nevertheless legitimate. (2014, 141)

But one might target the first premise instead. One might claim that you cannot have an objective reason to bring about something unless you can bring it about, a view I favor (see, e.g., Streumer 2007; 2010). So this premise is not true without qualification. Or, if one wishes to preserve the association with the axiological (or ideal) "ought" and objective reasons, one might explore the suggestion that there are different sorts of objective reasons, some that imply "can," and others that do not. To elaborate, if there are different sorts of moral "ought," and some sorts do not entail "can," why can't analogous things be true about reasons-wise "ought"? For example, why may it not be the case that if the "ought" of axiological recommendation is tied to objective reasons, these objective reasons are of a kind that do not entail "can"? In partial support of this view one might propose that if the ideal "ought" did not imply "can," but the sort of reasons-wise "ought" to which the ideal "ought" is supposedly tied did, there would be an implausible incongruity. I don't mean to be endorsing this view. I simply offer it as something for one to consider if one believes that since some sorts of moral "ought" do not imply "can" (whereas others do) these "oughts" that do not imply "can" must be a different species of moral "ought." A person drawn to this sort of view might also be drawn to an analogous view concerning reasons-wise "ought," to wit, if one sort of reason-wise "ought" does not imply "can" but another sort does, these are different sorts of reasons-wise "ought." It remains unclear to me, then, why one should favor rejecting line (2) of the argument above over renouncing line (1).

I leave this section with some comments on the axiological "ought." It may be suggested that even if determinism undermines traditional morally deontic obligation, this isn't a big deal because there are other sorts of moral "ought," in particular, the axiological "ought," that can take the place of the traditional deontic "ought." However, it appears that the axiological "ought" differs markedly from the traditional deontic "ought," and this may give us reason to pause about the proposed "replacement."

Assume, first, something not evident, that prescriptions (or proscriptions) of the axiological "ought" are just like those of the moral "ought" in that they take the form of prescribing or proscribing, whatever the case may be, actions, omissions, or states of affairs. This is not obvious because Pereboom often speaks of what is axiologically prescribed as a *recommendation* (e.g., 2014, 140). There are some recommendations that are optional in the sense that these are "take it" or "leave it" suggestions or proposals; we are free not to do as recommended without doing anything wrong or being at fault. Other recommendations are prescriptions or proscriptions of some sort of "authoritative" normative standpoint, such as the legal or the moral standpoint. If it is recommended that one not speed, the context may make it abundantly clear that this is tantamount to saying something like one legally ought not to exceed the speed limit. On the one hand, one may think that if a world does not accommodate moral obligation, the "moral" recommendations of the sort associated with the axiological "ought" are of the "take it" or "leave it" variety. On the other hand, Pereboom seems to want more; perhaps the recommendations of the "axiological standpoint" are somewhat like the recommendations of the morally deontic standpoint (but then one wonders why they do not entail "can"). Be that as it may, assume that axiological recommendations are not of the optional variety; they are more like the prescriptions or proscriptions of the morally deontic "ought." Given this assumption, one concern with the axiological "ought" mirrors the ones that arise with Nelkin's novel interpretation of *Kant's Law* (*New-OIC*). Revisit the case in which the best course of treatment for Ted is to receive two consecutive doses of medicine A, but instead the doctor settles for the second best course and gives two doses of medicine B. Unbeknownst to the doctor, he could not have given two doses of A owing to the presence of a Frankfurt-style counterfactual intervener who ensures that the doctor could not but give two doses of B. Given all he knows, at a time prior to which treatment has begun, it is open to the doctor to give a first dose of A and then a second; that is, it is epistemically open to the doctor that he give two doses of A, even though he cannot bring it about that he give two doses of A.[20] It seems that this is true: Doc axiologically ought to give two consecutive doses of A (even though he cannot bring it about that he give two doses). If he axiologically *ought* to give the first dose of A on Monday, then (presumably) it is axiologically impermissible for him to give B instead, and this even though he *can* bring it about that he gives B on Monday but *cannot* bring it about that he gives A on Monday.

Although I will not undertake the exercise here, I believe the axiological "ought" does not respect the prerequisites principle either. Simply adapt the example I used to show that Nelkin's novel interpretation of "can" in *Kant's Law* generates problems with the prerequisites principle to confirm that there will be an analogous problem with the axiological "ought." The problem, once again, ultimately traces to the condition that the axiological "ought" does not entail "can bring about." It appears, then, that the axiological "ought" is radically different from the traditional deontic "ought."

To scrutinize, further, the assumption that the "ought" of axiological recommendation prescribes actions, omissions, and so forth just as the "ought" of moral obligation does, the justification and goal of what Pereboom calls "forward-looking blameworthiness," broadly conceived, is to moderate or eliminate dispositions to misconduct. This is one sort of blameworthiness that Pereboom believes survives even if determinism (or its falsity) precludes desert-entailing blameworthiness. In what does this misconduct consist? Pereboom proposes that if "S is blameworthy for A in the forward-looking sense, then it is appropriate for a relevantly positioned respondent T to tell S that he ought, in the sense of axiological recommendation, not perform actions of A's type" (2014, 143). I introduce some terminology: If one is blameworthy for something in the forward-looking sense, then one is *forwardly blameworthy* for this thing. It appears that just as some tie desert-entailing moral blameworthiness to moral wrongness, Pereboom ties or suggests tying forward-looking blameworthiness to what one axiologically (or ideally) ought not to perform. In other words, the misconduct at issue appears to be associated with proscriptions of the ideal "ought." Assume that it ought to be that no children starve, or it ought to be that each person lives a life that it is intrinsically good for her to live. Take these "ought" judgments to be essentially bound to ideals, the first to the ideal that no children starve, and the second to the ideal that each person lives a life that is good in itself for her to live. How precisely are we to understand the recommendation that enjoins us to achieve these ideals? What sorts of thing from the standpoint of the ideal "ought" ought we to be doing when it is recommended to us that we achieve the former ideal (if, indeed, this is the sort of thing that is being recommended)? Should we strive to see to it that no children starve? Should we contribute to suitable charities that help needy children?

Assume this problem solved, that is, assume that with all judgments of the form, *it ought to be that X*, where substituents of X are ideals, there is a clear specification of things one should be doing or failing to do to achieve the ideal. Now, one can fall short of achieving an ideal without doing anything morally wrong or doing anything one nonculpably believes is morally wrong. (One might want to be more cautious and claim that if one falls well below achieving something that the ideal "ought" specifies one should achieve, one may end up doing things or failing to do things that it is morally wrong for one to do.) Maybe fault of some sort attaches to an agent who falls short of achieving an ideal. However, assuming other conditions for the fault at issue are not in question, it is difficult to see how this sort of fault could be anything like desert-entailing blameworthiness in every instance in which the agent falls short of living up to an ideal. In this respect, worlds devoid of desert-entailing blameworthiness but accommodating forward-looking blameworthiness would be quite different from worlds with room for the former sort of blameworthiness.

Pereboom claims that he proposes to ground his account of forward-looking blameworthiness not in basic desert but in three nondesert-invoking moral desiderata: protection of potential victims, reconciliation to relationships both personal and with the moral community more generally, and moral formation. Immoral actions are often harmful, and we have a right to protect ourselves and others from those who are disposed to behave harmfully. Immoral actions can also impair relationships, and we have a moral interest in undoing such impairment through reconciliation. And because we value morally good character and resulting action, we have a stake in the formation of moral character when it is plagued by dispositions to misconduct (2014, 134).

It does not seem unreasonable that it ought to be that one go beyond the call—for example, one perform actions it is supererogatory for one to perform—and that one avoid permissibly suboptimizing, for instance, one avoid doing things that it is suberogatory for one to do. If these are ideals, then if one fails to supererogate or one fails to avoid suberogating, from the standpoint of the ideal "ought," one will be doing wrong. Would one be forwardly blameworthy for such failings? Presumably the answer to this question turns partly but pivotally on whether such failings are properly associated with the aims of future protection, future reconciliation, and future moral formation. It is not evident how they are necessarily so connected.

Perhaps some might claim that I am guilty of making things much more complicated than they are. The import of prescriptions of the ideal "ought"—exactly what one is one committed to doing to fulfill such an "ought" prescription—has nothing essential to do with ideals but much to do with an appropriate ranking of alternatives, or, more generally, with the appropriate normative theory that specifies when acts are *axiologically* right, wrong, or obligatory. Even in the sort of possible world of interest—a world in which one has no alternatives perhaps because determinism is true at that world—arguably although this world would not accommodate *moral* obligation, it would accommodate "axiological obligation."

What, then, are the necessary and sufficient conditions for an act to be axiologically obligatory? We may start with a simple candidate to tease out various concerns.

Suppose one proposes that what one axiologically ought to do depends on the relevant value—"recommendation value" or "R value"—of one's options. It appears that Pereboom is not averse to ranking alternatives in some way. He seems to approve of the following.

> The core of Alastair Norcross's (2006) proposal for a purely axiological ethics involves specifying for each action-relevant situation the possible options for acting ranked in order of value realized. An option for acting might then be counted as morally wrong when its value is low enough in this ranking for it to be morally justified (on whichever free will skeptic friendly normative ethical theory is endorsed) for a relatively situated interlocutor to blame the agent in the forward-looking sense. (2014, 146)

If one's options are to be ranked in terms of R-value, we need to understand what determines R-value. One may co-opt the axiologies normative theories such as act utilitarianism presuppose. For instance, we might conceive of the R value of some alternative in this way: Take the total amount of pleasure it would produce if performed and subtract from this the total amount of pain it would produce if performed. Then we can say that a person axiologically ought to perform an act if and only if its R value exceeds that of all her alternatives. Forward-looking blameworthiness would then be tied to axiological impermissibility.

One problem with this way of conceiving R-value should be obvious: It inherits all the problems that afflict traditional act utilitarian theories. For example, there is Castaneda's (1968) formidable concern: If one axiologically ought to perform the conjunctive act (A and B), then one axiologically ought to perform each conjunct. But then each of A and B would maximize R value, an impossibility. Proponents of the axiological "ought" could not evade this problem by opting for a world utilitarian theory of Feldman's (1986) variety, because this sort of theory entails that if one ought to do something, there is a world *accessible* to one in which one does this thing. For another example, an act that framed a person for a crime that she did not commit may well maximize R-value. A more general problem is that there would be no guarantee that in every instance in which an act is axiologically impermissible, that act would be essentially associated with the aims of protection, reconciliation, and moral formation.[21]

One may, of course, strive to develop rival views about what makes axiologically obligatory acts obligatory. These views will have to be disassociated from any pertinent considerations of desert. It would be premature to speculate what such a view would look like. I simply call attention to the fact that the proponent of the axiological "ought" has a burden to discharge.

When Pereboom proposes that the justification and goal of forward-looking blameworthiness is to moderate or eliminate dispositions to misconduct, I may well be mistaken about how to conceive of the misconduct. Maybe the misconduct has nothing to do with ideals or with the sort of view sketched above regarding what makes axiologically impermissible acts impermissible (a view that invokes recommendation value). But then what *does* such misconduct have to do with?

There is a different sort of concern with the axiological "ought." Maybe this concern is not so much with this sort of "ought" as it is with the view that a significant correlation between obligation and rights cannot, it appears, be maintained if the kind of obligation in question is axiological obligation. To explain: Claim rights are rights that one person (or any entity that is the subject of such rights) holds against another person or persons (or "right bearers" if things other than persons can be such bearers). Many believe that this thesis that associates *such* rights with morally deontic obligations *owed* to persons is plausible:

> *Correlativity-1*: One person, *S*, has a claim right against another, *T*, that *T* perform some act if and only if *T* has a moral obligation owed to *S* to perform that act.

One can have a moral obligation to some persons but not to others. I may promise Tim's mother but not his father that I will attend her son's graduation ceremony. In virtue of promising, I have an obligation to Tim's mother—in this sense I "owe" her but not the father—an obligation to attend. Some obligations are not owed. One may have an obligation to do some voluntary work, but this obligation may not be owed to anyone. The correlativity thesis is usually understood to assert that claim rights (as opposed, for example, to other sorts of rights, such as liberty rights or powers) are correlative to prima facie as opposed to overall moral obligations that are owed to others. The distinction between prima facie and overall moral obligation will be of minimal import to the relevant discussion to follow as long as it is borne in mind that the morally deontic prima facie "ought" also implies "can."

Envision a world, "Perboom's world" or the "PB-World," that fails to accommodate the truth of morally deontic judgments but does accommodate the truth of axiological "ought" judgments. If the correlativity thesis is true, then the PB-World will be shorn of claim rights as no one in this world has a moral obligation (prima facie or overall) owed to anyone to do anything, or so it seems. I introduce the "so it seems" cautionary qualification because one may propose that there is a correlativity thesis that holds that there is a tight correspondence between claim rights and not moral obligation but *axiological* obligation:

Correlativity-2: S has a claim right against T that T perform some act if and only if T has an axiological obligation to S to perform that act.

I confess to not knowing how to interpret this second thesis, given my previous remarks on the axiological "ought." In particular, I am unsure what it is for one person to have an axiological obligation to another (or owed to another) to perform some action. One thought is that if one person has such an obligation to another to perform an act, then there is a recommendation ("deriving" from the standpoint of the axiological perspective) that the former perform the relevant act. But it seems that claim rights cannot be strictly correlated with recommendations if recommendations are not even prima facie obligations. Suppose in virtue of the promise that I make to Tim's mother, it is *recommended* that I attend Tim's graduation ceremony. Why should it be that I *owe* it to Tim's mother to attend bearing in mind that in the PB-World, it is false that in virtue of making a promise to anyone to do something, I incur a (moral) obligation to do that thing? At best, I "incur" a "recommendation." It is not credible to suppose that if it is *recommended* that one person do something that involves or concerns another, then the latter has a claim right against the former that the former do this thing.

An alternative thought is that, roughly, if one person has an axiological obligation to another to perform some act, then there is an "obligation" ("deriving" from the standpoint of the ideal "ought"— the "ought to be") that the former perform the relevant act. Again suppose, on the basis of the promise I make to Tim's mother, it ought to be that I attend Tim's graduation ceremony. Why should it true that I *owe* it to Tim's mother to attend, this time bearing in mind that the ideal "ought" does not imply "can"? It is implausible to suppose that if one "ideally" ought—that is, if one ought from the standpoint of the ideal "ought"—to do something that involves or concerns another, then the latter has a claim right against the former that the former do this thing. If it ought to be that I feed some starving children, how can these children have a right against me that I feed them if I am as destitute as they are and, hence, unable to feed them?

The primary moral to which I am calling attention is that, for whatever reason, if a world, such as the PB-World does not accommodate moral obligation, that world will not accommodate claim rights either (on the presumption that the correlativity thesis—*Correlativity-1*—is true).

Finally, I briefly address the connection between, first, axiological impermissibility and avoidability, and, second, forward-looking blameworthiness and avoidability. Regarding the former, suppose one endorses the following.

Axiological Impermissibility: As of t, it is axiologically impermissible for S to do A at t only if there is some time t^* at which S can refrain from doing A (or A-type actions), and t^* is not earlier than t.[22]

Pereboom allows for cases in which at t it is axiologically impermissible for S to do A at t when S cannot refrain from doing A at t. With this in mind, *Axiological Impermissibility* generates what seems to be an implausible result. You perform an act, A, at t that you cannot at t refrain from performing at t. Between t and future time $t10$ you can acquire the motivation not to perform A-type acts at $t10$ or times after $t10$. We may assume that at t it is axiologically impermissible for you to perform A at t. Now alter the case in this way: You die unexpectedly just after doing A at t. Then it would turn out if *Axiological Impermissibility* is true that it's false that it's axiologically impermissible for you to do A at t. Roughly, if A is bad, and it is recommended that you don't do A-type actions, why should there be something improper with this recommendation if you die shortly after doing A?

With respect to being forwardly blameworthy, Pereboom writes:

> While it's plausible that an agent's blameworthiness in the basic desert sense for an action is not explained per se by the fact that he could have avoided it, for an agent to be blameworthy for an action in the forward-looking sense it must be open that he refrain from performing actions of this type in the future. The Frankfurt-defender can accept this conclusion. It's intuitive that the agent in a typical Frankfurt example is blameworthy in the basic desert sense, but also in the forward-looking sense. But such an agent will then retain a general ability to refrain from performing the action at issue . . . This leaves it open that he will exercise that ability in the future. When a Frankfurt case is constructed as to permanently preclude the exercise of this ability . . . then it is evident that the agent is not blameworthy for performing the action in the forward-looking sense. (2014, 143–44)

It appears, then, that Pereboom accepts this principle:

Forward Blameworthiness: S is forwardly blameworthy for doing A at t only if there is some time t^* at which S can refrain from doing A (or A-type actions), and t^* is not earlier than t.

Imagine that in your Frankfurt predicament, you cannot refrain from doing A at t. But there is some later time at which you can refrain from doing an A-type action. We may suppose that you may be forwardly blameworthy for doing A at t. But now imagine, further, that you die unexpectedly just after doing A at t. Then *Forward Blameworthiness* yields the problematic result that you are not forwardly blameworthy for doing A at t.

My overall conclusion is that although some may believe it is controversial that a precondition of obligation is that one have alternatives, none of the objections considered in this chapter refutes this view.

NOTES

1. See, e.g., Feldman 1986, 43; Zimmerman 1996, 26–27; Haji 2012a, 61.
2. I rejected this argument in my 1993 paper. I still believe that this argument is not sound.
3. The rational abilities view mirrors Susan Wolf's "Reason View" of moral responsibility that also implies *Asymmetry*. See Wolf 1980; 1990. Fischer and Ravizza advance *Hero* and *Villain* to undercut the Reason View.
4. Others have ascribed a similar ability to agents such as Joe in Frankfurt cases. See, e.g., Vihvelin 2004; 2013; Fara 2008.
5. Vihvelin (2013) disagrees that holding fixed the past and the laws determinism precludes agents from being able to do otherwise.
6. Further discussion of this sort of issue occurs in Haji 2002.
7. One may, instead, prefer (roughly) this formulation of the prerequisites principles: If B is a necessary means of doing A, and one ought to do A, then one ought to do B. See, e.g., Persson 2013, 230; Zimmerman 2014, 55–56.
8. I owe this formulation of settling to Randy Clarke, whom I thank.
9. For discussion, see, e.g., Davidson 1963; Brand 1984; Bishop 1989; Sehon 1994; Audi 1997; Mele 2003a.
10. See, e.g., Melden 1961; Nagel 1986; Velleman 1992.
11. Some might prefer explicating the relevant issue concerning "can" in this way: What sort of possibility does "can" express? Elsewhere (Haji 2002), I have proposed that the "can" in *Kant's Law* does not imply that S has a dual ability to do A and to refrain from doing A; it is the "can" of ability and

opportunity and not the "can" of metaphysical or physical possibility; and the ability at issue is not a general but a specific ability to do *A*. Here, I focus on this last feature.

12. In the relevant discussion to follow concerning general ability, the pertinent considerations that tell against construing the "can" in *Kant's Law* as expressing general ability also tell against construing "can" in this law as expressing any broad ability that entails that in this Frankfurt predicament, Augustine has the broad ability to refrain from pushing the child off the cliff although he cannot (in his situation) bring about his refraining from pushing the child.

13. See also Urmson 1958; Feldman 1978, 48; Heyd 1982; and Mellema 1991, 17, 125–29.

14. In previous works (2002, 177–80), without an analysis of the supererogatory, I proposed that it is possible for one to do something that is supererogatory for one without being praiseworthy for doing this thing. But given McNamara's analysis, this proposal is false. What I should have said, roughly, is that one need not be praiseworthy for performing something akin to a supererogatory action. The idea is that, to the extent this is possible, imagine an action that has all the features of a supererogatory one save (roughly) that the agent performs it "from" base motives. Then we may have a supererogatory-like action for which an agent (such as Marion in our example) is not praiseworthy. McNamara also discusses various interesting cases in which an agent can be blameworthy (and praiseworthy) for doing something that was either precluded by doing the minimum or precluded by doing the maximum in, e.g., 2011a; 2011b; 2008.

15. On owed favors, see, e.g., Driver 1992, 289.

16. See also, e.g., Chisholm 1963; Mellema 1991; and Driver 1992.

17. Again, previously, not having an analysis of the suberogatory, I suggested that it is possible to do something that is suberogatory for one without being blameworthy for doing this thing (2002, 178–79). If McNamara's analysis is correct, this is false. What I should have said, roughly, is that one need not be blameworthy for performing something akin to a suberogatory action.

18. I say "some variety of" obligation because Pereboom's text does not make it clear whether he has moral or reasons-wise obligation in mind.

19. Also see Pereboom 2014, 139.

20. Pereboom concedes that in standard Frankfurt examples, it is open to an agent not to do something that she cannot avoid doing in her Frankfurt predicament (2014, 144).

21. Perhaps it may be suggested that the axiological "ought" need not be connected to these aims.

22. I don't know whether Pereboom endorses this principle. My recommendation is that he should not.

Chapter 4

Obligation Under Threat

In this chapter, I begin by drawing an important lesson from Frankfurt examples. They reveal that obligation is susceptible to luck because obligation requires alternatives, and whether one has alternatives in apt Frankfurt or Frankfurt-like cases is beyond one's control. I then refine and defend principle *Motivation/Ability* that links motivation to do something with ability to do it. Next, I argue that in many ordinary situations in everyday life, it appears that we lack alternatives as a result of luck's affecting the way we are. As in the Frankfurt examples called upon to expose luck's effect on obligation, in many mundane situations we cannot do otherwise ultimately because of luck's influence on our having alternatives. This finding, together with *Motivation/Ability*, is then used to underpin a primary conclusion of this book: Luck constrains the range of things that it is obligatory, permissible, or impermissible for us to perform.

4.1 FRANKFURT EXAMPLES, LUCK, AND OBLIGATION

Quite apart from casting doubt on the principle of alternate possibilities (PAP), Frankfurt examples, if cogent, are significant for a number of other reasons including the following. First, if freedom to do otherwise is not the sort of control that moral responsibility requires, then the search is on for a one-way or avoidability-free conception of control. Second, the examples motivate an "actual sequence" account of both the freedom that moral responsibility requires and moral responsibility itself according to which responsibility-level freedom and responsibility depend on features of the actual sequence that unfolds—these things depend on appropriate causal, modal, or dispositional features of the etiology of the pertinent behavior—and not on whether one had access to alternatives. Third, the examples go a long way (although not all the way) to shore up semicompatibilism regarding responsibility, the doctrine that even if determinism is incompatible with freedom to do otherwise, determinism is not incompatible with moral responsibility (Fischer and Ravizza 1998, 53). Fourth, as already outlined, the examples bring into relief a tension between a proposed control (or freedom) requirement of moral responsibility and a putative moral requirement. Fifth, as I explained in the previous chapter, the examples may be used to lend credibility to the view that suberogation is possible. I now want to discuss a sixth reason having to do with lack of control or luck.

Frankfurt examples are significant because they may be used to display how moral obligation is subject to luck in an instructive fashion. Revisit *Theft*, the Frankfurt example in which Augustine steals the pears. Suppose Ernie is not a principled counterfactual intervener in that sometimes he is on Augustine's case, but at other times he is not. Nor, when Ernie is on the scene, is it within Augustine's power to influence any of Ernie's activities. If Ernie is not on the scene, it is impermissible for Augustine to steal the pears or so we may safely assume; he could have refrained from stealing. If Ernie is on the scene, it is not impermissible for Augustine to steal the pears even though Ernie's presence or absence makes no difference *whatsoever* to how Augustine acts. Again, it is false (in Stage 2) that Augustine ought to refrain from stealing the pears because impermissibility requires avoidability. Moreover, whether or not Ernie is on the scene is a matter of luck for Augustine. The presence of such a counterfactual intervener "changes" an otherwise mundane situation from one in which Augustine has a moral obligation to refrain from performing an action to one in which he has no such obligation. The "change" is accomplished by eradicating alternatives. We may summarize this result as follows. (1) Necessarily, an action, A, is morally obligatory for an agent, S, only if S can refrain from performing A. (2) Whether the principal agent (like Augustine) in a Frankfurt situation can refrain from performing the relevant action, A, is a matter of luck. This is because it is beyond his control whether the counterfactual intervener, who has the power to ensure that he cannot do otherwise, is on the scene. More generally, it is beyond his control whether the fail-safe mechanism is "in place" and properly functioning. (3) If (1) and (2) are true, then in a Frankfurt situation, it is a matter of luck whether A is obligatory for the principal agent. So, in a Frankfurt situation, whether A is obligatory for this agent is a matter of luck.

I have appealed to Frankfurt examples to tease out a lesson concerning luck and obligation largely for these reasons. First, it is interesting in its own right that such examples may be invoked to show that moral obligation can fall prey to luck. Second, and more significantly, these examples help, fairly perspicuously, to underpin the view that moral obligation may be subject to luck *because* whether one could have done otherwise is or can itself be susceptible to luck. Again, from the vantage of an agent like Augustine, it is a matter of luck whether Ernie is alert or inert on the job, and so whether Ernie ensures that Augustine could not have refrained from stealing the pears. I want to exploit this key second point to show that one has a moral obligation to do something only in a narrow range of cases.

LUCK'S MISCHIEF

The basic argument for this view is this. (1) For any action, A, one has a moral obligation to do A only if one can refrain from doing A. (2) For any A, one can refrain from doing A only in a narrow range of cases. Hence, (3) for any A, one has a moral obligation to do A only in a narrow range of cases.

4.2 PRINCIPLE *MOTIVATION/ABILITY*

To support the second premise, I introduce a principle that links motivation to perform an action with ability to perform it. Action requires some sort of pro-attitude; that is, something with motivational force. It is a plausible conceptual claim that it is impossible for a person to perform an action without having some pro-attitude—desire, for short—to perform that action. For example, beliefs standardly construed do not have motivational force. Here is a first stab at the principle:

> *Motivation/Ability-1*: If S believes that it is morally impermissible as of $t1$ for S to perform A at $t2$, and S lacks any desire to perform A at $t2$, and in the relevant temporal interval (between $t1$ and $t2$), S cannot acquire a desire to do A at $t2$, then as of $t1$ S cannot do A at $t2$.[1]

The principle's basic idea is straightforward: If you believe that it is morally impermissible for you to do something, and you do not have any desire to do it (you have no motivation to do it), and, moreover, you cannot in the relevant time interval acquire any motivation to do it—you cannot, that is, acquire any pro-attitude to do it—then you cannot do it. This principle should not be conflated with the following (principle *Motivation/Ability-2*) that is false: If you believe that it is morally impermissible for you to do something, and you do not have a desire to do it, then you cannot do it. As John Fischer and Mark Ravizza explain, *Motivation/Ability-2* has counterexamples. Here is one:

> Just about anybody can summon up the worry that he is not free to do otherwise ... This worry can then generate *some* reason (perhaps, a desire) to do otherwise simply to prove that one can do so. Thus, barring special circumstances ... even an agent who actually does not have any desire to do other than A can have the power to generate such a desire (during the relevant temporal interval). And insofar as: (i) the agent *can* generate some desire to do other than A, (ii) the agent can try to act on this desire, and (iii) if he were to try to act on this desire, he would succeed, then we believe that the agent *can* (during the relevant temporal interval) do other than A. The leading idea here is that there is no reason to suppose that agents *generally* lack the power to generate (in some way or another) reasons to do otherwise, the power to try to act on those reasons, or the power to succeed in so acting. (1992b, 434, notes omitted)

Now for some refinements, first, it seems an agent who satisfies the conditions in the right hand side of *Motivation/Ability-1* may be able to A accidentally. If so, *Motivation/Ability* should be taken to be a principle about A-ing intentionally.[2] This is all for the good, especially since it is moral obligation that is of concern. Recall, direct obligations are restricted to intentional actions that one can perform (although this is not so with indirect obligations). We may take the relevant parts of the argument in chapter 2 to support the view that direct obligations are restricted to actions that one both can intentionally perform and intentionally refrain from performing.

Second, *Motivation/Ability* should also include the clause that if *S* believes that it is morally impermissible at *t1* for *S* to perform *A* at $t2$, in the relevant temporal interval between $t1$ and $t2$, S cannot cease to believe that it is morally impermissible for S to perform A at $t2$. The resulting principle is:

> *Motivation/Ability-3*: If S believes that it is morally impermissible as of $t1$ for S to perform A at $t2$, S lacks any desire to perform A at $t2$, and in the relevant temporal interval (between $t1$ and $t2$), S can neither acquire a desire to do A at $t2$ nor cease to believe that it is morally impermissible for S to perform A at $t2$, then as of $t1$ S cannot intentionally do A at $t2$.

Third, the principle as it stands is insensitive to side-effect actions.[3] Suppose you know that by B-ing you will A; furthermore, you have no desire to A, you can't acquire a desire to A over the span at issue, and you intentionally B. As you intentionally B, you do A as a side-effect action (even though you cannot acquire motivation to A in the relevant temporal interval). There are two ways to handle such actions. First, one might plausibly think that one does not *intentionally* perform the side-effect action; although one intentionally B-s, one does not intentionally A. However, suppose one believes to the contrary that in such cases, one does intentionally A. Then restrict *Motivation/Ability* to cases in which it is false that you know or even believe that by B-ing, you will A:

> *Motivation/Ability*: If (a) S believes that it is morally impermissible as of $t1$ for S to perform A at $t2$, (b) S lacks any desire to perform A at $t2$, (c) in the relevant temporal interval between $t1$ and $t2$, S can neither (ci) acquire a desire to do A at $t2$, nor (cii) cease to believe that it is morally impermissible for S to perform A at $t2$, and (d) it's false that A is a side-effect action; that is, it's false that S knows or believes that by B-ing at some time S

will A at $t2$, S has no desire to A, and S intentionally B-s, then as of $t1$ S cannot intentionally do A at $t2$.

At the heart of *Motivation/Ability* is the thought, roughly, that one can't intentionally do something if one has no reason or cannot acquire a reason to do it. This invites a first objection: the freedom to act crazily. Some existentialists (e.g., Camus 1946; Sartre 1953, 617–18) have proposed that it is conceivable that one can do something even in the absence of any reason to do it—what is rationally inexplicable is not impossible. If we take a desire (as we have broadly characterized it) to be a constituent of any reason, then this sort of existentialist concern speaks against *Motivation/ Ability*. Maybe the existentialists are right; perhaps there are occasions on which we can act crazily. Even so, this sort of freedom to do other than what one reasonably or rationally does is not the sort of freedom that obligation demands. The two-way control that direct obligation requires—the freedom to do and to refrain from doing something—is, minimally, two-way *intentional* control. Acting crazily does not give us this sort of dual intentional control. Compare what I have said about the two-way intentional control that obligation demands with what Robert Kane says about the sort of two-way control he believes responsibility requires. Concerning self-forming actions, which for Kane are paradigmatic free actions, he writes:

> They must be undetermined by the agent's pre-existing will and the agents must have what I call *plural voluntary control* . . . over them. That is, agents must have the power to voluntarily and purposefully perform them and the power to voluntarily and purposefully do otherwise (where "voluntarily" here means that actions are not coerced or compelled and "purposefully"

means that they are not done merely by accident or mistake, inadvertently or unintentionally). (2013, 61)

A second objection to *Motivation/Ability* turns on the alleged causal work of desires in action explanation. Regarding their causal role in explaining rational action, desires are generally thought to have intensities. Suppose Tim has a desire to do *A* to degree .9 and a desire to refrain from doing *A* to degree .1. Does Tim have a desire to refrain from doing *A* in such a scenario? The relatively weaker desire might not count as an overall desire, or an overall pro-attitude, toward refraining from doing *A*, but insofar as *Motivation/Ability* is plausible, it seems that Tim cannot refrain from doing *A* in this case, assuming Tim cannot muster a *sufficiently* strong desire to refrain from doing *A*.

Note, first, that principle *Motivation/Ability* focuses on cases in which one *lacks* any desire to perform some action during the relevant temporal interval. So cases in which one has conflicting desires—a desire of some intensity or strength to do one thing and a desire of some strength to refrain from doing it—do not undermine this principle. Second, in any case a more complicated variant of the principle can yield the desired results in cases of conflict. Here is an outline, and merely an outline, of such a variant: If *S* believes that it is morally impermissible as of *t1* for *S* to perform *A* at *t2*, and *S* has a desire to degree *i* to refrain from doing *A* at *t2*, and a desire to degree *h* to perform *A* at *t2*, and *i* is greater than *h*, and in the relevant temporal interval (between *t1* and *t2*), *S* cannot sufficiently strengthen the motivational force of the desire to do *A* at *t2*, then as of *t1* *S* cannot do *A* at *t2*.[4] (In the interests of brevity, I have omitted the other clauses about belief, and so forth.) It suffices for our concerns to work with the original principle because attention will primarily be confined to cases in which agents lack the relevant desires.

Third, some may think that there are counterexamples to *Motivation/Ability* such as the following. Sam has the ability to do fifty push-ups in a row from a rested state. If someone were to test him, he would pass the test every time. He does thirty planned consecutive push-ups and then stops because he strongly desires to relax, much more so than he desires immediately to complete another ten push-ups, which, had he wanted to, he could have accomplished. (Again, he could pass the test if challenged). In fact, he has no desire to do any more push-ups within the next five minutes. Furthermore, he cannot acquire a sufficiently strong desire to do so (a desire stronger than his desire to rest and relax) within the next five minutes. According to *Motivation/Ability* Sam cannot do another ten push-ups in the next five minutes, but—in what seems like the sense of "can" relevant to moral possibilities—he can.

Is it indeed the case that Sam intentionally can do ten more push-ups during the five-minute interval when it is true that he cannot acquire any relevant pro-attitude to do ten more push-ups in this interval? Some may think he can because he has succeeded in doing fifty push-ups in a row from a rested state on several occasions before, and this occasion is *not* relevantly different from these others. However, the occasion in question does seem to be pertinently different insofar as on this occasion Sam strongly desires to relax after having done thirty push-ups, he has no desire to do ten more push-ups in the next five minutes, and he cannot acquire a sufficiently strong desire to do more push-ups in the next five minutes. This difference cannot be discounted as insignificant or irrelevant on pain of begging the question against *Motivation/Ability*. Others may think that Sam can do ten more push-ups within the next five minutes because "can" is to be interpreted in a traditional, conditional way: One can do *A* at *t* if and only if had one wanted (or chosen or intended) to do *A* at *t*, one would have done *A* at *t*. However, we know that there are problems with this sort of conditional analysis.

Suffering from aquaphobia, Maria cannot jump into the children's pool, although it is true that if she had wanted to, she would have jumped into the pool. One of the lessons of counterexamples of this sort to the traditional analysis is revealing: It's not sufficient to analyze "one could have done otherwise than relax" as "one would have done otherwise than relax had one wanted to." We need minimally this augmentation: "and one *could* also have wanted to do otherwise."[5] As the push-up example is described, Sam could not, in the relevant temporal interval, have acquired a desire to do ten more push-ups.

A final response to this concern is to revert, again, to the distinction between a sense of "can" that merely expresses a general ability to do something, and a sense that requires both a specific ability and the opportunity to do something. We may admit that Sam can, in the former sense of "can" do ten more push-ups in the next five minutes, but he cannot, in the latter sense of "can" pertinent to direct obligation, do ten more in the relevant period.

4.3 DIMINISHED OBLIGATION

Motivation/Ability may next be mobilized to show that the range of obligations is narrow. Imagine that the devoted mother in the example above, Ann, must attempt to rescue her son immediately to prevent him from drowning. She believes that she ought to save her son, and it would be impermissible for her not to do so. Can she refrain from saving him? Assume that in most—if not all—such situations Ann has no desire to refrain from saving her child. Given *Motivation/Ability*, the pertinent question is whether she can, during the relevant time interval, acquire the desire not to save him (*Dr*). Remember that "desire" is an umbrella term for some apt pro-attitude.

If she can acquire *Dr*, she can do so intentionally or unintentionally. Regarding the first option, she cannot intentionally acquire a particular desire unless she has a conscious thought concerning that desire. In the situation, she does not have any such thought about the desire to refrain from saving her child. In addition, she cannot intentionally acquire the thought on the basis of any choice she makes, perhaps by engaging in practical reasoning with the goal of acquiring the thought. To acquire the thought in this way either she must have the thought already, or she performs some other action as a result of which the thought in question unintentionally occurs to her. The first apparent option is not an option. Regarding the second, as Zimmerman (1990) explains, it is very unlikely in any situation, for one immediately, or during the relevant temporal interval, to acquire the thought. For, first, the number of independent conscious thoughts any one of which one is in principle capable of having at one time is extremely large; and second, the maximum number of independent conscious thoughts all of which one is capable of having at one time is very small. So if all thoughts were equiprobable, the likelihood that on some occasion a particular one of them should occur would be exceedingly low. Second, however, not all thoughts are equiprobable; some are far more likely to occur than others, given the agent's past history, character, circumstances, and so forth. But even if this is so for some thoughts, it will not be so for many others. Indeed, it *cannot* be; for, given that at most some independent thoughts can occur at once, the increased likelihood of one thought tends to render others less likely (Zimmerman 1990, 350). Here is the relevant and astute passage from Zimmerman 1990:

> Consider, first, that the number of independent conscious thoughts any one of which one is in principle capable of having at one time is extremely large (call it *N*); and second, that

the maximum number of independent conscious thoughts all of which one is capable of having at one time is very small (five to seven ... call it n). Thus, if all thoughts were equiprobable, the likelihood that on some occasion a particular one of them should occur would be n/N—i.e., very low indeed. Now, of course, we cannot assume that all thoughts are equiprobable; some are far more likely to occur than others, given the agent's past history, propensities, circumstances, etc. For example, one is much more likely to think of what to have for dinner than to wonder how much wood a woodchuck could really chuck. Indeed—and this is the possible exception—it may be that having a certain thought at t' is personally necessary for someone at t *because of some choice* made by him or her *prior* to t. In such a case it may even be *likely* (from a perspective prior to t'), rather than unlikely, that the thought in question will occur at t'. But even if this is so for some thoughts, it will not be so for many others. Indeed, it *cannot* be; for, given that at most n independent thoughts can occur at once, the increased likelihood of one thought tends to render others less likely. Thus, ironically, *whatever exceptions there are prove the general rule.* This is so even if we ignore "irrelevant" thoughts altogether and concentrate only on those that are of potential concern to the agent; for the number of such thoughts is still very large (call it N^*) and hence n/N^* is still very small. (1990, 350, notes omitted)

Regarding the second option—Ann's unintentionally acquiring the desire to refrain from saving her child—often we do acquire desires unintentionally. For example, strolling in the park on a hot, sunny day, you chance upon an ice cream cart. You find yourself with a desire for a strawberry sundae. The cart, or your perception of it, is a stimulus that triggers your acquisition of the relevant desire. Or sometimes we unintentionally acquire desires on the basis of the way we feel. On hearing about the fall of the stock market, you are doleful. Your feeling of impending doom causes you to acquire a desire to puff on your pipe. Your acquisition of this desire is unintentional. Reverting to the scenario in which the son is drowning, it is not true that there is some stimulus, relevantly analogous to the ice cream cart or Ann's perception of it, which might contribute to her unintentionally acquiring the desire to refrain from saving her child (*Dr*). Nor is it true that Ann has relevant feelings that trigger her acquiring *Dr*. One cannot, however, dismiss the possibility that Ann acquires *Dr* by sheer chance. But the probability of Ann's doing so, as Zimmerman cautions, is exceedingly low inasmuch as the pool of relevant candidate thoughts is very large and the number of thoughts that can be had at any one moment is very small.

In the passage reproduced above, Fischer and Ravizza propose that just about anyone can muster the worry that he is not free to do otherwise. We may readily agree with Fischer and Ravizza that there *are* contexts, such as the one discussed in their passage, in which this is true. But it should also strike us that there are many contexts in which we would not be able to summon up the thought that we are free to do otherwise. Ann's context is just of this sort. To explain, presumably, *intentionally* to summon up the thought that she is free to do otherwise, Ann must have this conscious thought. But on the occasion Ann does not have any such thought. Nor does it seem plausible, for the reasons already canvassed, that Ann can intentionally acquire the germane thought by any choice she makes. Similarly, for the reasons previously discussed having to do with the very large pool of candidate thoughts and the very small number of thoughts that can be had at any one time, it is not credible to suppose that Ann can unintentionally acquire the conscious thought that she is free to do otherwise.

So it is reasonable to think that Ann cannot (during the relevant temporal period) acquire the desire to refrain from saving her son. Recall *Motivation/Ability*:

Motivation/Ability: If (a) S believes that it is morally impermissible as of $t1$ for S to perform A at $t2$, (b) S lacks any desire to perform A at $t2$, (c) in the relevant temporal interval between $t1$ and $t2$, S can neither (ci) acquire a desire to do A at $t2$, nor (cii) cease to believe that it is morally impermissible for S to perform A at $t2$, and (d) it's false that A is a side-effect action, that is, it's false that S knows or believes that by B-ing at some time S will A at $t2$, S has no desire to A, and S intentionally B-s, then as of $t1$ S cannot intentionally do A at $t2$.

Concerning the elements of this principle's antecedent, Ann satisfies (a) with the trivial qualification that she lacks any desire to *fail* to perform a certain action (she lacks the desire to refrain from saving her son). She also satisfies (b), (ci), and, we may safely assume, (d) as well. What about (cii), though? Is it credible to suppose that she cannot, during the relevant temporal interval, cease to believe that it is morally impermissible for her to refrain from saving her son? Surely so, for unless the circumstances are extraordinary, we simply cannot shed deeply ingrained beliefs over at least a short temporal span. Second, assuming we are rational, we would need to acquire reasons to shed deeply ingrained beliefs under ordinary conditions. It seems that an argument parallel to the one to show that Ann cannot, during the relevant time span, acquire the desire to refrain from saving her son, can be deployed to show that she cannot, during this time span, acquire reasons to shed her belief that it is impermissible for her not to save her son.

With its antecedent satisfied, *Motivation/Ability* generates the result that Ann cannot, during the relevant temporal period, refrain from saving her child. One noteworthy, intermediary conclusion is apt: If Ann cannot but save her child, then this act which one initially may plausibly take to be obligatory for her is not in fact obligatory for her insofar as obligation requires control, and such control entails that one could have done otherwise.

We highlight one more observation. Factors beyond her control preclude Ann from being able to refrain from saving her son. She is unable to refrain from saving her son because she is unable intentionally or unintentionally to acquire the desire (Dr) to refrain from saving him during the relevant temporal span. Take each of these options in turn. Ann is unable intentionally to acquire this desire because she lacks the conscious thought concerning it, and, moreover, she cannot acquire this thought. In many situations Ann will not have any conscious thought concerning desire Dr because of the sort of person she is. Furthermore, in many situations, the sort of person she turns out to be is inextricably associated with factors beyond her control, such as her genetic makeup, the sorts of parents she had, the education she received as a child, and the social culture in which she was nurtured. In her situation, Ann cannot intentionally acquire the conscious thought to possess desire Dr because the candidate pool of relevant thoughts is very large and the number of thoughts that can be had at any one moment is very small. Both these factors are beyond her control.

Ann is unable unintentionally to acquire desire Dr because there is no relevant stimulus that would trigger her acquiring Dr, or she has no apt feelings that would contribute to her acquiring Dr, or the probability of acquiring Dr by chance is excessively low. Each of these things—lack of a proper stimulus, apt feelings, or the low probability—and, as one credibly suspects, any other reasonable candidate as well, is something not within her control. So we may now draw a second intermediary conclusion: In many situations Ann is unable to refrain from saving her child because of factors beyond her control.

Finally, some may worry that Ann's example of saving the child is somewhat special—it reveals something about her "deep" nature; it is an expression of who she really is, or what she really "stands for."[6] In this way it contrasts with other mundane actions, such as, perhaps, Ann's contributing to a charity. So whereas it may be plausible to suppose that Ann cannot but save her child, it seems far more contentious that, for example, she cannot but donate to a charity on those occasions when she donates to a charity. However, this (apparent) distinction is simply a distinction without a difference. There is, it appears, nothing special per se about the sort of example—Ann's saving her child—in that many seemingly obligatory acts are acts of the sort that their agents are unable to refrain from performing in the relevant temporal interval. For instance, suppose you very strongly believe that you ought to contribute to feeding the starving children in East Africa, or you ought to aid the elderly person to cross the street, or you ought to show gratitude to your colleague for her staunch support over the years, or you ought to be loyal to your spouse, and so on. Given pertinent circumstances and the sort of person you are, if you believe that it is impermissible for you not to perform each of these acts, and you have no desire not to perform them, then, it may well be far more probable that in the relevant temporal interval, you cannot acquire the desire to refrain from performing them than that you can acquire the desire. Again, the previous discussion sheds light on why, if you cannot acquire the germane desires, your inability to do so may well be something beyond your control. Drawing on our two intermediary conclusions, we may infer the following: Many acts that one initially may plausibly take to be obligatory (or for that matter, impermissible or permissible) for one are not in fact obligatory (impermissible or permissible) for one insofar as obligation requires freedom to do otherwise, but factors beyond our control preclude us from being able to do otherwise.

4.4 OBJECTIONS AND REPLIES

Now, for some objections, suppose Ann has made herself into a certain sort of person; she has taken deliberate steps to see to it that she would protect or come to the aid of her children or others when called upon. Furthermore, suppose she has molded herself to become the kind of person who cannot do or refrain from doing various things (such helping her children in germane circumstances). This sort of character formation should not undermine obligation or impermissibility. Even if she cannot refrain from saving her child, it is still obligatory for her to save her child because she has freely made herself into the kind of person who cannot but rescue or attempt to rescue her child from impending danger.

Whether agents freely mold themselves or to what extent they do so to become the adults they are is controversial. I will not linger on this concern. Rather, the objection can be parried by recognizing that it is a variation of the "self-imposed impossibility" objection to *Kant's Law*, and appreciating that this objection leaves much to be desired. Imagine that you promise Fred to return a book, which you borrow from him on Monday, not later than Friday morning. In virtue of promising, assume that you ought to return the book by Friday. Now suppose that on Wednesday, you sell the valuable book because you are short on cash. Against *Kant's Law*, some may object that you still have an obligation to return the book by Friday even though, as of the time you have sold it, you cannot return it. However, friends of *Kant's Law* may rejoin that what is in fact true is that prior to selling the book, you ought to return it by Friday, in part, because you can, before selling it, keep your promise. After selling it, though, and so no longer being able to return it, it is not true that you ought to return it by Friday. Of course, one can maintain that you ought, up to the time of selling the book, to return it later, and as this (remote) obligation is *not* satisfied, a wrong *is* done. But this is consistent with holding that as of the time you sell it, your returning the book is not obligatory for you, and, moreover, as of this time you acquire new obligations, such as the obligation to apologize and make reparation. Notice, in addition, that obligations do expire. If you ought to return the book not later than 9:00 a.m. and it is now 9:32 a.m., even if you have not sold the book, *this* obligation has expired. At 9:32, you no longer have an obligation to return the book at 9:00, and you do not have this obligation because as of 9:32 you cannot return the book at 9:00. If obligations can expire after the proper time of discharge (9:00 a.m. in the example), why suppose that they cannot expire before the slated time of discharge if the relevant inability has set in prior to this slated time? It is, then, perfectly in order to conclude that once you have sold the book, and thus the relevant inability sets in, your obligation to return it by Friday expires (see, e.g., Zimmerman 1996, 98–100; Haji 2002, 47–52, and Vranas 2007, 175–79).

For whatever bizarre reason, suppose you have made yourself into the kind of person who will not return a borrowed book on time. The prior considerations lend support to the view that once the pertinent inability sets in, you do not have an obligation to return the book even if it is assumed that before this inability sets in you did have such an obligation.

Another objection, affiliated to the previous one, to the conclusion that we have (perhaps many) fewer obligations than we are typically inclined to believe starts with questioning the principle that impermissibility requires alternatives:

(IA): Necessarily, if it is impermissible for one to do *A*, then one is able to do and to refrain from doing *A*.

It may be proposed that examples such as the following falsify (IA). When Zack drinks alcohol it makes him do bad things, for instance, hit innocent people. Thus, if Zack is drunk now, he cannot refrain from striking an innocent person he sees in front of him. If (IA) is true, Zack has no obligation to refrain from hitting this person. But this is absurd. We rightly blame and punish people for injuring others in these circumstances, and we do this partly because we believe that they have failed to live up to their obligations toward others in harming them.

It could be said that in this scenario the drunk *can* refrain from hitting the innocent person in the sense that had he not made himself drunk he could refrain. If we understand the ability to refrain in these terms, then maybe it is plausible that the drunk is still obligated to refrain from hitting the innocent person. But if (IA) is defended in this way, then it is no longer clear that Ann lacks an obligation to save her child. For this pathway around the objection implies that Zack still has the obligation not to hit innocent people when drunk because it is up to him whether he makes himself drunk. However, analogously, it is up to Ann whether she makes herself into the sort of person who cannot refrain from saving her child. Assuming it is up to her—assuming she is responsible for her character—then just as Zack is responsible for becoming drunk and thereby still obligated not to hit innocent people when drunk, so too is Ann obligated to save her child. At best, then, the line of reasoning for the conclusion that our range of obligations is narrow sustains only the weaker conclusion that if our characters (or large parts of them) are not up to us, then the range of our obligations is much smaller than we typically think.

In reply, first, the objection seems to assume that if we duly overtly blame an agent for doing something, we blame partly because we believe that the agent is blameworthy, and the agent is blameworthy only if the agent has done something impermissible. Or perhaps the thought is that we cannot rightly overtly blame a person for doing something unless it is impermissible for the person to do that thing. However, as I have suggested, the blameworthiness-requires-impermissibility principle is questionable. Second, when we assess Zack's case, we should bear in mind the double temporal indices of "ought" statements, and one lesson of the reply previously discussed to the self-imposed impossibility objection that obligations can change with the passage of time. Prior to getting drunk, Zack ought to refrain from hitting the innocent person at some later time, but when he loses obligation-relevant control (by being unable to refrain from hitting the person), it is no longer true that as of this time, he ought to refrain from hitting the innocent person (just as it is no longer true that as of this time, it is permissible for him to hit the innocent person). Furthermore, the objector's proposal to circumvent the objection suggests a sort of "tracing principle" for obligation (or impermissibility) that is captured in this reworked version of *Kant's Law*:

> *Kant's Law-1:* S ought at *t1* to do A at *t2* only if S has the power at *t1* to do A at *t2*, or it would have been in S's power at *t1* to do A at *t2* had S not done something, B, that it was impermissible for S to do at a time, *t0*, before *t1*, the doing of which prevented S from A-ing at *t2*.

Kant's Law-1, however, will not do. Assume all other conditions for its being the case that S has an obligation at *t1* (5:00 p.m.) to do A at *t2* (6:15 p.m.), save the condition expressed in *Kant's Law-1*, are satisfied in the following scenario so that if *Kant's Law-1* is met, S does have an obligation at *t1* to do A at *t2*. We are to ponder whether this assumption is tenable, as it would be, if it were true that, given the facts of the scenario, as of 5:00 p.m., I ought to visit Vick in the hospital at 6:15. The relevant facts are the following. At 4:30 p.m., on the way to the hospital, I drop in at Cheers and get so drunk that I am no longer able to make it to the hospital. I don't get drunk in order to avoid seeing Vick; I just get carried away with the song and drink. Had I not stopped at the bar, I would have visited Vick. As *Kant's Law-1* is met (its second but not first disjunct is satisfied), I have an obligation, as of the time I am intoxicated and, hence, unable to make it to the hospital at 5:00 p.m., to visit Vick at 6:15 p.m. This result is untenable. I'm inclined to think that, as of the time I am inebriated, I have no obligation to visit Vick, although at an earlier time, I did have this obligation. As a (remote) obligation was not fulfilled, I did (remote) wrong. Further, I may well be blameworthy for failing to visit Vick.

One may try yet again:

Kant's Law-2: S ought at *t1* to do *A* at *t2* only if S has the power at *t1* to do *A* at *t2*, or it would have been in S's power at *t1* to do *A* at *t2* had S not done something, *B*, with the intention of preventing S from being able to do *A* at *t2*, that it was impermissible for S to do, at a time, *t0*, before *t1*, the doing of which prevented S from *A*-ing at *t2*.

Again, assume that if *Kant's Law-2* is met, S does have an obligation at *t1* to do *A* at *t2*. But *Kant's Law-2* is problematic as well. Suppose I borrow Carl's watch and promise to return it on Sunday. The question this time is whether it is true that as of 8:00 a.m. on Sunday (*t1*), I ought to return the watch at 10:00 a.m. (*t2*) on the same morning. I'm aware that Carl highly values the old watch that once belonged to his father. I hear some nasty (but false) rumors about Carl at Cheers on Saturday night. I believe these nasty things. Later that night, I throw Carl's watch into the river partly to prevent myself from being able to return it the next day. As *Kant's Law-2* is met (its second disjunct is satisfied), I have an obligation, even as of the time I've thrown the watch into the river, to return the watch to Carl at 10:00 on Sunday. Again, I find this result unacceptable. Surely, as an advocate of *Kant's Law*, one wants to say that, as of the time I toss the watch into the river, I do not have an obligation to return the watch to Carl because I can no longer return it. I did, though, earlier have an obligation to return it, and as this obligation is not fulfilled, a (remote) wrong has been committed. So it seems that the interesting objection can be resisted.[7]

A final objection is that the considerations advanced for the view that, oftentimes, we cannot do otherwise in mundane situations in life rests on a psychological assumption (PA): We are so constituted that frequently we cannot (during the apt temporal interval) acquire motivation to do other than what we in fact do in many ordinary situations in life. Some people may want to challenge this psychological assumption.

In reply, support for PA derives partly from the following two theses which seem reasonable: (i) One cannot *intentionally* acquire a particular desire unless one has a conscious thought concerning that desire. (ii) The number of independent conscious thoughts any one of which one is in principle capable of having at one time is extremely large; and the maximum number of independent conscious thoughts all of which one is capable of having at one time is very small. In addition, speaking for myself, and for many others who have chatted with me about PA, it seems that the way many of us conduct ourselves in day-to-day situations bears out this assumption. Under mundane circumstances, it appears that very many of us would not betray confidences, not refrain from coming to the aid of a child who is drowning when we could easily save, not walk away from the nursery with a plant without making payment even though we could effortlessly do so, and so forth, and, moreover, we could not acquire the apt motivation to do or to refrain from doing (whatever the case may be) such things.

Suppose, however, that PA is false. Would the putative result that our range of obligations is narrow be of little significance? No because what would be brought to light is that obligation hangs on a thread in this way: It is not hard to imagine that we can easily succumb to factors over which we have no control (because, for instance, we may not even be aware of them) that preclude us from doing otherwise. It seems that it is just a matter of luck whether or not such factors do affect us in the relevant way. (Each of us is either a winner or loser of the Rawlsian natural lottery where one can think of the prizes as ranging from such things as genetic constitution, the sort of family in which one was born, whether one had a benevolent and constructive upbringing, and so forth, to the sorts of decisions one makes and actions one performs that are appropriately causally connected to the latter sorts of prize.) If they do affect us in the pertinent way—they preclude our being able to do otherwise—our range of obligations will narrow considerably; if they do not affect us in the relevant way, then again it will simply be a matter of luck that they fail to affect us in this way. It is disconcerting, to say the least, that whether our range of obligations is narrow or expansive turns on whether the pertinent factors (that are beyond or largely beyond our control) affect us in the germane way.

4.5 ANOTHER FRANKFURT EXAMPLE

Principle *Motivation/Ability* may be exploited to construct a novel sort of Frankfurt example that does not involve counterfactual interveners nor dual pathways (as in Pemba's case). Mario's spouse, Bella, never misses to record events of the day she deems important in her personal diary each night before retiring for the day.

Suppose, on a Saturday night, his eye falls on Bella's diary just as he is about to turn off the reading lamp on his side of the bed. He wonders about Bella's most recent entry, but he intentionally refrains from peeking. The story so far may be taken to be the Stage 1 correlate of *Theft*. In Stage 2, simply imagine that clauses (a) to (d) in *Motivation/Ability*, properly interpreted to incorporate the facts of this story, are all satisfied: Mario believes that it is morally impermissible as of 10:30 p.m. for him to peek into the diary a few minutes later at 10:34; (b) he lacks any desire to peek at 10:34; (c) in the relevant temporal interval between 10:00 and 10:34, he can neither acquire a desire to peek at 10:34 nor cease to believe that it is morally impermissible for him to peek at 10:34, and so forth. Imagine, furthermore, that Mario has no idea that he is unable to acquire the desire to peek during the relevant temporal interval. It appears that Mario may well be praiseworthy for refraining from peeking even though he could not have done otherwise.

The anticipated objection is that this case is straightforwardly question-begging. Why should friends of PAP accept the verdict that Mario is praiseworthy for not peeking when it is clear that between 10:00 and 10:34 he could not have done otherwise? The reply, once again, is to start with not passing initial judgment or not already making up one's mind on PAP. In *Theft*, the presence of counterfactual intervener, Ernie, and his mind-reading equipment do not affect conditions of responsibility *other* than the one in question, PAP. For example, if Augustine steals the pears while nonculpably believing that it is morally impermissible for him to steal them, Ernie's appearance in Stage 2 has no impact on this belief or its role in the etiology of Augustine's action. Similarly, in Stage 2 of Mario's case, Mario's being unable to acquire the pertinent desire during the germane temporal interval has no influence whatsoever on the other conditions for his being praiseworthy for not peeking other than the alternate-possibilities condition that is up for assessment. This should quell concerns about question-begging.

4.6 OBLIGATION AND SELF-CONTROL

Let's record a consequence of diminished obligation. Roughly, self-controlled individuals are motivated to conduct themselves in accordance with their best or better judgments against actual or anticipated competing motivation. (The clause "or better" will henceforth be assumed but suppressed.) In many contexts, what creatures like us judge best to do is customarily informed by our beliefs about what is morally obligatory, permissible, or impermissible. Assuming that self-control and akrasia are two sides of the same coin (Mele 1995, 5), some akratic individuals freely and intentionally fail to do what they judge morality requires of them. Call the self-control effectively exercised when the behavior of the self-controlled agent conforms to his best judgment concerning moral prescriptions or proscriptions, "morally focused self-control." If our best judgments regarding moral obligation turn out more often than not to be false, then the putatively morally self-controlled person's exercises of self-control will be defeated insofar as such a person will have acted in conformity with best judgments that are false. The failure would be somewhat unusual in this respect: It would not be the person who is weak-willed. Rather, it would simply be that the exercise in self-control would be in vain because she would be acting in conformity with what is not in fact a moral prescription (or proscription).

One of morality's "functions" is to constrain behavior. We may suppose that a morally conscientious person, who heeds the "call of morality," frequently forms best judgments that align themselves with what is morally obligatory or permissible for her to do, and attempts to act (continently) in accordance with these judgments. This is a way in which morality keeps her behavior in check. If, however, the range of obligations for persons is narrow, then their instances of morally focused self-control will diminish as well.

To conclude, luck infuses our lives in many different ways. I have argued that it is a matter of luck whether we can avoid performing garden-variety sorts of acts in everyday life that are seemingly obligatory for us. But if this is so, then the range of obligations for each of us is narrower—perhaps unsettlingly far narrower—than we may have hitherto believed.

NOTES

1. A principle roughly along these lines is discussed in Van Inwagen 1989 and Fischer and Ravizza 1992b.
2. An insightful paper on abilities and intentional action is Mele 2003b.
3. I thank Mele for this point.
4. See Mele 1992, ch. 3 for a highly illuminating discussion on how this sort of principle might be refined.
5. Needless to say, even so augmented, the analysis is defective. Some may find this objection to the conditional analysis less compelling than Keith Lehrer's (1968) objection.
6. Frankfurt (1994; 1999) speaks of volitional necessities.
7. For more on obligation and tracing, see Haji 2002, 47–52. Kane (2014, 183–86) appears to endorse both the view that moral obligation presupposes that we have strong, incompatibilist alternatives, and that some sort of tracing principle concerning this sort of obligation is true.

Chapter 5

Blameworthiness Under Threat

In this chapter I argue that the first primary conclusion of this book—our range of obligations is narrow—in conjunction with principles that associate obligation and being to blame, ratifies the second primary conclusion—we are blameworthy for perhaps far less than what many may plausibly believe. I also advance additional arguments to support this second conclusion. Finally, I propose that the reach of nonmoral blameworthiness—prudential blameworthiness, for instance—is reduced too, and for the same sorts of reason for which moral blameworthiness is constrained.

5.1 BLAMEWORTHINESS AND IMPERMISSIBILITY

Moral blameworthiness has a freedom (or metaphysical) requirement and a deontic (or moral) requirement as well. The most prominent skeptical arguments designed to show that no one has been, is, or ever will be blameworthy—and more generally, morally responsible—for anything centrally appeal to the freedom precondition. In contrast, the considerations I advance for curtailed reach of blameworthiness turn crucially on the moral requirement.

Let's distinguish three candidates for the moral requirement, the objective view, the simple subjective view, and the complex subjective view.

5.1.1 The Objective View

The objective view is simply the familiar view that blameworthiness requires impermissibility:

> *Objective (or Blameworthiness/Impermissibility)*: Necessarily, an agent, *S*, is morally blameworthy for doing something (or refraining from doing something), *A*, only if it is morally impermissible for *S* to do *A* (or to refrain from doing *A*).

This view is widely endorsed by many including various philosophers who advance what they take to be avoidability-free accounts of blameworthiness (see, e.g., Mellema 1991, 87; Smith 1991, 271; Widerker 1991, 223; Fields 1994, 408–09; Copp 1997; 2003, 286–87; Fischer 2006, 218; Arpaly 2006, 91, n. 3; Campbell 2011, 33–34). In addition, it is a view favored by some who are compatibilists about responsibility, others who are libertarians, and yet others who are skeptics. So, for example, Pereboom, a skeptic about responsibility, proposes the following:

> In my view, an agent's being blameworthy for an action is in fact entailed by his being morally responsible for it . . . together with his understanding that his action was in fact morally wrong. This is because for an agent to be morally responsible for an action in this sense is for it to be hers in such a way that she would deserve to be the recipient of overt blame if she understood that it was morally wrong. (2014, 89)

One may take this passage to be an affirmation of the objective view (although, see Pereboom 2014, 142). I have raised doubts about the objective view, but even if it is true, the gamut of things for which we are blameworthy—the "scope of blameworthiness" as I'll say—diminishes.

5.1.2 The Simple Subjective View

The simple subjective view (or, more properly, family of views) ties moral blameworthiness not to moral impermissibility but to relevant beliefs concerning impermissibility:

> Simple Subjective: Necessarily, S is morally blameworthy for doing something (or refraining from doing something), A, only if S does A (or S refrains from doing A) while nonculpably believing that it is morally impermissible for S to do A (or to refrain from doing A).

A variation of simple subjective is that one is blameworthy for doing something only if one does it on the basis of the nonculpable belief that it is morally impermissible for one to do it (Zimmerman 1988; Haji 1998).[1] This more involved variant entails the simpler view (Simple Subjective). When focusing on the family of simple subjective views, it will suffice to confirm that the scope of blameworthiness is reduced to work with the simpler view.

Simple Subjective, however, is not trouble-free either. The possibility of being blameworthy for doing something it is permissibly suboptimal for one to do appears to cast doubt not just on the objective view but on Simple Subjective as well. In Delivery, I need not be deluded that each of my options of calling you and delivering the parcel personally is permissible for me. Despite not taking myself to be doing anything *impermissible*, it may well be the case that I am blameworthy for calling you. Appreciating this problem leads us to our third deontic candidate.

5.1.3 The Complex Subjective View

In *Reason's Debt to Freedom* (2012a, 185), I tentatively suggested the following principle:

> *Complex Subjective-1*: Necessarily, one is morally blameworthy for doing something only if it is either nonculpably believed that it is impermissible for one to do it, or it is nonculpably believed that it is morally deontically inferior to something else one could have done instead.

I said (in the book) that the proposal is strictly tentative. Why was I so cagey? *Complex Subjective-1* countenances counterexamples if there are ranked permissible options. For instance, as McNamara insightfully illustrates, there are cases of graded supererogation. There may be two people in danger; it is supererogatory to rescue either one alone, and still better and supererogatory to rescue both (McNamara 2011a, 229–30). Then to rescue only one, despite being heroic and highly praiseworthy, will, on *Complex Subjective-1*, be blameworthy if the person realizes she could do better and rescue both but does not do the best possible (again, assuming other conditions of responsibility are met).

However, I still believe that something like *Complex Subjective-1* is in the right ballpark. If you do something while nonculpably believing that it is impermissible for you to do it, then you take yourself to be doing something it is morally deontically amiss for you to do. Similarly, in *Delivery*, it is not merely that I believe I could have done something it is (deontically) better for me to do. Presumably, if I am rational and not mistaken about the primary moral statuses of my relevant actions, I do believe that but I also take myself to be doing something it is deontically improper for me to do. I realize that it is permissible for me to phone or permissible for me personally to deliver the parcel. I (nonculpably) take the former option not to be morally deontically impermissible, of course, but (for lack of better expression) I do take it to be morally deontically subpar or untoward.

Now I suppose one may claim that in the case of graded supererogation, if you rescue one rather than both, you may take yourself to be doing something morally subpar, and, stronger still, you may even nonculpably take yourself to be doing something morally subpar. But then wouldn't the proposed sketch of how *Complex Subjective-1* is to be adjusted still deliver the incorrect verdict: You are blameworthy for saving only one? Here, however, I would urge caution in rejecting the proposed adjustment. After all, I have already motivated the view that one can be blameworthy for performing a supererogatory-like action. Just as one can be blameworthy for doing something that it is obligatory for one to do (if, for instance, one does it in the nonculpable although mistaken belief that it is impermissible for one to do it), so, one can be blameworthy for doing something that is precluded by doing the permissibly minimum if one nonculpably believes (perhaps mistakenly) that in doing this thing, one nonculpably takes oneself to be doing something it is morally amiss for one to do. I am drawn, then, to the view that moral blameworthiness is associated with nonculpable belief in either doing the impermissible or in doing something that is denotically morally amiss:

Complex Subjective: Necessarily, S is morally blameworthy for doing A only if either S nonculpably believes that it is impermissible for S to do A, or S nonculpably believes that it is morally deontically amiss for *S* to do *A*. (It goes without saying that short of analytic confusion anyone who believes the first disjunct also believes the second, so believing the second weaker clause will suffice for any rational agent as a necessary condition for blameworthiness.)

Unfortunately, I have little to offer by way of an analysis of deontic amissness. In her insightful discussion on suberogation, Julia Driver characterizes suberogatory actions as those that are permissible though bad (1992, 291). One's suboptimal permissible options, however, need not be bad, if we take "bad" to denote overall intrinsic badness. Driver's characterization, nonetheless, is in keeping with the spirit of my suggestion that one nonculpably takes oneself to be doing something that is deontically amiss—bad—when one is blameworthy for doing something it is permissibly suboptimal for one to do. W. D. Ross (1930) lists as one of the main kinds of prima facie duty, duties of gratitude: If someone has previously benefitted me, and I can now repay the past kindness, I have a prima facie duty to do so. In *Delivery*—and more generally, with owed favors—I have a prima facie duty to repay the person for the no-strings-attached favor when I am in a position to do so. Suppose, as in *Delivery*, I do have the opportunity to repay, but I don't, and have no good excuse (or justification) for not reciprocating. Although it is permissible (albeit suboptimal) for me to call you to collect the parcel, my calling you is something it is morally amiss for me to do perhaps because I thwart a prima facie obligation (which is not a duty proper) that I could easily have discharged. A related thought is that if you nonculpably believed you could have done something else that, in a broad sense of "benefit" would have benefitted others (or more others) with little or no additional cost to yourself, and you deliberately failed to do this thing, then if you did something it was permissibly suboptimal for you to do, you did something it was morally amiss for you to do.

Let's revisit Marion's case. She rescues the child from the flames only to satisfy her intention to exploit him for personal gain. Marion does something it is permissibly beyond the call for her and for which she is blameworthy. Why, exactly, is she blameworthy for this deed? One suggestion is that at the time she rescues the child, she nonculpably believes that she is violating a prima facie obligation of intending to harm an innocent person (we assume that all other conditions of blameworthiness are satisfied). There are, however, doubts about whether there is any such prima facie obligation. Another concern is that Marion's intending to harm the child may well be impermissible for Marion, and Marion may nonculpably believe that this state of affairs is impermissible for her.

We previously noted that a Strawsonian suggestion is that Marion is blameworthy for saving the child because she expresses ill will in her conduct. One may further venture that if one expresses ill will in one's action, then it is morally amiss for one to perform that action. Recall, McKenna's proposal is that the quality of will one expresses in one's action manifests the worth of the moral regard one has toward others (or oneself), and toward the relevance of moral considerations. However, there are complications with this quality-of-will view as well.

Suppose Tim, unlike Tony, believes that morality is not overriding. Or suppose Tony suffers from a type of akrasia—he frequently does what is contrary to his consciously held best judgment concerning what he morally ought to do—whereas Tim has no such failing. Or suppose Tim has a much better appreciation than Tony of the various modes of moral evaluation and the wide-ranging items that are possible candidates for moral evaluation. Or suppose that frequently, when Tim does what it is morally obligatory or permissible for him to do, his act causally arises from mixed motivations, whereas when Kantian Tony does what it is permissible for him to do, he always does what he does simply for the sake of doing something permissible. Do these differences give us reason to believe that Tony shows more regard toward moral considerations than Tim or vice versa? In addition, it seems that there can be numerous relevant factors that might pull in different directions when it comes to the overall moral worth of one's will. These may nonexhaustively include: (a) the many and varied modes of moral appraisal, such as, on the positive side, being good, right, virtuous, and commendable, and, on the negative side, being bad, wrong, vicious, and reproachable; (b) certain pertinent interests of various parties; (c) one's relationship with others; (d) one's psychological capacities to do (or not to do) something, or to feel or not to feel something; and (e) one's motives in performing certain acts. How do these disparate factors "combine" to give us an overall rating of the worth of one's will as deficient, or adequate, or commendable? To bring out this problem, it is reasonable to assume that "requirements" of love can conflict with morally deontic considerations of obligation, permissibility, and impermissibility. Maybe it isn't too much of a stretch to think that, in certain circumstances, considerations of love require that a mother save her own child, and not someone else's, when she can only save one, but moral considerations require that the mother save the other. From the standpoint of love, the mother ought to save her child; from the standpoint of morally deontic considerations, she ought to save the other. One deep concern that may stand in the way of combining these two considerations to arrive at a judgment of overall worth is incommensurability of the values at issue.

As another illustration, consider this sort of example that Richard Brandt advances. Suppose Sam nonculpably believes "some things no decent person will believe to be right" (Brandt 1959, 473); he nonculpably believes that it is right for him to do *A* even though no decent person would believe that. Imagine that Sam does *A* on the basis of this belief. Some, many, or all "decent" others may condemn *him* for doing *A* or may condemn his *act*. Here, it seems that there is an appropriate conflict of judgments: There is a positive judgment concerning an excuse—after all, Sam *did* nonculpably believe that he was doing right—and there is a negative judgment concerning condemnation. What, then, is the overall regard that his act *A* expresses? One option, of course, is that the conflicting judgments do not prohibit the appropriateness of a single, comprehensive judgment concerning regard. Ross, for example, proposed that an act's being both prima facie right and prima facie wrong does not exclude an overall judgment of the act's being all-things-considered right (or wrong). But Brandt's case (and numerous relevantly similar others) suggests that in many scenarios no comparison is possible, and so no overall judgment can be made. This is as it should be. There is no reason to disavow the complexity of morality, and to deny that in virtue of this complexity, it is reasonable to suppose that on many occasions there will simply be no judgment concerning a person's overall regard when it is regard for others or moral considerations at issue. The person may score high on some scales and low on others, and that is exhaustive of what a fair assessment of the case calls for.[2]

Here is an alternative suggestion regarding moral amissness. Suppose one does something it is permissible for one to do, but only because one believes that doing it is a prerequisite to doing something else that one nonculpably believes it is morally amiss—morally impermissible, for instance—for one to do. Then although one does what it is permissible for one to do, one does something that, if one is rational, one believes it is morally amiss for one to do. Marion saves the child only because she cannot do what she nonculpably believes it is impermissible for her to do—subject the child to severe harm unless she saves the child. She thus does something that she nonculpably believes it is morally amiss for her to do.

Maybe the notion of moral amissness has to do fundamentally with one's motives, the core idea being that it is morally amiss for one to do something if one's primary motivation for doing it is morally problematic. Ponder this example: Let $M1$ be the motive of Marla's wanting to sell the child, $A1$ be the act of Marla's saving the child, and $A2$ the act of Marla's saving the child with motive $M1$. Suppose, unbeknownst to Marla, Marla can save the child only if she acts with motive $M1$. Assume that, as of time, t, it is obligatory for Marla to save the child. If she ought to see to the occurrence of her saving the child, and she cannot see to the occurrence of her saving the child without seeing to the occurrence of her wanting to sell the child, then she ought, too, to see to the occurrence of the latter. But then she ought to see to the occurrence of $A2$. Suppose, further, that Marla performs $A1$ with motive $M1$. Suppose she nonculpably but falsely believes that it impermissible for her to see to the occurrence of $M1$ (her wanting to sell the child); she doesn't believe that she can save the child only if she has motive $M1$. Then although it is obligatory for her to save with the motive of wanting to sell the child, it is morally amiss for her to save with this motive. Roughly, it is morally amiss for her to save with this motive because she nonculpably believes that it is morally impermissible to have this motive. If an act that it is morally obligatory for an agent to perform can be morally amiss for this agent to perform, then there is no reason to deny that an act that it is morally permissible for an agent to perform can be one it is morally amiss for this agent to perform.

5.2 RESPECTING SUBJECTIVE VIEWS

To put it rather mildly, some people look askance upon subjective views. Under suspicion is the crux of such views that responsibility has to do with nonculpable *belief* in what it is impermissible for one to do in the case of blameworthiness, and nonculpable belief in what it is obligatory (or permissible) for one to do in the case of praiseworthiness. Again, I restrict discussion to blameworthiness.

5.2.1 Subjective Views Defended

Frequently, I have encountered the complaint that if one has done no wrong, one cannot be deserving of blame. As one commentator put it to me, if you think that blameworthiness is associated not with impermissibility but with what one nonculpably takes to be impermissible, you need some "theory," some special justification for this subjective view; those who opt for the objective view need no such theory.

I am unsure what lies behind such a demand. Suppose one keeps in mind that responsibility appraisals are "agent-focused" appraisals—they are first and foremost appraisals of the person. Morally deontic assessments of obligation, permissibility, and impermissibility, in contrast, are "act-focused" appraisals, being first and principally appraisals of actions (or "actional" states of affairs). Intuitively, why should we think that a person is less at fault, or not at fault at all—when the personal fault is of the sort that blameworthiness marks—if the person freely does something she nonculpably takes to be impermissible for her to do but which, fortuitously, turns out *not* to be impermissible for her? It appears that Augustine is no less at fault for stealing in those instances in which counterfactual intervener Ernie is awake and kicking, thereby ensuring that it is amoral for Augustine to steal, than in those instances in which

Ernie falls asleep, and so in which it is impermissible for Augustine to steal. Augustine's "inner ledger" seems to be equally tainted in either variation of the Frankfurt case.

It may be thought that proponents of subjective views marshal unmerited support for such views by failing carefully to differentiate actions or states of affairs for which one is supposedly to blame. Specifically, in all cases in which it is thought that some person is blameworthy for an action that is *not* impermissible for her, there is some *other* action—some action in the "vicinity"—that *is* impermissible for her and for which she may well be to blame. Consider, for instance, *Deadly's Defeat* that I have elsewhere advanced as a problem for the objective view. I proposed that this case goes against principle *Blameworthiness/Impermissibility*: One is blameworthy for performing an action only if one ought not to perform it. Deadly injects hospitalized Ernie with drug, C, for the purpose (or with the intention) of killing Ernie. But because of an error in diagnosis of which Deadly is unaware, C is actually the cure for Ernie's malady. Indeed, we may assume that it is obligatory for Deadly to inject Ernie with C. Intuitively, Deadly is blameworthy for giving Ernie C even though it is not impermissible for him to give C.

Friends of the objective view might rejoin that if Deadly ought to inject Ernie with C, then he is not blameworthy for giving C. Rather, he might be blameworthy for *something else*, such as attempting to kill Ernie, that *is* impermissible for Deadly. So *Deadly's Defeat* does not defeat their view. However, I proposed that it may also be true that Deadly ought to attempt to kill Ernie. This may be because Deadly may not be able to inject Ernie with C without attempting to kill Ernie. Given the prerequisites principle, if Deadly ought to inject Ernie with C, and Deadly cannot do so unless he attempts to kill Ernie, then he ought, too, to attempt to kill Ernie.

As Justin Capes recently queries, why, though, might it be thought that Deadly cannot intentionally inject Ernie with C without attempting to kill him? Capes says, "I see no reason what-soever to accept . . . [this] claim and, moreover, it seems straight-forwardly false" (Capes 2012, 424). But it's relatively easy to think of an apt reason to accept this claim. Imagine that Daisy is squea-mish about needles, and, ordinarily, is psychologically incapable of injecting anyone. It is only in the exceptional situation where she has no recourse to attempting to save her child but by injecting him with an antivenom that she can thrust a needle into him. Similarly, suppose Deadly is just like Daisy when it comes to needles. It is only under the special circumstances in which he has the purpose or intention of killing his bitter, foe, Ernie that he can muster sufficient motivation to force the injection containing C into Ernie. There is no more reason to believe that this story is incoherent than there is reason to believe that Daisy's story is incoherent.

Capes advances his own counterexample to the blameworthiness-requires-impermissibility principle.

> Beatrix freely shot and killed Bill. She did this despite believing that it was objectively wrong to kill Bill, that it was within her power to avoid killing him and, indeed, that it was within her power to avoid wrongdoing altogether. Why, then, did Beatrix kill Bill? . . . A significant role was played by her hatred of Bill and her (no doubt morally unjustified) desire to rid the world of him. Unbeknownst to Beatrix, however, Bill was just about to torture and kill her daughter, and the only way she could have prevented him from doing this was to shoot and kill him. Call this case "Kill Bill." (2012, 428–30)

Now of course, the advocate of the objective view might insist that just as Deadly is *not* blameworthy for his attempt to kill Ernie if Deadly *ought* to attempt to kill Ernie, so Beatrix is *not* blameworthy for killing Bill if it is true that Beatrix *ought* to kill Bill. How do we move this debate (other than appealing to subjective views)? One might attempt to persuade the advocate to come around by advancing considerations that support the view that Deadly or Beatrix are indeed blameworthy for doing what it is obligatory for them to do. Here is Capes's suggestion reminiscent of McKenna's views:

> According to what I will refer to as the Quality of Will View, necessarily, if S is blameworthy for A-ing, then A manifested a morally objectionable quality of will on the part of S . . . An agent has a morally objectionable quality of will just in case the beliefs, desires, values, intentions, plans, etc. in light of which the person acts exhibit a morally unjustifiable degree of ill will, indifference, or lack of due regard for others or for the moral considerations that bear upon her situation . . . An action A manifests (or expresses) a morally objectionable quality of will only if the attitudes in which the objectionable quality of will consists are among the non-deviant causes of A. According to the Quality of Will View, then, the only actions for which a person is to blame are those that express a morally objectionable degree of ill will, indifference, or lack of due regard for others or for the moral considerations that bear on the situation. (2012, 432)[3]

Focus on these elements of the Quality of Will View (for simplicity, I omit blameworthiness for omissions): If S is blameworthy for doing A, then, (i) A expresses a degree of "ill will, indifference, or lack of due regard for others or for the moral considerations that bear on the situation," and (ii) this degree is morally objectionable. Presumably, frequently, one's behavior can express both what is intuitively "good regard" and "ill regard" in an act. The Quality of Will View, apparently, presupposes that there is some way to tally the regard that an act expresses to arrive at some overall measure of this regard. Assume that overall regard may be either positive—in which case, we may call it "good will"—or negative, in which case it is "ill will." Assume, further, that ill will and good will come in degrees. If one's act expresses ill will to a degree that is morally objectionable, then according to the Quality of Will View, one will have satisfied a necessary condition for blameworthiness.

This view, though, countenances difficulties. We have already remarked on one of its problems having to do with factors that purportedly determine the value or worth of one's will, one's regard for others (or oneself) or for moral considerations. Capes's Quality of Will view has another shortcoming. Just what sort of normative appraisal is at issue when it is proposed that the degree of ill regard that one's action expresses is *morally objectionable*? One candidate is moral impermissibility: The degree of ill regard that an agent's, S's, action, A, expresses is morally objectionable if and only if the state of affairs, *S's doing A and A's expressing ill regard to degree n* is morally impermissible for S. But if this is Capes's view, it faces two hurdles. First, it seems that blameworthiness would, ultimately, be tied to impermissibility, something Capes wishes to reject. Second, in the end, Capes agrees that Deadly is blameworthy for injecting Ernie with C. In his estimation, "Deadly's action, it seems clear, manifested an objectionable quality of will . . . So according to the Quality of Will View, it is something for which . . . [Deadly] may legitimately be to blame" (Capes 2012, 433). Consider, however, this state of affairs:

> D*: Deadly's injecting Ernie with C with the purpose (or intention) of killing Ernie.

It may credibly be assumed that D* is an "actional" state of affairs that captures Capes's view that Deadly's act of injecting Ernie expresses overall ill regard. But Deadly *ought* to see to the occurrence of D* because in *Deadly's Defeat*, Deadly ought to attempt to kill Ernie, and he cannot attempt to kill Ernie without bringing about D*. After all, plausibly, D* just *is* the relevant attempt. Some may rejoin that Deadly *can* attempt to kill Ernie without bringing about D* because the needle might break during the attempt and not pierce Ernie's skin. To guard against this concern, simply imagine that the needle is made of titanium or some such substance that just won't break.

Given the proposal under consideration—the degree of ill regard that S's action A expresses is morally objectionable if and only if the state of affairs, *S's doing A and A's expressing ill regard to degree n* is morally impermissible for S—it would follow, contrary to Capes, that the degree of ill will that Deadly's act of injecting Ernie with C expresses is *not* morally objectionable. Perhaps it would be judicious to conclude that moral objectionability is not tantamount to moral impermissibility. The proponent of the Quality of Will View owes us a convincing account of moral objectionability.

Yet against subjective views, some might think that if we simply understand blameworthiness—if we come to grips with its nature, if we are clear on its analysis—then it should become evident that blameworthiness has essential ties not with what one takes to be impermissible for one but with what is in fact impermissible for one. I have strong doubts that this is so. Consider, for instance, the following brief sketches—and only sketches—about the nature of blameworthiness or responsibility in general. On a Strawsonian view to which I have already alluded, appealed, or invoked, to be morally responsible just is to be the appropriate object of the reactive attitudes—evaluative reactions to people's behavior—such as, gratitude, resentment, indignation, and the like. Strawson explains that it matters to us whether the actions of other people "reflect attitudes towards us of good will, affection, or esteem on the one hand or contempt, indifference, or malevolence on the other" (Strawson 1962, 63). The reactive attitudes are "natural human reactions to the good or ill will or indifference of others towards us as displayed in *their* attitudes and actions" (1962, 67); and they express "the demand for the manifestation of a reasonable degree of good will or regard, on the part of others, not simply towards oneself, but towards all those on whose behalf moral indignation may be felt" (1962, 71). On such an account, when one is blameworthy for an action, one expresses ill will in one's action (roughly, it may be proposed, as McKenna does, one does not show sufficient regard for others or moral considerations), and others react to the perceived ill will with appropriate reactive attitudes. However, McKenna, who has an elegant development of such an account of the nature of blameworthiness, aptly remarks that this sort of account is consistent with the subjective view.

According to ledger accounts, to be morally responsible is to be such that one's moral standing or record as a person is affected by some episode in, or aspect of, one's life. Zimmerman explains that the Strawsonian and ledger accounts are allied. The difference between the two is that "whereas the former identifies responsibility with susceptibility to certain reactive attitudes, the latter identifies responsibility with that in virtue of which one is susceptible to such attitudes" (Zimmerman 2002, 555; see also Zimmerman 1988, 38–39.) On the ledger account, when a person is praiseworthy, her moral standing has been enhanced in virtue of some episode in her life; when blameworthy, her moral standing has been diminished. Metaphorically speaking, when blameworthy, a negative mark has been entered into her appropriate moral ledger. The ledger account has it that it is because one's moral standing has been diminished that one is a suitable candidate for things such as resentment and indignation. So this second account denies that one's being susceptible to the reactive attitudes is *constitutive* of responsibility. Once again, the ledger account does not entail that the subjective view is false.

Timothy Scanlon summarizes his "relations-impairment" account of blameworthiness in this way:

> Briefly put, my proposal is this: to claim that a person is *blameworthy* for an action is to claim that the action shows something about the agent's attitudes toward others that impairs the relations that others can have with him or her. To *blame* a person is to judge him or her to be blameworthy and to take your relationship with him or her to be modified in a way that this judgment of impaired relations holds to be appropriate. (2008, 128–29, note omitted)

The general idea of Scanlon's account is fairly easy to grasp. Suppose two people stand in some sort of relation to one another; maybe they are friends. Among other things, various attitudes, intentions, feelings, expectations, and dispositions of the two constitute this relationship. We may think of friendship as governed by, or subject to, certain norms or standards of behavior. Suppose I, as one of the parties, intentionally do something that violates one of these standards; I break trust, for instance. Such conduct expresses a certain attitude of mine—not being sufficiently sensitive about things you have disclosed to me in confidence—that may well blight our friendship. You may not want to confide in me anymore or you may be much more reserved about what you decide to confide in me. Scanlon's account (together with the germane facts of the example) entails that I am blameworthy for my conduct in virtue of its expressing attitudes toward you that impairs my relationship of friendship with you.

A key constituent of Scanlon's account is that as long as the attitudes one's conduct expresses are or can be revealing of whether one's behavior is or is potentially damaging to the pertinent relationship, one can be blameworthy for this behavior. Imagine that

I take myself to be doing something it is morally impermissible for me to do; I think I am disclosing something to another person that you revealed to me in confidence. But I am in fact doing no wrong. I am simply misremembering. You *did* tell me about this thing but not in confidence. It may still be that my germane behavior expresses attitudes of mine that may impair my relation of friendship with you. There is, then, nothing in this sort of account that prevents it from being paired with subjective views.

Some people may be averse to *Simple Subjective* (and its more complex variation) because they believe that if it is true, there will be implausibly few cases in which persons are responsible for their negligent behavior. It is not hard to see why. Randolph Clarke gives this sort of example. Suppose you have promised your wife to buy some milk on the way home from work, and in virtue of promising you have an obligation to do so. (In Clarke's version of the story, your wife calls and asks that you pick up some milk.) But as you are driving home, you start to think about a paper you're writing on omissions, and you simply forget to stop at the store for the milk. As you pull into your driveway, you realize your mistake. It may be proposed that you are blameworthy for not buying the milk (Clarke 2014, 164–65). We may imagine that it's false that you nonculpably believe you're doing anything wrong in failing to stop at the store as you drive by it. At the time, you have no such belief at all. Despite not having this belief, some may suggest that you *ought* to have had this belief. Since you are blameworthy for failing to have this belief, and your not buying the milk is suitably related to this failure, you are blameworthy for failing to buy the milk too. However, if the subjective view is true, then you are blameworthy for failing to have this belief only if you nonculpably believe that it is impermissible for you to fail to have (or acquire this belief), and it would be rare indeed if this condition were met.

Is this an embarrassing consequence for the subjective view? I don't think so. Here, I will consider Clarke's interesting suggestion about why you may well be to blame for failing to buy the milk. Clarke proposes that in scenarios of this sort, blameworthiness for the omission in question need not derive from blameworthiness for any prior actions or omissions.

> [A] case of this sort can be imagined so that there's no prior blameworthy action or omission—from which blameworthiness for my failure might derive. Since I was on my way out of the door when my wife called, it was reasonable of me to entrust my plan to memory. I *could* have taken time to enter a reminder into my phone, with an alert to be sounded at the estimated time of my approach to the store. But in the circumstances, it would have bordered on compulsion to do such a thing, and I'm not blameworthy for not doing it. (2014, 165)

So why, according to Clarke, am I blameworthy for the failure? He explains:

> As the case might be imagined, my forgetting my plan on this occasion was substandard. It fell below a cognitive standard, not just for people generally and not just for me generally, but one applicable to me, with my specific cognitive and volitional powers, in the situation I was in. I can recall things of this sort in situations like this—indeed, I almost always do. I remember my plans for minutes, hours, even days! I remember them even when between making them and carrying them out, I think about other things, including my work. And no extraordinary circumstance—no horrifying car crash, no exploding bomb, no apocalyptic news story on the radio—taxed my ability to recall mundane plans on this occasion. Further, I can reinforce

my memory, as I see fit, by, for example, asking myself whether I'm remembering what I've planned to do. That I forgot my plan on this occasion falls below a standard that, given my cognitive and volitional abilities and the situation I was in, applied to me. (166)

Clarke gives the following sufficient condition for basic blameworthiness—blameworthiness that does not derive from the blameworthiness for other actions or omissions—for a wrongful omission that is not intentional and of which the agent is (at the relevant time) unaware:

> Provided that the agent has the capacities that make her a morally responsible agent, she is blameworthy for such an omission if she is free in failing to doing the thing in question and if her lack of awareness of her obligation to do it [or her lacking the belief that she ought to do it]—and of the fact that she isn't doing it—falls below a cognitive standard that applies to her, given her cognitive and volitional abilities and the situation she is in. (167, notes omitted)

Clarke suggests that a virtue of this proposal is that it yields intuitively correct results in a host of other cases, some involving actions. For instance, he considers this example that Gideon Rosen advances:

> In the ancient near East in the Biblical period the legitimacy of chattel slavery was simply taken for granted. No one denied that it was bad to be a slave, just as it is bad to be sick or deformed. The evidence suggests, however that until quite late in antiquity it never occurred to anyone to object to slavery on grounds of moral or religious principle. So consider an

ordinary Hittite lord. He buys and sells human beings [one of them is Annittas], forces labour without compensation, and separates families to suit his purposes. Needless to say, what he does is wrong. (Clarke 2014, 182, quoting Rosen 2003, 64–65)

As Rosen describes the case, it's plausible that the lord is blameless for believing that there is nothing impermissible with enslaving Annittas. If so, assume that the lord is blameless for buying Annittas (or separating Annittas from the rest of his family). Rosen says that the example supports the view that one is not blameworthy for wrongdoing if one blamelessly believes that one is doing nothing wrong (the subjective view). But granting that the lord is blameless for believing that there is nothing impermissible with slavery, Clarke offers an alternative explanation of the lord's nonculpability for buying Annittas.

Suppose we agree with Rosen that the Hittite lord is blameless for believing there's nothing wrong with slavery. If that is the case, then something further seems to be true: In so believing, the lord doesn't fall below any cognitive standard that, given his cognitive and volitional capacities and the situation he is in, applies to him. As Rosen puts it, "Given the intellectual and cultural resources available to a second millennium Hittite lord, it would have taken a moral genius to see through to the wrongness of chattel slavery" (2003, 66). The lord's failure to do so isn't substandard (Clarke 2014, 183).

Reverting to the milk case, it seems Clarke agrees that even if you freely fail, and it is wrong for you to fail, to buy the milk you need not be blameworthy for failing; and this is surely plausible. Moral blameworthiness calls for something more than freely doing wrong (or freely failing to do something you ought to do). Clarke submits that this something more is violation of certain cognitive standards that apply to one, given one's cognitive and volitional abilities and the situation one is in. The thought is that but for the violation of these standards, you would have been aware of your obligation to buy the milk or you would have had the belief that you ought to buy the milk. Let us say that if you violate *such* standards, then you do something it is cognitively wrong for you to do—you do something that is "substandard." Something it is cognitively wrong for you to do—for instance, forgetting to stop at the store—need not be morally wrong for you to do as is so in the milk case. If freely failing to do something it is *morally* wrong for you to fail to do is not sufficient for blameworthiness, it is unclear how supplementing this first moral wrong with something it is cognitively wrong for you to do suffices for blameworthiness (agreeing that freedom conditions for blameworthiness are not in question). I assume that violation of cognitive norms is pertinently like violation of moral norms of right, wrong, and obligation; the violation would "reflect" first and foremost on the relevant act or omission and not primarily on the agent. In this way, the violation would primarily be act- and not agent-focused. A fault that comprises such a violation would differ from a fault that comprises blameworthiness. Appraisals of blameworthiness (or praiseworthiness) reflect, in the first instance, on agents and only derivatively on actions (or omissions)—these appraisals are agent-focused. The issue to be pondered is this: Let's suppose, again, that in the milk case, freely omitting to do what it is morally impermissible for you to omit to do is not sufficient for your being to blame for not buying the milk. If we are now told that not buying the milk is also derivatively cognitively wrong for you in that, roughly, forgetting to buy the milk is cognitively wrong for you, and it is in virtue of this cognitive wrong that the former (your not buying the milk) is cognitively wrong for you, the additional fault comprised by violation of the cognitive standard is act- and not agent-focused. Why, then, are you morally *blameworthy*? Why is this sort of agent-appraisal apt when you add to the mix of a fault that is *not* a fault of blameworthiness—your omitting to do what you ought to do—another fault—violating cognitive standards—that is also not a fault that pertains first and foremost to agents?

One may propose that as you drive home, if you violate the apt cognitive standards that apply to you, you are blameworthy—not morally but let's say "cognitively"—partly in virtue of your violating these standards. Then it may further be added that but for being so blameworthy, on your way home you would have had the relevant belief that you ought to stop for the milk. And then, perhaps, one could work one's way to the conclusion that you are morally to blame for failing to buy the milk. But this sequence of reasoning is not convincing either. First, even supposing that there is a species of blameworthiness that is cognitive blameworthiness, one may wonder why you are cognitively *blameworthy* for violating the cognitive norms that apply to you in the milk case. We may admit that you have (freely) done something it is cognitively wrong for you to do, but this would not suffice for cognitive blameworthiness (just as freely doing something it is morally wrong for you to do does not suffice for moral blameworthiness). It would be implausible to submit that in the milk case you are cognitively blameworthy for failing to do something—whatever it is—that it is cognitively wrong for you to fail do because you nonculpably believe it is cognitively wrong for you to fail do this thing. Second, even if you are cognitively blameworthy for, for instance, forgetting to stop at the store, this fact, in conjunction with the fact that you freely failed to do something you morally ought to have done—buy the milk—seems not to sanction the claim that you are thereby *morally* to blame for not buying the milk.

In sum, although Clarke's proposal for why you are blameworthy for failing to buy the milk in the milk case is engaging, I don't believe it provides uncontroversial grounds to launch a successful attack against the subjective view.

While some might not be perturbed by this original variation of the subjective view,

Subjective-1: Necessarily, S is morally blameworthy for doing something, A, only if S does A while nonculpably believing that it is morally impermissible for S to do A,

they would shun the following.

Subjective-2: Necessarily, S is morally blameworthy for doing something, A, only if S does A on the basis of nonculpably believing that it is morally impermissible for S to do A.

What might motivate the move from *Subjective-1* to *Subjective 2*? The crux of the matter is that one can do something one nonculpably believes it is impermissible for one to do despite one's inner, apt "ledger" remaining untainted. A "Jackson-like" case nicely brings this out. Jill's evidence correctly indicates that giving John drug A will effect a partial cure, and giving him no drug will leave him permanently incurable. But the evidence leaves it open whether giving John drug B or C would cure him completely or giving him B or C would kill him. Assume that B would cure completely and C would kill (Jackson 1991). What ought Jill to do?

Among other things, this case has given rise to discussion concerning whether what we morally ought to do is to maximize actual or expected value. Ingmar Persson has advanced an intriguing answer. He proposes that we ought to do both (2008; 2013, 232). He distinguishes between what one ought to try (choose or decide) to do and what one ought to do. Regarding the former, one should act on the evidence accessible to one—one should do what maximizes expected value. With the latter, one should do what maximizes actual value. He writes:

> In support of this distinction [between what one ought to try to do and what one ought to do], suppose that Jill decides or chooses to prescribe A, writes down the prescription on her computer and sends off an email with this prescription. During the transmission of her message, however, there occurs some kind of totally unforeseeable failure such that the message received is a prescription of B. Consequently John gets B and completely recovers. It seems clear that in this case, *Lucky failure*, Jill has not failed with respect to anything she ought. She has decided and tried to prescribe A, and this is the responsible course to take. . . . But, owing to totally unforeseeable fortuitous circumstances, she has in fact achieved what she wished that she could achieve, to prescribe—or at least bring it about that he gets—the drug which causes John's complete recovery. . . . Surely there is no reason to regret that this transmission failure occurred, though there would have been such a reason if the transmission failure had caused her to fail to do something that she ought. (2013, 223)

However, Jill's lacking regret for failing to try to do what she ought is no reason to believe that she has fortuitously done what she ought to do.

Sometimes Persson suggests that there are two senses of "ought," the evidential sense ("e-ought"), which is to maximize expected value, and the factual ("f-ought"), which is to maximize actual value (2013, 229–30). On this view, one may propose that Jill e-ought to give A, and f-ought to give B. But Persson also insists that although Jill ought to try to give A, she ought not to give A.

If one agrees that Jill ought to give B (and so ought not to give A) because giving B is one's best option, why not simply endorse the Moorean view that Jill ought to give B? Supplement this view with the proposal that in situations when one does not know what one ought to do because of lack of appropriate evidence or some other factor, one rely on subsidiary considerations, such as a policy not to take what one deems to be unacceptable risks, to decide what to do. In situations of this sort a conscientious agent would willingly do wrong by giving A because this is what the policy requires. One may indeed take Jackson-like cases to cast suspicion on the principle that, necessarily, if one acts morally conscientiously, then one does not deliberately do something one believes to be overall morally wrong. What dictates the choice of the sort of subsidiary policy that I proposed? I haven't the faintest idea. What I do affirm is that when one doesn't know which option is best, one ought still to choose that option which is best. Should this strike the reader as less than satisfying, reflect on the following. Some may take a Jackson-like case to *impugn* the view that one ought to do the best one can (e.g., Zimmerman 2008; 2014). For example, convinced that these sorts of case do indeed undermine the view that one ought to perform an act if and only if it is the best option one has, Zimmerman offers a powerful and highly insightful defense of the alternative that one ought to perform an act if and only if it is one's prospectively best option. The prospectively best option constitutes the "best bet" regarding what is morally at stake, where this notion of a best bet is to be construed (roughly) "in terms of the probabilities of the various possible outcomes of one's options and the probable values of these outcomes" (2014, 92). Of relevant interest is Zimmerman's concession that if the prospective view expresses the truth of the nature of overall moral obligation, in those cases in which one doesn't know which option is prospectively best, one ought nonetheless to choose that option which is prospectively best

(2014, 110–11, 113). Zimmerman aptly adds that unfortunately, "there is no easy solution in the offing here" (2014, 113).

In addition Persson is aware of the following potential objection to his proposal that we distinguish between what one ought to try to do and what one ought to do. Suppose Jill could give B only by trying to give B. Then she ought to try to give B if (roughly) it is true that if x is a necessary means to doing y, one can avoid doing x, and one ought to do y, then one ought to do x too. For then it would follow that Jill ought to try to give A and she ought to try to give B although she cannot try to do both. Persson's way out is to deny that trying to do an action can be a necessary means of doing it (2013, 230). However, this is controversial. Suppose that, given your phobia, you can pick up the grass snake only if you try to pick it up. It does not seem incoherent that trying to pick up the snake is a necessary means of picking it up.

Or perhaps the view is that there is a single sense of "ought." What one ought to try to do is to maximize expected value, and what one ought to do is to maximize actual value. To his credit Persson says nothing to commit him to this dubious view. Choosing or trying to do something—giving drug A—is an action as is doing something—giving B. I see no plausible reason to treat these differently in that expected value should be considered with the former and actual value with the latter, when the issue is what one ought to try to do or do.

However this issue is resolved—whether one ought to maximize expected or actual value—Persson agrees that Jill is *not* blameworthy for doing what she realizes is impermissible for her—giving A (2013, 226).[4] The necessary requirements for blameworthiness include a control or freedom requirement, a moral requirement, and a more controversial ownership requirement. Regarding this last requirement, roughly, the choice or bodily action for which one is responsible must issue from germane springs of action with respect to which one is autonomous (Haji 1998; Haji and Cuypers 2008). We may assume that the first and the third of these requirements are satisfied in Jill's case when she gives A. If these three conditions suffice for blameworthiness, then if the objective view is true—one is blameworthy for doing something only if it is impermissible for one to do it—Jill *is* blameworthy for giving A (for she knows that it is impermissible for her to give A). But she is *not* blameworthy for giving A or so I suppose, again, siding with Moore here. One may rejoin that these three conditions are not sufficient—blameworthiness also requires satisfaction of some quality of will condition. Jill does not express ill will in giving A—indeed, she has the best interests of John in mind. But as I have discussed (and will discuss further), I have strong reservations about this condition.

Interestingly, if the three requirements—the freedom, moral, and autonomy requirements—are sufficient for blameworthiness, then if *Subjective-1* is true, Jill is once again blameworthy for giving A, for she gives A while believing that it is impermissible for her to do so. But in favor of *Subjective-2*, she does *not* give A on the basis of the nonculpable belief that it is impermissible for her to give A. That it is impermissible for her to give A is not a constituent of her reason for giving A.[5]

Perhaps people are averse to subjective views because they believe that these views have counterintuitive consequences. However, it is hard to see why objective views escape this very sort of complaint. One ought not to choose between these views, or among the objective, subjective, and complex subjective views merely on the basis that one or more of them has disturbing implications, since each of them has such implications. To arrive at an overall assessment of a principle, one thing one should do is to balance, or at least attempt judiciously to balance what are deemed to be undesirable substantive implications of the principle against its other strengths. In short, I don't think subjective views should be dismissed so easily.

5.2.2 Subjective Views and the Principle of Alternative Expectations

Finally, some may endorse the core element of subjective views—blameworthiness requires nonculpable belief in impermissibility—but claim that this element cannot rationally be held in tandem with what I and many others take to be a lesson of apt Frankfurt examples: It is not a precondition of blameworthiness that one have alternatives. This is because the core element itself is derived from a more fundamental principle that entails that blameworthiness requires alternatives. In short, the challenge is to explain how commitment to the core element fails to strike a death blow to Frankfurt examples that seemingly show that blameworthiness does not require avoidability.

To elaborate, in an illuminating paper, Widerker invokes the principle of alternative expectations (PAE), among other things, to impugn Frankfurt examples. This principle says:

PAE: An agent S is morally blameworthy for doing A only if, in the circumstances, it would be morally reasonable to expect S not to have done A. (Widerker 2000, 92)

The notion of moral reasonability is left largely unanalyzed except for the following. One might wonder to whom it must be morally reasonable to expect S not to have done A. Widerker proposes that it must be morally reasonable "for someone who is morally competent and knows all the relevant nonmoral facts pertaining to the situation the agent is in" (2005, 297, n. 20). In a Frankfurt case, it would not be morally reasonable to expect the star character, such as Joe in *Villain*, not to have refrained from doing what he did simply because if one were competent and aware of the pertinent nonmoral facts concerning Frankfurt situations, one would know that this character could not have refrained from doing what he did. But then, given, PAE, contrary to the Frankfurt defender, Joe would not be blameworthy for pushing the child off the pier.

Perhaps Widerker should have said more to clarify PAE because if one is aware of Joe's "Frankfurt predicament," it would be reasonable to expect Joe not to do otherwise, but one may wonder what *this* sort of reasonability—predictive expectation—has to do with moral reasonability. I revert to this distinction below.

In any event Frankfurt defenders might invoke Frankfurt examples to undermine PAE itself. They might propose that since a good prima facie case can be made for the view that, in *Villain*, Joe is blameworthy for pushing the child despite his not being able to do otherwise, Frankfurt cases show that something is wrong with PAE, just as they show that something is wrong with PAP-Blame (the principle that persons are blameworthy for having done something only if they could have done otherwise). We may have, then, a sort of stalemate. PAE defenders may propose that PAE overturns Frankfurt examples; Frankfurt defenders may rejoin that Frankfurt examples undermine PAE. One way to break this deadlock is to offer additional, independent support for PAE. Building on certain comments of Widerker, this is precisely what David Palmer has recently done.

Widerker suggests that PAE "is a more general principle than PAP, since it can be used to explain why we exonerate an agent in situations in which his wrongdoing was avoidable" (2000, 192). Developing this suggestion, Palmer invites us to ponder these cases:

> Suppose a person, Grace, flips a switch to what she assumes is the light as she first enters a hotel room. . . . Unbeknownst to her, this switch activates the fire alarm . . . There's no sign to say that it's the fire alarm rather than the light switch. In this situation, it seems clear that Grace is not blameworthy for

setting off the fire alarm . . . even if we assume that she *could* have done otherwise and not flipped the switch . . . A reason to think that . . . [PAE] is true is that it gives a natural explanation as to *why* Grace is not blameworthy. Given her circumstances, it would surely be morally *unreasonable* to expect Grace not to have acted as she did. (2013, 561)

Suppose a young infant, Jake, knocks over a valuable antique vase. Jake would not be blameworthy for breaking the vase in the way in which a fully grown adult might be . . . [PAE] provides a natural explanation as to why not. Given the circumstances, it would be morally unreasonable to expect Jake not to have acted as he did . . . even if Jake *could* have acted differently. It would be morally unreasonable to expect Jake not to have acted as he did because he did not know any better and, unlike fully grown adults, we wouldn't think that he *should* have known any better. (2013, 561)

Palmer thoughtfully considers alternative explanations of why these two individuals are not blameworthy. In particular, he entertains the suggestion that "what explains why Grace and Jake are not blameworthy is that (i) they didn't believe that it was wrong for them to behave as they did, and (ii) it wasn't the case, albeit for different reasons, that they *should* have believed this" (2013, 562). In short, the alternative invokes the core element of subjective views, *Simple Subjective* (or at least a principle close enough to *Simple Subjective*). I shall simply take it that *Simple Subjective* is the principle under consideration.

However, Palmer believes that PAE still wins the day because PAE justifies *Blameworthiness/Belief*:

Even if we grant, for the sake of argument, that this epistemic condition [*Blameworthiness/Belief*] on blameworthiness *does* explain why both Grace and Jake are not blameworthy, then this helps to *confirm*, rather than to disconfirm, . . . [PAE]. This is because even if we suppose that this epistemic condition on blameworthiness is true and that it explains why Grace and Jake are not blameworthy, these two cases still support . . . [PAE]. They just do so *indirectly* rather than directly, by virtue of . . . [PAE] justifying the epistemic condition itself . . . Why should we think that people are blameworthy for their actions only if they believe it would be morally wrong for them to perform those actions (or, if they don't believe this, that they should have done so)? A natural answer . . . is . . . that . . . if it's the case that they *don't* believe their actions are wrong (and it's *not* true of them that they should believe this), then it's difficult to see how it could be morally reasonable, under the circumstances, to expect them not to have acted as they did. After all, if someone *doesn't* believe that acting in a particular way is wrong and it's not the case that he *should* think that this is wrong, then how can it be morally reasonable, given the circumstances, to expect him not to do the thing in question? (2013, 562)

We may extract the following argument from this passage.

(2-1) If S is blameworthy for A-ing, then it is morally reasonable to expect S to refrain from A-ing.

(2-2) If it is morally reasonable to expect S to refrain from A-ing, then S nonculpably believes that it is morally impermissible for S to A.

Therefore, (2-3), if S is blameworthy for A-ing, then S nonculpably believes that it is morally impermissible for S to A. (2-3 is *Blameworthiness/Belief.*)

The second premise, however, may be questioned on several grounds. First, suppose you nonculpably believe you face a genuine moral dilemma. (Henceforth, unless otherwise specified, assume that the beliefs in question are nonculpable). That is, you believe you ought to do each of two things but you cannot do both; you believe that in this situation, wrongdoing is inescapable no matter what you do. It may be proposed that it is morally reasonable to expect you to refrain from performing at least one of these alternatives despite your not believing that it is impermissible for you to perform the alternative that you refrain from performing.

Second, the Overridingness Thesis says, roughly, that overall moral obligation is supreme in this way: If ever, one ought morally to do some act, and one ought nonmorally (for example, legally or prudentially) to do some incompatible act, then one "just plain ought" to do the former.[6] The key idea here, roughly, is that from the overarching standpoint of plain "ought" this thesis presupposes, a standpoint that delivers verdicts on the relative normative stringency of "narrower" normative obligations such as moral, legal, or prudential ones, moral obligation reigns supreme. Suppose, upon philosophical reflection, you believe that this thesis is false, and you believe, too, that the prudential "ought" is supreme. In instances in which nonprudential narrow "ought" prescriptions "conflict" with what prudence requires, you have adopted the policy of doing what you prudentially ought to do. Now imagine that on some occasion you morally ought to do A, you prudentially ought to do B, but you can't do both A and B. In this sort of situation, it seems that it is morally reasonable to expect you to refrain from doing A even though you don't believe it is impermissible for you to do A.

Maybe some will object that in these first two cases, although it is *reasonable* to expect you to do something that you do not believe it is morally impermissible for you to do, it is not *morally* reasonable to have this expectation. It is, however, difficult to evaluate this objection without an analysis of moral reasonability.

In any event, third, seemingly moral obligation can conflict with considerations of justice. What we ought morally to do may well depend on considerations other than justice; for instance, it might depend upon total utilities as well. Suppose you believe this is so. Suppose, further, that on some occasion, you believe that you ought to do A but it is unjust to do A. Overall, you care more to avoid injustice than to do what it is obligatory for you to do. Again, it may well be that it is morally reasonable to expect you to refrain from doing A even though you believe you ought to do A.

Fourth, and finally, if one can have ranked permissible alternatives, then it can be morally reasonable to expect you to refrain from performing some alternative even though you believe it is permissible for you to perform that alternative. In McNamara's *Contact*, each of the alternatives available to contact your friend, either writing a letter or stopping by, is permissible for you, but stopping by is better. Suppose I know you always strive to do the (morally) best you can, and you are in a situation analogous to the one *Contact* describes. Then although it is morally reasonable to expect you to refrain from writing, it is false that you nonculpably believe it is morally *impermissible* for you to write.

Reverting to a distinction to which I previously alluded, here is a template of a general objection to each of these four examples. Distinguish between *predictive* expectation or reasonability and *moral* expectation or reasonability. In each of the four examples, the claim that the thing it is morally reasonable to expect the agent to refrain from doing is mistaken. Rather, it is merely predictively reasonable to expect the agent to refrain from doing this thing. In the example involving what is taken to be a moral dilemma, it is not morally reasonable to expect you not to perform one of the actions you deem obligatory. Rather, predictively, one can expect that you won't perform one of them. But predictive expectation is different from moral expectation. In the second example involving prudential obligation, it's not morally reasonable to expect you not to do what you morally ought to do, even though, predictively, this is just what one expects you will do (since you believe that the prudential "ought" is supreme). In the third example, it is not obvious that it's morally reasonable to expect you not to do A (because you believe you ought to do A). It's true that since you think it's unjust to do A, and you care more about justice than obligation, one predictively expects that you will not do A. But that's a different matter. In the fourth example, if all the options are permissible, it is not obviously morally reasonable to expect you to refrain from performing one of them. Again, it is merely predictively reasonable to expect you not to perform the least best of them. In summary, the examples are compelling if we use predictive expectation. But this is not the relevant sense of "expectation" Widerker or Palmer have in mind.

My response to this general strategy is forthright. I've already confessed to not having a good handle on the concept of being morally reasonable. I'm perfectly willing to concede that moral reasonability may well be different from predictive reasonability. Anyone who accepts this difference, though, owes us an explanation of why, in a Frankfurt case such as *Villain*, it would not be merely predictively reasonable, as opposed to being morally reasonable, of one who is aware of the Frankfurt setup to expect Joe not to have refrained from doing what he did.

There are good reasons, then, to reject the proposal that the principle of alternative expectations justifies *Simple Subjective*. There is, consequently, nothing improper in both endorsing the core element of subjective views (that blameworthiness requires nonculpable belief in impermissibility) and defending Frankfurt examples involving blameworthiness.

Although I am partial to *Complex Subjective*, and have given some reasons to favor this view over its competitors (*Simple Subjective* and *Objective*), my aim is to show that no matter which of these views is correct (or no matter which combination of these views is correct if one conceives of the deontic requirement as a hybrid of two or more of these views), the scope of blameworthiness diminishes. It may be worth stressing that at least some parties, Pereboom for example, may not be averse to accepting the hybrid view that blameworthiness requires both relevant belief and impermissibility. Witness, for instance, this passage:

> Once it is settled that an agent is morally responsible, it then needs to be determined whether what the agent did was wrong, and also whether he understood that it was wrong, and if he did not, whether he could have or should have understood that it was. But if it is clear that the agent is morally responsible for the action . . . and that performing the action was wrong, and he understood that it was, then I claim that it is entailed that he is blameworthy for it. (Pereboom 2014, 90)[7]

5.3 DIMINISHED BLAMEWORTHINESS

It remains to bring together the primary result of the past chapter—the range of things it is obligatory (or permissible, or impermissible) for us to perform is narrow owing to our frequently lacking alternatives—and the three candidates for the morally deontic precondition of moral blameworthiness, to show that we are blameworthy for less, perhaps far less, than what we may have hitherto believed.

Interestingly, arguably the most popular of the three competitors, *Objective*, if true, imperils the reach of blameworthiness fairly directly. If the objective view is true, then since blameworthiness requires impermissibility, and impermissibility requires avoidability, agents who cannot refrain from doing what it is seemingly impermissible for them to do will not be blameworthy for such deeds. Alternatively, if we frequently lack alternatives because of luck, then, it will often be false that it is impermissible for us to do what we do. This result, together with the objective view, yields the further result that, repeatedly, it will be false that we are blameworthy for what we do.

Suppose, second, that *Simple Subjective* is true; one is blameworthy for an action only if one nonculpably believes that it is impermissible for one to perform it. Then a person may erroneously but nonculpably believe that many actions she cannot refrain from doing (due ultimately to luck) are impermissible for her to do, and so may be blameworthy for doing them. However, if rational and enlightened about her mistake concerning the moral statuses of her actions, she would not be blameworthy for pertinent seeming wrongdoings. Blameworthiness would hinge on "deontic irrationality" in this sense: One would be blameworthy for doing (or refraining from doing) something only if one harbored false beliefs about the primary moral status of doing (or refraining from doing) this thing; whether one is blameworthy would depend on whether one falsely believed that it is impermissible for one to do (or not do) this thing.

Finally, what if *Complex Subjective* were true? This principle says one is morally blameworthy for doing something only if one nonculpably believes that it is morally impermissible or morally amiss for one to do it. In many cases, one might take what one is doing to be morally amiss for one because one takes it to be morally impermissible for one. In all such cases, it will be deontic irrationality that sustains blameworthiness, assuming that one could not have done otherwise on such occasions. But there will be other cases, such as

Delivery, in which one nonculpably takes some action to be morally amiss but *not* because one nonculpably takes it to be *impermissible* for one. Here, one may well be blameworthy without being deontically irrational. One may have the true belief that it is amoral—not morally obligatory, permissible, or impermissible—for one to perform the action while nonculpably believing that it is morally amiss for one to perform this action. Still, "rational" blameworthiness would diminish in that in all other cases in which one nonculpably believed one was doing wrong, it would be deontic irrationality that would sustain blameworthiness.

Assume that the objective view is false, and either one of *Simple Subjective* or *Complex Subjective* is true. It would not, of course, immediately follow that the scope of blameworthiness in our world is considerably narrow, even supposing that the scope of obligation in this world is significantly restricted. To sustain skepticism about the reach of blameworthiness, we require the additional assumptions that people don't have false beliefs regarding the primary moral statuses of their intentional actions or omissions, and when they act (or intentionally fail to) they do not do so in the belief that they are doing anything it is morally impermissible or amiss for them to do. So whether the scope of blameworthiness turns out to be wide or narrow again pivots on empirical considerations concerning relevant moral beliefs of people. However, if it were to become general knowledge that our range of obligations is narrow, then we would expect that (in the fullness of time) if either variant of the subjective view were true, the scope of blameworthiness would diminish.

Some may still dissent. They might insist that our "commitment" to obligation, and to blameworthiness (or to responsibility more generally) runs very deep. Strawson (1962), for example, proposed that we are psychologically incapable of renouncing the reactive attitudes. One might similarly propose that even if it were true that the range of our moral obligations is limited, people for the most part would still behave *as if* they were doing what it is morally right or wrong for them to do, given their dedication to obligation.

However, I continue to remain suspicious about this sort of claim. I believe that the importance of morally deontic considerations, demands, or concerns in the lives of very many of us has been greatly exaggerated. We are frequently devoted, or more deeply devoted, to other goals, cares, or ideals. Pertinent examples and reflection on what people actually care about in the relevant sense of "care" supports this view.

Both Bernard Williams and Michael Slote have described cases in which a "morally concerned individual might consider a given project to be of greater importance, for him, than all the harm to other people than that particular project" (Slote, 1983, 78).[8] Slote develops one of Williams's examples involving a somewhat fictionalized Gauguin:

> We are all to a greater or lesser extent familiar with the fact that Gauguin deserted his family and went off to the South Seas to paint. And although many of us admire Gauguin, not only for what he produced and for his talent, but also for his absolute dedication to (his) art, most of us are also repelled by what he did to his family . . . I believe that we can persuade ourselves of the wrongness of that desertion and we can do so without losing our sense of admiration for Gauguin's artistic single-mindedness. Single-minded devotion to aesthetic goals or ideals seems to us a virtue in an artist; yet this trait, as we shall see, cannot be understood apart from the tendency to do such things as Gauguin did to his family, and so is not—like daring or indeed like Gauguin's own artistic talent—merely "externally" related to immorality. (1983, 80)

One lesson Slote wishes to draw from cases of this sort is that "morality need not totally constrain the personal traits we think of as virtues and there may indeed be such a thing as admirable immorality" (Slote 1983, 78). My interest in the case resides in something different. Spinning the tale as he does, Slote provides convincing grounds for the view that it was morally impermissible for Gauguin to desert his family and Gauguin believed it was so. Nevertheless, Gauguin's passion for art, his zealous devotion to the realization of an "impersonally valuable good," the production of great art that supposedly is of benefit to everyone, took precedence for Gauguin over his concerns for morality (really, immorality) and for his own health or safety. Fictionalized Gauguin is similar in this respect to scores of novelists, sculptors, composers, poets, philosophers, or other scholars. In like manner, some spectacularly (and not so spectacularly) successful business persons, political leaders, professors, or athletes, seeking to accomplish their "professional" goals give less than reasonable weight to their own well-being, and little or no weight at all to morally deontic concerns. Their devotion to their projects is not "grounded in," nor does it stem from, any moral obligation or moral concern.

Great artists, novelists, sculptors, and politicians aside, consider one aspect of the relationship among parents and their young. It would be incredulous to believe that the importance to parents of their children's well-being derived in any way from specifically moral obligations to care for them. We care for our children because we love them. As Harry Frankfurt explains,

> Moral obligation is not really what counts here. Even if parents are somehow morally obligated to love or to care about their children, it is not normally on account of any such obligation that they do love them. Parents are generally not concerned for their children out of duty, but simply out of love; and the love,

needless to say, is not a love of duty but a love of the children. To account for the necessities and the authority of parental love, there is no reason to invoke the moral law. (1994, 140)

Similarly, in addition to parental love, there is love among friends and love between spouses, and with love there is the associated care, respect, and trust. For many, there is love for, or devotion to, God. Again, it seems that, at root, moral obligation is not what really matters here. It would false to the facts to suppose that our concern for the well-being of our friends or loved ones somehow derives from specifically moral duties. Here we would do well to remind ourselves of Mill's perceptive remark that ninety-nine hundredths of all our actions are not performed "from" or "out of" moral duty. (Mill [1863] 1989, 23)

The notion of acting from duty is enormously complex. For immediate interests, I comment on one of its central features when it is, first, *moral praiseworthiness* or *blameworthiness* or, in short, moral responsibility, that is of concern. One is morally praiseworthy for something only if one acts narrowly from moral duty. One acts narrowly from moral duty only if one's act is intentional and the concept of moral duty, understood to encompass moral obligation or moral permissibility, figures pivotally in the representational content of one's intention. So, for instance, a mother acts narrowly from moral duty in giving up one of her kidneys to some child only if she intends to do what she (nonculpably) believes it is morally obligatory or permissible for her to do. One can act narrowly from moral duty but not purely so as when the mother's act issues partly from an intention to do what she morally ought and to care for the child, where the caring is divorced from any morally deontic association. There are broader conceptions of acting from moral duty. Suppose Theresa, a benevolent person, frequently acts out of kindness, and she has the standing belief that she ought morally to act out of kindness. Now suppose she gives alms to the poor, and in so doing acts out of kindness, but not with any intention to do what she believes morality requires or permits. Her act of giving alms is intentional, but the representational content of the intention Theresa executes when she gives alms is disassociated from any moral concerns. There is a sense in which Theresa acts from moral duty, given her standing belief that she ought morally to act out of kindness. But she does not narrowly act from moral duty when she gives alms. Theresa, then, is not morally praiseworthy for giving alms, although other normative assessments, such as she is virtuous or her act expresses kindness, are entirely proper.

Still, one might worry that even if we often do not act narrowly *from* moral duty or concerns (and, hence, are often not morally praiseworthy), this alone does not show that we are often not morally responsible. It needs to be argued, additionally, that we often do not act *despite* moral concerns; for then it would follow that we are often not morally blameworthy—unless we are morally to blame for not "accessing" the relevant concerns or beliefs in the first place.

But this objection can be met. For, first, there are numerous circumstances in life in which we fail to have the relevant moral beliefs—perhaps for the simple reason that we have not thought about what morality requires or forbids in such circumstances. Juan may skip class (indeed, he may form a habit of doing so) without a thought about morality's "informing" his action or cultivation of his habit; a business person may feel that it is "professionally wrong" to divulge company secrets or to take extended coffee breaks but still fail to act, when she deliberately avoids divulging certain sensitive information or avoids prolonging her breaks, out of or despite *moral* duty or concerns. Second, even in cases in which people have the appropriate sorts of moral belief, they are not morally responsible for what they do, because these sorts of belief are frequently not "accessed" when they perform the relevant actions. Franz may harbor the dispositional belief that it is morally impermissible for him to be impolite but may, when completely engrossed in his work, snap at interrupters without in any way "accessing" this belief. When discourteous, he acts just as he would have in the absence of having the standing belief; he does not act, even partly, on its basis. Since the counterfactual scenario in which Franz lacks the germane belief but snaps is presumably not one in which he is morally blameworthy for his impoliteness, and it is a scenario relevantly analogous to the actual one in which he is impolite (an appropriate belief is not accessed because it is not even possessed), Franz is not morally blameworthy for being impolite. This is perfectly compatible with Franz's being morally to blame, say for failing to access the belief that being impolite is wrong or for failing to muster self-control. Third and finally, even in cases involving acting out of love or friendship, or nonmoral *concern* for some other individual—such cases are common enough—the agent simply fails to act *despite* moral concern, again for the reason that the agent's behavior in the circumstances is entirely divorced from *any* sort of moral regard or interest.

Suppose we grant that the importance of moral obligation in our lives is limited: Very many of our concerns or cares are not in any way derivative from moral duty, and when we act, we often fail to act *from* or *despite* moral duty. Moral concerns—beliefs regarding what is right, wrong, or obligatory, or beliefs that what one is doing is of some moral import—frequently play no role at all in the actual sequence of events that generate our actions. Then the scope of moral responsibility—moral blameworthiness or praiseworthiness, whatever the case might be—is significantly narrow because moral responsibility requires that we act from or despite moral duty or act "out of" moral concern.[9] Although not morally responsible for many of our everyday actions, this still leaves open the possibility that we may be nonmorally but normatively responsible for them because we act, for example, from or despite love.[10] Recall the example of the loving mother who is not morally praiseworthy but is nonmorally normatively praiseworthy for giving up her kidney. It is (among other things) what we take to be important normative interests in our lives that both restrict the scope of moral responsibility and widen the horizons of nonmoral normative responsibility provided these sorts of nonmoral varieties of praiseworthiness or blameworthiness are free of other concerns, something to which I will briefly return below.

Even setting aside pessimism about the importance of moral obligation in our lives, it would still remain that blameworthiness hangs on an all too fragile thread: False beliefs about the primary moral statuses of our actions (or omissions) would sustain blameworthiness.

In sum, have it any way you want. Pick any one of the three competing candidates (*Objective*, *Simple Subjective*, or *Complex Subjective*) as the frontrunner for the moral requirement of blameworthiness. This candidate, together with luck's ensuring that frequently we are unable to do otherwise, shows that if we are not mistaken about the primary moral statuses of our actions—whether they are obligatory, permissible, or impermissible for us—the range of things for which we are blameworthy diminishes.

5.4 CHANGING OBLIGATIONS, BLAMEWORTHINESS, AND IMPERMISSIBILITY

Let's complement the line of reasoning for the reduced scope of blameworthiness which proceeds from luck's frequently eviscerating alternatives with a second set of arguments. This supplemental set appeals to the changeability of obligation over time, and the principle (the *"Luck Principle"*) that degree of blameworthiness cannot be affected by what is not in one's control (or, if one wants, degree of blameworthiness cannot be affected by luck).

To enthuse the luck principle, if we accept the view that one cannot be blameworthy for something that is not in one's control—and here the sense of "control" is the personal one moral responsibility presupposes—then it is hard to see why we should not also accept the view that degree of blameworthiness is immune to what is beyond one's control. Suppose that in *Killer-1* you are blameworthy to a certain degree for killing Sam. You take careful aim and the bullet smatters her brain. *Killer-2* is just like *Killer-1* except that a few seconds before you fired the gun, Sam expired because of an aneurism; although you didn't know it, you shot into the body of a dead person. You are no less blameworthy (or, if one prefers, no more blameworthy) in *Killer-2* than you are in *Killer-1*, although as Zimmerman cautions, in these sorts of circumstance you may be blameworthy for more things in the one case than in the other (Zimmerman 2011, 129–30). For example, in *Killer-1*, you are blameworthy, among other things, for the attempt to kill and the death, whereas in in *Killer-2* you are not blameworthy for the death.

Frankfurt examples also give us reason to endorse the luck principle. In *Theft*, it is not in Augustine's power to influence any of Ernie's activities. If Ernie is not on the scene, as is so in Stage 1, it is assumed that Augustine is blameworthy to some degree for stealing the pears. If Ernie is on the scene as in Stage 2, Augustine is just as blameworthy for stealing the pears in this stage as he is for stealing them in the former. Ernie's presence makes no difference to his degree of blameworthiness because Augustine has no control over Ernie's comings or goings or his conduct.

The luck principle may provisionally be regimented in this way:

Luck Principle: If one's doing a certain sort of thing in a certain way is sufficient for being blameworthy for doing that thing in that way, then something with respect to which one had no personal control cannot affect one's degree of blameworthiness for doing the sort of thing one did in the way in which one did it.

To appreciate better this principle, consider some objections to it. According to the first one may concede that in *Theft* Augustine is blameworthy in both stages but still renounce the luck principle. For it may be proposed that the following principle—the "degrees principle"—is true: Other things equal, one is more blameworthy for doing something it is impermissible for one to do (if one does it while nonculpably believing it is impermissible for one to do it) than for doing something it is amoral—not permissible, impermissible, or obligatory—for one to do (while nonculpably believing it is impermissible for one to do it).[11] So something regarding which one has no control—roughly, in *Theft*, the presence of the counterfactual intervener in Stage 2 and his activities—*can* affect one's degree of blameworthiness.

One concern with this objection is its seeming, implicit presupposition that blameworthiness *does* require impermissibility or impermissibility per se augments degree of blameworthiness. Without this presupposition, why believe that Augustine is more to blame for stealing the pears in Stage 1, where it is impermissible for him to steal them, than he is in Stage 2, where it is amoral for him to steal them? But presupposing the principle that blameworthiness requires impermissibility or enhances impermissibility would be dialectically improper in this context—it is this very principle that, in the end, is one of the principles at issue.

A second concern is that, as I have already underscored, responsibility appraisals are agent- and not act-focused; they are first and foremost appraisals of the agent, and only secondarily if at all, appraisals of the agent's activities. Roughly, if an agent is blameworthy, her moral worth has been diminished in virtue of some episode in her life. As Augustine acts no differently in Stage 1 than he does in Stage 2—nothing about *him* is morally different—there is no reason to believe that his moral worth diminishes to a greater degree in Stage 1 than it does in Stage 2. To put the point somewhat differently, if you are blameworthy for something, it is in virtue of something about *you* that you're blameworthy for this thing. Similarly, if you're blameworthy to a greater degree for doing (or refraining from doing) one thing than you are for doing (or refraining from doing) another, it is in virtue of something about *you* that you are more blameworthy for the one than you are for the other (call this principle the "worthiness principle"). The worthiness principle gives us reason to affirm that Augustine is just as blameworthy for stealing the pears in Stage 1 as he is in Stage 2. Hence, if you accept this principle, and reflect carefully on *Theft*, then you should deny the degrees principle.

The second objection (to the luck principle) appeals to the following two cases. In Case 1 Augustine intentionally steals some pears in a certain way and does so freely. He is blameworthy to some degree for this action. In Case 2 Augustine performs the same sort of action that he does in Case 1 but solely as a result of God's covertly manipulating him to do so. We may even allow that God sees to it that the event that is *Augustine's stealing the pears* is deterministically caused. Assume that Augustine has no personal control over any of God's activities. The luck principle (together with these facts of the case) implies that this kind of interference with Augustine's agency cannot affect his degree of blameworthiness for his deed. But this is implausible. Doesn't manipulation of this sort undermine blameworthiness?

The objection, however, is insufficiently sensitive to the luck principle's constraint that the agent who is subject to luck do the sort of thing that she did *in the way in which she did it*. If you do something in a way sufficient for your being to blame for doing it, then you do it freely (provided what you do is directly free). The objection presupposes that the manipulation at issue is responsibility-undermining. Let's suppose it is so because, broadly, manipulation (of this sort) undermines freedom. Then we don't have a case where something with respect to which one had no personal control affects one's degree of blameworthiness for doing the sort of thing one did in the way (*including freely*) in which one did it. Perhaps this elucidation of the luck principle will help:

> Luck principle (elaborated): If one's doing a certain sort of thing in a certain way, including freely doing it, is sufficient for being blameworthy for doing that thing in that way, then something with respect to which one had no personal control, cannot affect one's degree of blameworthiness for doing the sort of thing one did in the way (including freely) in which one did it.

Consider a third objection to this principle. Assume that Augustine freely helps himself to some peanuts while nonculpably believing it is morally impermissible for him to take them. But it turns out that this belief is false; it is in fact permissible for him to walk away with a handful. To simplify, assume further that freely taking the nuts in light of the nonculpable belief that it is impermissible for him to take them suffices for being blameworthy for taking them. Now modify the case in this respect. The belief that it is permissible for him to help himself to some nuts indeterministically comes to Augustine's mind prior to his pocketing the nuts; he has no control over the acquisition of this belief. Shouldn't this affect his degree of blameworthiness for his germane deed?

The correct answer will turn on pertinent details. One possibility is that Augustine takes the nuts while nonculpably believing that it is permissible for him to do so. This should, presumably, influence his degree of blameworthiness. Perhaps freely taking the nuts in light of the nonculpable belief that it is permissible for him to take them suffices for not being to blame for taking them. But then there is no counterexample to the luck principle. Yet again, we don't have a case in which something beyond his control affects Augustine's degree of blameworthiness for taking the nuts in the manner in which he took them in Case 1. In the former but not the latter case, Augustine takes the nuts while nonculpably believing that he ought not to take them. A second possibility is somewhat unusual. Augustine suffers from irrationality: He has the nonculpable occurrent belief that it is impermissible for him to take the nuts and, let's suppose, the unconscious belief that it is permissible for him to take the nuts (a belief that, using the following somewhat opaque terminology, indeterministically came to his "unconscious" mind). Assume, in addition, that the belief that is "veiled" from his conscious mind plays no role whatsoever in the etiology of his taking the nuts. He still freely walks away with the peanuts while nonculpably believing it is impermissible for him to do so. Then, once again, I don't see how his acquisition of the "permissibility belief" can have any effect on his degree of blameworthiness for his pertinent deed.

Something not in your control may affect one among a number of conditions that are jointly sufficient for your being to blame for some choice, action, or intentional omission. If that's so, then it is uncontroversial that this thing that is not in your control may affect your degree of blameworthiness. You may not be blameworthy at all for stealing some plums if you steal them only because you have been covertly manipulated to steal them. But if you are blamewor-thy for some choice, C, and you are to blame for C in virtue of satis-fying sufficient conditions for being to blame, then it is hard to see how something that is not in your control can affect your degree of blameworthiness for a C-type choice when this thing has no effect whatsoever on any of the conditions that suffice for your being to blame for C, and these conditions *are* satisfied when you make C.

We remind ourselves that obligation can "change" with the pas-sage of time. Revisit our stock example that illustrates such change. Imagine that on Monday, it is impermissible for you, the doctor, to give medicine B to a patient on Wednesday because medicine A, which is also available, will cure the patient with no unpleasant side effects. Assume that there are no other remedies for the cure. However, suppose you deliberately plan on doing wrong by giv-ing B, and you do give B on Wednesday. Next, initiate the follow-ing change in the case: Unbeknownst to you, and owing to events entirely beyond your personal control, the supply of A is exhausted on Tuesday. Some unfortunate alcoholic, desperate to get her hands on some "good stuff," guzzles all the A in the belief that A is some exotic intoxicant. And because of this, as of Tuesday it is no longer impermissible for you to give B on Wednesday; indeed, you ought, as of the time A is unavailable, to give B on Wednesday, as this is the only way in which your patient will be cured. It seems that such scenarios in which owing to luck—that is, owing to factors beyond one's control—the rights and wrongs in the scenario "change" with the passage of time are not uncommon in our day-to-day dealings with others.

The changeability of obligations over time is interesting, among other reasons, because it provides another basis for arguing against the blameworthiness-requires-impermissibility principle (*Blameworthiness/Impermissibility*). Suppose this principle is true. In *Cure-1*, the doctor's case proceeds exactly as before save that, you, the doctor, could still have given A instead of B to the patient on Wednesday. We may assume here that it is impermissible as of the time you give B—time t—for you to give B at t, and you are blameworthy, to a certain degree, for giving B. *Cure-2* is just the original case in which no A is available because the alcoholic has gulped it all down. In *Cure-2*, it is no longer true that as of the time you give B—time t—it is impermissible for you to give B at t. If *Blameworthiness/ Impermissibility* is true, then although you are blameworthy for giving B in *Cure-1*, you are not blameworthy for giving B in *Cure-2*. If you are not blameworthy for giving B in *Cure-2*, things with respect to which you have no personal control—the activities of the alcoholic, for instance—*do* have a bearing on your degree of blameworthiness. But this is not as it should be if the luck principle is true. It is false, then, that you are not blameworthy for giving B in *Cure-2*. As the only relevant difference between *Cure-1* and *Cure-2* is that in the former but not in the latter, it is, as of t, impermissible for you to give B at t, it is the blameworthiness-requires-impermissibility principle that is the culprit.

Frankfurt examples expose an interesting asymmetry: Luck affects obligation in a way in which it does not affect degree of blameworthiness. Augustine has no control regarding any of Ernie's behavior. We have assumed that if Ernie is not on the scene, it is impermissible for Augustine to steal the pears. But if Ernie *is* around and is doing his job properly, it is not impermissible for Augustine to steal the pears. Again, when Ernie is on the scene it is false that Augustine ought to refrain from stealing the pears because impermissibility requires avoidability. Ernie's presence "changes" the scenario from one in which Augustine ought to refrain from performing an action to one in which he has no such obligation. So, obligation falls prey to luck.

The same is not true, however, of moral blameworthiness. With a finicky counterfactual intervener like Ernie, assume that Augustine is to blame to some degree for stealing the pears in Stage 1 (or when Ernie is on the scene but has dosed off). In Stage 2 (or when Ernie is awake and alert), Augustine conducts himself in just the manner in which he does in the prior scenarios. If, in Stage 2 or when Ernie is fastidious, Augustine is not blameworthy to any degree, as the proponent of the blameworthiness-requires-impermissibility principle would have us believe, because it is not impermissible in this stage for Augustine to steal the pears, then yet again we would have violation of the luck principle. Some things—the presence of Ernie and his being awake—with respect to which Augustine has no personal control would affect his degree of blameworthiness. But as nothing over which Augustine has no personal control can affect his degree of blameworthiness, Augustine is just as blameworthy in Stage 2 as he is in Stage 1. So whereas Frankfurt examples show that obligation is susceptible to luck, they also suggest that degree of blameworthiness is not or, minimally, not in the way in which obligation is.

Another sort of consideration validates this asymmetry. It seems that, frequently, we do what we nonculpably take to be impermissible for us to do even though it may well not be impermissible for us to do these things. One should believe this if one favors the analysis of obligation (MO-2) according to which, as of some time, you morally ought to perform an act if and only if you can do it, you can refrain from doing it, and (simplifying) it occurs in all the best worlds accessible to you at this time. In all your best life histories, you perform this act at the relevant time. On each occasion when you do something, whether or not it is obligatory or impermissible for you to do this thing depends on which sort of world you make actual when you do this thing. The deontic value of the world you actualize when you do something, however, depends on what many others do (or fail to do) in the world as well; it depends on the occurrence of a plethora of events over which you have no personal

LUCK'S MISCHIEF

control. We may help ourselves to this conversant line of reasoning. In *World-1*, suppose as of *t*, you take yourself to be doing wrong. As of *t*, you do something, you give medicine B to your patient at *t* (even though you could have given medicine A), and giving B fails to occur in any of the best worlds accessible to you at *t*. In *World-2*, again you do what you believe it is impermissible for you to do; at *t*, you give B at *t*. But this time, given what others do—for instance, the alcoholic exhausts the supply of A—as of *t*, you make actual the best world accessible to you at *t*. In *World-2*, it is no longer impermissible, as of *t*, for you to give B to your patient at *t*. Suppose that you are blameworthy to some degree for giving B in *World-1*. Then, on pain of violating the luck principle, you should be blameworthy for giving B in *World-2* too.

It seems that replete in everyday life are scenarios in which owing to luck—owing to factors beyond one's control—the rights and wrongs of the scenario "change" with the passage of time. This phenomenon of changeability also contributes to sustaining the view that the range of things for which we are blameworthy is narrow. If blameworthiness requires impermissibility, then as of Tuesday, you are not to blame for giving B to your patient (because, as of Tuesday, it is not wrong for you to give B). If one is blameworthy for doing something only if one does it while nonculpably believing that it is impermissible for one to do it, then if you're cognizant of the moral status of your pertinent action—as of Tuesday, it is no longer impermissible for you to give B on Wednesday—again you won't be blameworthy for giving B (assuming you now give B in the nonculpable belief that you ought to give B). Frequently, what we take to be obligatory (or impermissible) for us turns out not to be obligatory (or impermissible) because of the "changeability" of obligations with passing time. Luck plays a heavy hand in this sort of changeability. Hence, we are led yet again to the conclusion that owing to luck the range of things for which we are blameworthy is more limited than what we may have thought.

5.5 A COSTLY WAY OUT: OBLIGATION AND BLAMEWORTHINESS RESCUED

Is there a way to rescue obligation and blameworthiness from luck's intrusion? To appreciate how one might attempt to escape the view that the reach of obligation and blameworthiness is imperiled, I need to digress somewhat. I first argue that forward-looking accounts of blameworthiness do not fit well with a consequentialist justification of a desert claim concerning overt blame. Just why this fact is relevant to understanding attempted "rescue operations" will emerge shortly.

Let's start with tightening up some terminology. In his 1962 article, Strawson refers to a variety of attitudes he calls "reactive"— gratitude, resentment, indignation, and forgiveness; moral approval and disapproval; shame and guilt—and of practices, such as punishment, that include these attitudes. We may add to this list overt blame and praise. According to a desert-entailing account of blameworthiness, one is to blame for something only if one deserves to be the object of some reactive attitude regarding that thing. To simplify, let's stipulate that this reactive attitude is overt blame. A nondesert entailing account is not a desert-entailing account. According to such accounts, when one is to blame for something, it is false that one is *deserving* of any reactive attitude. Such views might allow that blameworthiness is importantly tied to overt blame but not via desert. Finally, we can say that an account of blameworthiness is forward-looking just in case there is, on this account, some nontrivial tie between being to blame and overt blame (a tie that may not involve desert), and the warrant or justification of overt blame appeals to the effects or consequences of such blame.

Next, it will be instructive to examine elements of Manuel Vargas's views of blameworthiness. His account of blameworthiness is doubly forward-looking. First, it is forward-looking insofar as it justifies overt blame on the basis of the effects of such blame, and, second, the account has it that overt blame can be deserved, and the justification for a desert claim in which what is deserved is overt blame appeals to the consequences of such blame.

Vargas explains that

> our responsibility-characteristic practices [such as overt blaming] can be justified if the norms of moralized praise and blame suitably contribute to the development of a special form of agency. I . . . [accept] the idea that norms of a broadly Strawsonian sort—that is, norms emphasizing a demand for a kind of quality of will, or concern for what morality demands—can plausibly serve such a function. Among moral considerations-sensitive agents, the currency of such norms fosters moral considerations-sensitive agency. (2013, 199)

Practices are justified if they "make good sense" (2013, 158–59) and we have reason to engage in them, or they are "well supported by our various interests and cohere with our not-indefensible commitments" (159). The justification sought is more than pragmatic; it must be "rooted in features with significant normative heft" (160).

In Vargas's view, ultimately the justification of overt praising and blaming is forward-looking; it turns on one of the outcomes of these activities. The crux of Vargas's "agency cultivation model" is that practices characteristic of responsibility are justified if they foster "*a distinctive form of agency in us, a kind of agency sensitive to and governed by moral considerations*" (173). Agents who are morally responsible for at least some of their behavior have the ability to recognize moral considerations, and to guide their conduct on the basis of these considerations. Vargas's view appears to be that we cultivate such agency by internalizing norms of "moralized praise and blame." The norms are of a broadly Strawsonian sort. In the Strawsonian view (Strawson 1962), central to our practice of holding morally responsible are

> our expectations about how we are to be treated, and our dispositions of reaction to violations of those expectations. That is, ordinary human adults are attuned to what Strawson called "the quality of will" evinced by others. When someone's actions fail to demonstrate a kind of concern for us that we expect, we react with anger, resentment, indignation, and so on. On this picture, when one acts with a bad will, one is blameworthy and where one acts with a good will, one is praiseworthy. Blameworthiness and praiseworthiness are statuses that simply reflect our assessments (or perhaps norms of assessment) that grow out of concern for quality of will. Judgments about responsibility express an underlying framework of attitudes built around inter—and intra-personal demands for concern. (Vargas 2013, 160–61)

Presumably, the norms will have something to say about, among other things, (i) the quality of will agents express in their conduct— "whether those agents were acting with the sort of concern due to agents in light of morality" (161); (ii) what is morally right, wrong, obligatory, supererogatory, and so forth; (iii) excuses; (iv) exemptions (whether the person in question is a morally responsible agent—an agent who can be subject to the quality of will-sensitive norms of praise and blame); and (v) the conditions under which it is permissible to express praise or blame.

Vargas theorizes that overt praise and blame "initially work by providing external motivation for agents to track moral considerations and regulate their behavior in light of them" (175). When the norms are internalized, they will be "experienced as intrinsically motivating" (175). Agents who have internalized these norms "will typically go on to both perpetuate and enforce those norms" (175).

In his interesting discussion of desert and blame, Vargas raises and responds to an apparent concern that seemingly arises when one wishes, as Vargas does, to combine a forward-looking account of blame that justifies overt blame on the basis of the effects of blaming with the view that people deserve blame. He says:

> [Forward-looking] accounts are sometimes regarded as lacking the resources to say why people can deserve blame. That is, one can allow that it is perhaps useful to blame, and that it has an important role to play in our becoming agents of a particular sort. Nevertheless, the critic can protest, these things do not constitute an adequate basis for desert. (249)

Vargas concurs that there are three essential elements in a basic fact about desert, the deserver—whatever it is that deserves something, the desert—whatever it is that is deserved, and the desert base—whatever property in virtue of which the deserver is deserving of the desert (249–50). (Presumably, a basic fact about desert will have additional elements such as, for instance, the strength of the deserver's desert, and the time of deserving. We may set these other elements aside.) The last quoted passage might lead one to believe that Vargas's concern is with what constitutes an adequate desert base for blame. Other passages, however, strongly suggest that he is interested in a different problem. Roughly, it is the problem that if someone deserves something, for example, overt blame, on the basis of having a certain feature, what accounts for or justifies this person's deserving blame on the basis of this feature? So, for instance, Vargas takes issue with the following view of Pereboom:

> For an agent to be morally responsible for an action in the sense at issue is for it to belong to him in such a way that he would deserve blame if he understood that it was morally wrong, and he would deserve credit or perhaps praise if he understood that it was morally exemplary, supposing that this desert is basic in the sense that the agent would deserve the blame or credit just because he has performed the action, given understanding of its moral status and not by virtue of consequentialist considerations. (251)

Vargas questions why we should "accept the exclusion of consequentialist normative ethical accounts, or any other approach to accounting for the desert base" (257). It is tempting to interpret him as wondering about why consequentialist accounts or justifications of desert statements are unacceptable as he, Vargas, seems to take Pereboom to be claiming.

Both issues—the desert base of overt blame when overt blame is deserved and the justification of desert claims—are significant and complex. I take Vargas to be primarily concerned with the latter. Regarding the former, he says that a "person deserves blame in virtue of being a responsible agent and doing something morally bad in a way that manifests bad quality of will" (250). Competitors to this candidate include (i) a person deserves blame in virtue of freely doing something it is morally impermissible for her to do; and (ii) a person deserves blame in virtue of freely doing something she nonculpably believes it is morally impermissible for her to do. Indeed, sometimes, it looks as though Vargas accepts something like (i). He writes:

> I find it more plausible to think that when we judge that Fitzgerald deserves Jackie's blame what we are mainly committing ourselves to is the idea that Fitzgerald has done something wrong, and that in light of that violation, blaming is called for. (253)

Regarding the justification of desert claims, Vargas says:

> [Passage 1] Acceptance of blame (via the concomitant of guilt) provides a path to improved self-governance in light of moral considerations. That is, blaming is ordinarily deserved because, in creatures like us, blaming plays a crucial role in our ability to self-regulate. Without blame, guilt cannot benefit the wrongdoer. Were we to opt out of blame, as the responsibility skeptic would have us do, we would thereby remove one of the vehicles by which others around us (and perhaps ourselves) undertake moral improvement. In short: in the ordinary case, a responsible agent's experience of guilt and repentance is beneficial *to the agent*. (263)

> [Passage 2] For blame to be deserved, it suffices that a system of praising and blaming really does contribute to the cultivation of moral considerations-responsive agency. (264)

Regarding Passage 1, the ability to regulate our conduct on the basis of moral considerations is an essential constituent of being a moral considerations-responsive agent. So, it seems that one of Vargas's proposals is this:

V1: S deserves overt blame on the basis of having property, P, if and only if S's being overtly blamed contributes to fostering in S a certain form of agency, moral considerations-sensitive agency (a sort of agency that has to do with having the capacity to recognize apt reasons for conduct and to translate these reasons into action).

Passage 2, however, suggests a slightly different view. Taking certain liberties about the concept of *some society's being an agent's society*, and the concept of *members belonging to an agent's society*, perhaps Vargas's thesis is this:

V2: S deserves overt blame on the basis of having property, P, if and only if S's being overtly blamed contributes to fostering in (at least some or many?) members of S's society moral considerations-sensitive agency.

Let's agree that when overt blame is deserved, it is deserved on the basis of the deserver having some property, P, whatever precisely P is. Maybe P is Vargas's candidate or maybe it is one of the other two competitors previously mentioned. It will be useful to review why typical consequentialist justifications of desert claims, when it is blame that is the desert, fail in order to evaluate V1 and V2. Consider the following consequentialist proposal.

C: S deserves overt blame on the basis of S's possession of P if and only if overtly blaming S on the basis of S's possession of P would maximize utility.

The utility of an act is the intrinsic good minus intrinsic evil that would be contained in the consequence of that act if it were performed. Suppose some person, Bert, has some alternatives at some time. Suppose one of these alternatives, a0, is such that no other has a higher utility that it has. Then a0 maximizes utility. It may be that among Bert's alternatives on some occasion is the alternative, a1, of overtly blaming S on the basis of S's possession of P. But it is surely possible that S deserves blame on the basis of the possession of P even when there is no person, like Bert, to overtly blame S. Maybe S is the only agent alive and she has done something for which she deserves blame. Revert to a situation in which Bert's overtly blaming S on the basis of S's possession of P—his alternative a1—maximizes utility. Among the common objections to consequentialist justifications of desert claims are the objections that in some cases a person can deserve something even though giving him what he deserves does not maximize utility, and that in other cases giving a person something he does not deserve may maximize utility. For example, it could happen that Bert's overtly blaming S on the basis of S's possession of P for stealing some prunes would fail to maximize utility even though S deserves the overt blame in virtue of possessing P. Simply imagine that if Bert were to blame S for stealing the prunes, S would lose her temper and commit a horrendous crime.

Now, to assess Vargas's V1, suppose that S, an extremely astute computer hacker, has pulled off many "hacking" offenses without being caught. She will enjoy several more hacking triumphs before she dies and will never be caught. With a character like S, it is not difficult to envision that even if she were overtly blamed for one of her computer crimes, this would not foster the relevant sort of agency in her (moral sensitive-considerations agency); she is set in her ways. Typically, mentally healthy, adult human beings do have the ability to recognize and react to moral considerations; they are suitably reasons-responsive. Why, then, suppose that when *such* agents overtly praise or blame others who, like themselves, are *already* reasons-responsive agents, they are contributing to fostering morally responsible agency? The issue here is not one of whether every instance of overt praise or blame contributes to the cultivation of the requisite form of agency. Rather, with the relevant members of a "moral community," it appears that the training period is over. In this sort of case, it seems that S is deserving of overt blame (on the basis of possessing P) for her crimes but V1 implies otherwise.

A slight modification of this example shows that V2 is defective as well. Suppose the spread of a virulent virus has resulted in the death of a very high percentage of the members of S's society. Of the members who are still alive, each is already the relevant sort of agent; overtly blaming would not contribute to fostering in any of them moral sensitive-considerations agency. Thus, overtly blaming S for her computer crimes would fail to cultivate in S or in any other member of her society this sort of agency. Still, contrary to the implication of V2, S is still deserving of blame for her hacking offenses.

I conclude that it would be prudent to divorce forward-looking accounts of blameworthiness from desert. I next turn to two such accounts, one advanced by Ingmar Persson (2013) and the other by Pereboom (2014).

Imagine the "Persson world"—the "P-World"—in which there is no desert-entailing but only forward-looking responsibility. One may suppose that desert-entailing responsibility requires that we be the ultimate originators of our actions in a strong way. To be responsible, for instance, for a choice, that choice must issue from the way one is—from one's character or motives for which one is responsible. But to be responsible, in turn, for the way one is, one must be responsible for yet prior choices that contribute to the way one is (Strawson 1986; 1994). Assume that in this world, however, actions can be morally permissible, impermissible, or obligatory. Suppose one further contends that responsibility in the P-World is forward-looking (but not desert-based) in that the prospect of overt blame or praise (or punishment or reward) can affect the outcome of practical deliberation; these things or the reactive attitudes can function as reasons to encourage or discourage us to behave in certain ways. Roughly, what we can be responsible for is whatever can be influenced by reasons for action (Persson 2013, 172–73).[12] Finally, assume that, with the exception of being an ultimate originator in the strong sense just outlined, the conditions required for one to be "forwardly blameworthy" or, more generally, "forwardly responsible" for something supposedly mirror those that are required for one to be responsible in the desert-entailing sense of "responsible." So, for instance, to be forwardly blameworthy for a decision, one must exercise control in making that decision, and the moral requirement (whatever it is, the objective view, the subjective view, or so forth) should be satisfied. It is this last assumption that I want to examine more closely. Focus, in particular, on control. If forward-looking blameworthiness is oriented to influencing behavior and not to registering anything about desert, then it is not clear why the sort of control that this type of blameworthiness requires should be the sort that desert-entailing blameworthiness requires. So, for instance, if strong incompatibilist alternatives are a prerequisite to be blameworthy in the desert-entailing sense for something, surely one need not require this sort of control to be forwardly blameworthy for this thing. Even if determinism is true, the reactive attitudes can influence behavior. Or suppose it is proposed that to be blameworthy in the desert-entailing sense for a decision, one must be aptly reasons-responsive; one must be able to recognize a suitably broad array of sufficient reasons to do otherwise, and be able to do otherwise for those reasons. But yet again, it seems that one could influence behavior even though one were not reasons-responsive in this way. One may recognize that if one does any one of a cluster of things, one will be adversely affected, and if one wants to avoid these detrimental consequences, one should not do these things. (Strict liability laws may function pretty well in channeling behavior.) It would seem, then, that the control forward-looking blameworthiness requires need be nothing like the control desert-entailing blameworthiness requires.

Suppose this is granted. Then one should be cautious about endorsing the luck principle:

Luck-Simplified: The degree to which one is blameworthy for something cannot be affected by what is not in one's control.

This is a principle, as we have seen, that is highly reasonable provided the blameworthiness in question is desert-entailing. With the species of forward-looking blameworthiness at issue, however, as the control it presupposes (whatever it precisely is) is not the sort that desert-entailing blameworthiness demands, a convincing rationale is required for supposing that *Luck-Simplified* is true even with forward-looking blameworthiness. If a strict liability law can effectively regulate behavior, then why should one think that *Luck-Simplified* is true with forward-looking blameworthiness?

If the luck principle fails in the P-World, this failure will undercut the argument against the objective view developed in the previous section. But as the P-World accommodates moral obligation, we may still invoke the considerations laid out in chapter 4 to show that our range of obligations in this world is diminished because of luck. If it is further assumed that a precondition of forward-looking blameworthiness is either the objective view or some variant of the subjective view, the scope of blameworthiness in the P-World will also be reduced.

Now let's entertain a different sort of world. We move from the Persson world—the P-World—to the Pereboom world (the "PB-World"). This world, like the P-World, is devoid of desert-entailing responsibility as Pereboom argues (e.g., 2001; 2014), but unlike the P-world, it is also bereft of moral obligation. Again, since rewards, punishments, and their likes in the PB-World are to be given a forward-looking justification in terms of their good effects, *Luck-Simplified* should be abandoned in connection with Pereboom's species of forward-looking blameworthiness.

Furthermore, it won't be true, or at least it appears that it won't be true in the PB-World that axiological obligation is subject to luck in the way in which moral obligation is (in a world that accommodates moral obligation). Assume that in Stage 1 of *Theft*, Augustine axiologically ought not to steal the pears. In Stage 2, even when he has no alternatives, it may be that he axiologically ought not to steal the pears either. Since the axiological "ought" does not imply "can," lacking alternatives because of luck will not undermine axiological obligation. In the PB world, then, neither axiological obligation nor forward-looking blameworthiness will hang on a thread. These consequences bring to light a feature of the PB-World: It is a demanding world. For example, "obligations" (or, perhaps, more aptly, "recommendations") may not change with the passage of time even though, as pertinent events unfold you may not be able to do what at a prior time you could have done. And you may well be forwardly blameworthy for a decision of yours even though you lack the sort of control in making this decision that desert-entailing blameworthiness requires.

The price of rescuing obligation and blameworthiness from the reach of luck, in the way envisioned, will be a "move" to a PB-World. Obligation will be replaced by "recommendation," and desert-entailing blameworthiness by forward-looking blameworthiness.

5.6 SEMICOMPATIBILISM AND NONMORAL VARIETIES OF BLAMEWORTHINESS

Aspects of the discussion in the previous four sections prompt some interesting questions about semicompatibilism and the scope or reach of nonmoral varieties of blameworthiness to which I now turn.

5.6.1 Semicompatibilism

I am partial toward Frankfurt examples, and I agree with Fischer (2006) that these examples go a long way, although not all the way, to sustaining semicompatibilism concerning moral responsibility, the view that although determinism may be incompatible with freedom to do otherwise, it is not incompatible with responsibility. I have argued that anyone who believes Frankfurt examples make a good case for the thesis that blameworthiness does not presuppose one's having alternative possibilities cannot rationally hold on to the principle that blameworthiness requires impermissibility. Frankfurt defenders, then, should renounce the objective view in favor of one of the subjective views, or at least in favor of a deontic candidate that is not in any way committed to one's having alternative possibilities.

Frankfurt examples, if cogent, also reveal that semicompatibilism concerning moral obligation is not defensible. It is false that even if determinism expunges alternatives, the thesis of determinism is compatible with the truth of morally deontic judgments of obligation, permissibility, or impermissibility since the truth of these judgments presupposes our having alternatives. So there is this interesting asymmetry involving semicompatibilism: Semicompatibilism concerning moral praiseworthiness and blameworthiness but not moral obligation is viable.

Needless to say, not everyone accepts this asymmetry. In this subsection, I respond to Widerker's recent criticism of semicompatibilism concerning responsibility. Widerker believes that a suitably modified variation of Frankfurt examples, such as *Theft*, sustains the view that blameworthiness does not require avoidability.[13] Indeed, Widerker develops a libertarian position that entails that free actions are not caused and having alternatives is not a precondition of blameworthiness. Setting aside their difference on whether some free actions arc uncaused, because semicompatibilists generally and Widerker are agreed on one alleged moral of Frankfurt examples—that blameworthiness does not require alternative possibilities—and, furthermore, because semicompatibilists regard such examples as largely sustaining semicompatibilism's implication that responsibility does not require avoidability, why does Widerker reject semicompatibilism concerning responsibility ("semicompatibilism-R")? First, he proposes that semicompatibilism-R cannot satisfy an adequacy constraint on a "plausible theory of moral culpability" (2009, 100). Second, he questions rationales that some proponents of Frankfurt examples have provided to support the judgment that an agent, such as Stage 2 Augustine, is morally responsible despite lacking alternatives (2009, 99–100). I have already addressed the second reason, at least indirectly, in section 2.3 in which I gave an explanation for this judgment that circumvents Widerker's concerns. So, I limit my comments to Widerker's first criticism.

Widerker develops this criticism by focusing on some of Fischer's semicompatibilist views. Widerker writes:

> Call a compatibilist a 'self-reflective compatibilist' if and only if he is aware of his compatibilist belief, i.e., that determinism is compatible with judgments of moral blame. Now, a plausible theory of moral culpability should allow for the possibility that

also a self-reflective compatibilist can correctly and justifiably regard himself blameworthy for his deeds. Normally . . . the mere fact that someone is aware that he subscribes to a certain theory of moral blame (assuming that this person is morally competent, etc.) should not be a reason for enabling that person to exculpate herself/himself for acting wrongly. Notice however that semicompatibilism does not satisfy this condition. To see this, let's assume that Bob in [case] Theft is a self-reflective semicompatibilist who knows that he lives in a deterministic world. Bob is aware that deciding to steal the watch is morally wrong. However, qua semicompatibilist, he is also convinced that which decision he will ultimately make, is determined ineluctably by the laws of nature and the state of the universe that obtained before humanity existed—factors for which he bears no responsibility. If that's the case, then (assuming that ultimately Bob decides to steal the watch) I simply cannot see how Bob could coherently regard himself blameworthy for deciding to steal the watch, or to use Fischer's terminology, regard himself a fair target for the reactive attitudes. How could he do so knowing that his decision was an ineluctable result of dumb luck, consisting in the primordial state of the universe and the laws of nature? (2009, 99–100, note omitted)

Reflect, preliminarily, on the proposal that a self-reflective compatibilist cannot plausibly regard herself as blameworthy for some decision if she realizes that this decision "was an ineluctable result of dumb luck" because it had its origins in distant states of the universe and the laws of nature. This problem of *remote* luck against compatibilism is well known. Having no wish to battle it here, I merely indicate that libertarian accounts of free action, including the noncausal variant that Widerker endorses, have frequently been accused of succumbing to a problem of *proximal* luck as well.

A central tenet of the noncausal account is that a directly free action is an action whose freedom is not inherited from the freedom of other actions to which it is suitably related. Widerker's noncausal libertarianism has it that directly free actions are not caused, not even by apt, proximal reason states of their agent. Briefly, the proximal luck problem on one understanding of this problem is that if one agent does one thing and another refrains from doing it, and there is nothing about the agents' powers, capacities, states of mind, moral character, and the like that explains this cross world difference, then the difference appears to be just matter of luck (Mele 1999a, 280).[14] Luck of this sort seems incompatible with free action and moral responsibility. It is not my intention here, either, to rule on the cogency of this luck objection (although I will have more to say about it in the last chapter).[15] I simply indicate that a self-reflective libertarian of Widerker's stripe, prima facie, fares no better vis-à-vis meeting Widerker's adequacy constraint than does a self-reflective compatibilist, *owing to concerns of luck.*

Next, however, suppose that you are a self-reflective compatibilist because you have carefully considered the various competing positions—semicompatibilism-R, event-causal libertarianism, agent-causal libertarianism, and so forth—on free action and responsibility, and you are convinced that your brand of semicompatibilism-R is in the right ballpark. Imagine that knowledgeable parties have discussed your elegant view because it is among the most prominent and promising compatibilist accounts on offer (I have in mind Fischer and Ravizza's 1998 view or Mele's 1995 view). You have defended your account against various criticisms, you have modified elements of it to handle certain objections, and there is general consensus that your view has a lot going for it. One then wonders why Widerker "simply cannot see" why you, as a self-reflective compatibilist, would not be able coherently to regard yourself to blame for some of your decisions.

Perhaps Widerker's skepticism derives from his "causal determinism exonerates" (CDE) principle:

> (CDE) If an agent's action was causally determined by factors for which he is not to blame, then the agent is not blameworthy for it. (2009, 93)

Why, however, should we accept CDE? On the face of it, CDE appears straightforwardly to beg the question against compatibilism? Responding, Widerker says:

> I confess that I do not have an answer to this question in the sense of being able to offer an independent or a transcendental argument for CDE. CDE strikes me as intuitively plausible, as being partially explicative of our notion of blame. I view myself as justified in holding CDE, simply because it seems to me to be true, and I am not aware of a good reason to the contrary. But perhaps the FF-libertarian [i.e., the Frankfurt-friendly libertarian] can . . . argue for CDE indirectly by showing that the position of those who reject CDE—compatibilists regarding determinism and moral blame—is problematic. I believe he can. (2009, 94–95)

In the present context, however, of assessing why Widerker finds it incredulous to believe that a self-reflective semicompatibilist could regard herself as blameworthy for some of her decisions that the distant past and the laws entail (call this belief "Widerker's Belief"), he could not duly avail himself of CDE: If *support* for CDE is to derive partly from *showing* that semicompatibilism-R cannot account for blameworthiness in a deterministic world (because of no independent argument for CDE), then support for Widerker's Belief cannot derive from CDE itself that *yet* awaits support.

In addition, CDE has another shortcoming. Event causal libertarians hold that a directly free action is nondeterministically caused by apt reason states (or their neural realizers) of its agent (e.g., Mele 1995; Kane 1996; Clarke 2000). Libertarians who are noncausalists aver that a directly free action is uncaused, but it is suitably "informed" by reasons states (Ginet 1990; Goetz 1998; McCann 1998). According to noncausalists, typically, when an agent acts freely, the explanatory relation between an agent's act and the reason for which she acts is teleological: The agent performs the act for the purpose or with the intention of attaining a goal, and regards the act as a means to securing that goal. If noncausal libertarians, such as Widerker, find CDE attractive, I see no reason why they would grudge event-causal libertarians from acceding to this principle:

(CDE Event-Causal) If an agent's action was nondeterministically caused by factors for which he is not blameworthy (or not morally responsible), then the agent is not blameworthy (or morally responsible) for it.

Furthermore, I see no reason why libertarians who find CDE compelling, should grudge noncausalists from also accepting:

(CDE Noncausal): If an agent's action was not caused but "informed" by factors for which he is not blameworthy (or not morally responsible), then the agent is not blameworthy (or morally responsible) for it.

After all, CDE and its siblings share a common kernel:

(CDE Common) If an agent's action was produced or "informed" by factors for which he is not morally responsible (or regarding which he has no responsibility-level control), then he is not the ultimate originator or source of this action; and one is blameworthy (or morally responsible) for an action only if one is its ultimate originator.

However, CDE and its event-causal and noncausal variants countenance this standard problem: Assuming with the libertarian that we sometimes perform actions for which we are morally responsible, consider the very first free action for which one is morally responsible. Presumably, it will causally derive from, or be informed by, factors such as reason states for which one is not morally responsible or regarding which one lacks responsibility-level control (see, e.g., Pereboom 2001, 48–49; Clarke 2003, 89–91). In addition, many compatibilists accept the common kernel of these principles—that one be the ultimate source of one's actions to be morally responsible for them—but these compatibilists defend accounts of ultimate origination that are compatible with determinism (see, e.g., Frankfurt 1971; Mele 1995; Fischer and Ravizza 1998; Haji and Cuypers 2008). It is far from settled whether these compatibilist accounts are inferior to libertarian competitors. We may conclude that Widerker's (first) criticism does not defeat semicompatibilism-R. So at least one hurdle against the symmetry thesis, the thesis that semicompatibilism concerning moral responsibility but not semicompatibilism concerning moral obligation is plausible, has been overcome.

This asymmetry, in turn, prompts the following question: Assuming semicompatibilism concerning responsibility can be defended, what is semicompatibilism's reach? Roughly, in asking this question I am asking what sorts of normative appraisal are such that the truth of their judgments does not presuppose the availability of alternative possibilities. How do we go about investigating semicompatibilism's scope? I aim to lend credibility to the position that normative appraisals essentially associated with reasons of the sort that moral obligation is affiliated with—objective reasons—are beyond semicompatibilism's reach whereas those appraisals essentially associated with subjective reasons may be admitted into semicompatibilism's domain.

5.6.2 Semicompatibilism's Domain

We said that objective reasons are facts dissociated from the agent's desires or attitudes that are intrinsically motivating. Such reasons provide support for one's attitudes or acts. One's objective reasons contrast with one's subjective reasons, reasons one *takes* to be one's objective reasons. One has a subjective reason to do something if and only if one believes that one has an objective reason to do it.

Again, I remind the reader that we use "it is O-reasons-wise impermissible, permissible, or obligatory to do something" to flag that such reason-wise appraisals are appraisals from the point of view of objective reasons. To help delineate semicompatibilism's domain, consider any variety of normative appraisal that sanctions or entails judgments of this form:

Normative Appraisal: It is N-impermissible (that is, it is impermissible from the perspective of the normative appraisal, which we label "N," in question), N-permissible, or N-obligatory that agent, S, do A.

Next, consider, all judgments of this type—all N-type judgments—that, in turn, entail:

NO: It is O-reasons-wise impermissible, permissible, or obligatory for S to do A (alternatively, it is impermissible, permissible, or obligatory from the perspective of objective reasons for S to do A).

Any NO-type judgment is true only if S can refrain from dong A because, assuming it is not O-reasons wise arational for S to do A, necessarily, if it is O-reasons-wise impermissible, permissible, or obligatory for S to do A, then S can refrain from doing A. The interesting consequence is that semicompatibilism concerning the sort of normative appraisal at issue—an N appraisal that entails NO-type judgments—is *not* sustainable. It is not sustainable because it is false that the truth of N-type judgments of, for example, the form "it is N-impermissible for one to do something," is compatible with causal determinism even if causal determinism is incompatible with freedom to do otherwise. And this, in turn, is simply because the truth of N-type judgments of this form (that is, N-type judgments that entail NO-type judgments) requires that one could have refrained from doing what one did. Briefly put, if some normative appraisal "involving" an agent is wedded to the view that the appraisal is true only if the agent O-reasons-wise ought not to have done something, (and it is not O-reasons-wise arational for the agent to have done it), then semicompatibilism concerning this sort of appraisal is out of the running.

To illustrate with a simple example, if one morally ought not to do something, then, it is O-reasons-wise impermissible, permissible, or obligatory for one to do it (assuming that it is not O-reasons-wise arational for one to do it). But then, given the connection between objective reasons and freedom to do otherwise, if one morally ought not to do something, one can refrain from doing it.

It should be stressed that my concern is with the part of semicompatibilism that says that the truth of judgments of the pertinent normative appraisal does not require *freedom to do otherwise*. Even if, for instance, moral impermissibility requires avoidability, it does not, of course, straightforwardly follow that determinism is incompatible with moral impermissibility because one might argue that the relevant notion of avoidability is compatible with determinism. As another illustration, there are other varieties of obligation in addition to moral obligation. For instance, it may be prudentially but not morally impermissible for one to do something. Furthermore, it is reasonable to suppose that if it is prudentially impermissible for one to do something, then one has an objective *pro tanto* reason to refrain from doing it. But if one has such a reason to refrain from doing something, then it is O-reasons-wise impermissible, permissible, or obligatory for one to do it (barring its being O-reasons-wise arational for one to do it). Hence, given the association between objective reasons and avoidability, semicompatibilism concerning prudential impermissibility is not viable.

To extend the example, it seems perfectly intelligible to suppose that one can be prudentially blameworthy for doing something (see, e.g., Haji 1998, ch. 11). If, contrary to what I believe, prudential blameworthiness, in turn, is tied to prudential impermissibility—one is prudentially blameworthy for doing something only if it is prudentially impermissible for one to do it—then semicompatibilism regarding prudential blameworthiness cannot be maintained.

Similarly, in opposition to what I have proposed, if moral blameworthiness *is* tied to moral impermissibility—if principle *Blameworthiness/Impermissibility* is true—then semicompatibilism concerning moral blameworthiness is ruled out.

In contrast, subjective accounts of blameworthiness, accounts that have either *Simple Subjective* or *Complex Subjective* as constituents, appear to be consistent with semicompatibilism concerning blameworthiness. *Simple Subjective* says that if one is morally blameworthy for doing something, then one does it while nonculpably believing that it is morally impermissible for one to do it. *Complex*

Subjective has it that if one is blameworthy for doing something, one does it while believing that it is either morally impermissible or morally amiss for one to do it. Pondering *Simple Subjective*'s consequent, suppose *S* believes it is morally impermissible for *S* to do *A*. Then, if rational, *S* believes that *S* has an objective reason not to do *A*. So, when the agents in question are rational, *Simple Subjective* is associated with subjective reasons: If one is morally blameworthy for doing something, then one believes that one has an objective reason not to do it.

We cannot duly infer from *Simple Subjective* that one is morally blameworthy for something only if it is morally impermissible for one to do it. So, we cannot duly infer from *Simple Subjective* that one is morally blameworthy for something only if it is O-reasons-wise impermissible, permissible, or obligatory for one to do it.[16] With this inference blocked, there is no straightforward route to the conclusion, if there is any route at all, that *Simple Subjective* is inconsistent with semicompatibilism concerning moral blameworthiness. Similar things are true of *Complex Subjective* too.

We have made some progress in mapping the reach of semicompatibilism. Normative appraisals that have or entail judgments of the form that it O-reasons-wise impermissible, permissible, or obligatory for some agent to perform some action are excluded from semicompatibilism's domain.

To make further headway, Fischer proposed semicompatibilism as a doctrine concerning moral *responsibility*. I have, for the most part, restricted attention to semicompatibilism concerning moral blameworthiness. But as we seen, there are other varieties of blameworthiness including prudential blameworthiness and etiquettical blameworthiness. Prudential blameworthiness, just like moral blameworthiness, should be dissociated from prudential impermissibility. After all, it seems that one can be prudentially blameworthy for doing something it is prudentially permissible but suboptimal for one to do. In *Ride Home*, you have been savoring several wines at Vinny Merlot's estate. By the wee hours of the morning, you have had a bit too much of the too fine vintages. You (prudentially) ought to get a ride home. You can secure safe passage in a number of permissible ways, some better than others. In increasing order of deontic-for-you value, (a1) get Vinny's chauffeur, Pinot, to drive you home (the distance home is fairly long, and old Pinot is a slow driver); (a2) ride the subway; or, (a3) take a cab. You don't particularly like Pinot. You know that he has had a busy night—he has driven several others (in states of inebriation similar to the one you are in!) home, and he is tired. Simply to irk him further, you ask for his services. You do so full well realizing that you are doing something it is prudentially deontically amiss for you to do. In this case you may well be prudentially blameworthy for doing (a1), an option that is (from the prudential perspective) permissibly suboptimal. I propose, instead, that prudential blameworthiness should be associated not with prudential impermissibility but with belief in doing something one nonculpably takes to be prudentially impermissible or (prudentially) deontically amiss. Once, again, given this doxastic association, there is no reason to believe that prudential blameworthiness is essentially associated with freedom to do otherwise.

We may now propose the following. If E is an evaluative perspective, such as the prudential, etiquettical, or morally deontic perspective, then as I will say, for some such perspectives, one can be E-blameworthy for some of one's conduct; one can, for instance, be morally, prudentially, or etiquettically blameworthy for some of one's actions. Consider any variety of E-blameworthiness that is dissociated from E-impermissibility, but (essentially) associated with the relevant sorts of belief; these varieties will include as a necessary condition for blameworthiness, an appropriately modified version of the condition that principle *Complex Subjective* specifies.

Semicompatibilism concerning any instance of these varieties of E-blameworthiness is viable.

To tie some ends together, suppose semicompatibilism concerning moral blameworthiness is true. Would this result be considerably less interesting if semicompatibilism concerning moral obligation were not so? I doubt it. For, as I have argued, agreeing with Fischer's insight, semicompatibilism has an extended reach. Although semicompatibilism concerning moral obligation is suspect, semicompatibilism concerning many varieties of blameworthiness is defensible. Semicompatibilism has resilience: Its primary domain is, roughly, the domain of responsibility but not merely moral responsibility.

As I will discuss in the last chapter, however, semicompatibilists about moral blameworthiness face real concerns about whether people are in fact morally blameworthy for their behavior if people are aware that, should it be true, they never have alternatives of any sort.

5.6.3 The Scope of Nonmoral Varieties of Blameworthiness

Finally, what of the scope or reach of nonmoral varieties of blameworthiness such as prudential blameworthiness? They would diminish, too, and for the very same sorts of reason that the scope of moral blameworthiness diminishes. For example, regarding prudential blameworthiness, if one is prudentially blameworthy for something only if it is prudentially impermissible for one to do it, prudential impermissibility requires avoidability, and luck constrains the range of things for which one can do otherwise, then luck also constricts the range of things for which one is prudentially blameworthy. Suppose, however, that a precondition of prudential blameworthiness is not prudential impermissibility

but noncuplable belief in something that is prudentially impermissible or prudentially amiss. Then in all those instances in
which one could not have done otherwise ultimately in virtue of
luck, and in which but for luck one would have done something
it was prudentially impermissible or amiss for one to do, and
one was aware that one did not do anything it was prudentially
impermissible or amiss for one to do, one would not be prudentially blameworthy for what one did. Prudential blameworthiness would, thus, go the way of moral blameworthiness: Its scope
would diminish.

In addition, prudential obligation, just like moral obligation,
can change with the passage of time. With simple adjustment, the
sort of argument that invokes the changeability of moral obligations
owing to luck to confirm that moral blameworthiness is restricted,
also shows that changeability of prudential obligation because of
luck restricts prudential blameworthiness.

5.7 TELEOLOGICAL THEORIES, OBLIGATION, AND BLAMEWORTHINESS

I end this chapter with brief remarks on whether espousers of teleological accounts of action—"teleologists"—should be concerned
about the sort of skepticism regarding the range of obligation and
blameworthiness for which I have argued. Teleologists propose
that behaviors that are actions, as opposed to mere events that
happen to agents, are actions in virtue of being directed toward
goals their agents have and value. Teleological explanations of an
instance of behavior, which qualifies as a choice or an overt action,
account for this behavior by citing a state of affairs or goal toward
which the behavior is targeted. Since they don't address the causes
of the pertinent behavior, such explanations need not cite any

antecedent mental states of the agent at all. Rather, these explanations illuminate what the behavior is aimed at accomplishing (see, e.g., Wilson 1989; Schueler 2003; Sehon 2005; n.d.). Teleological accounts stand opposed to causal accounts according to which behaviors are actions if, roughly, reason states of their agents nondeviantly cause them (see, e.g., Davidson 1963; Bishop 1989; Mele 1992; 2003a). Teleologists may allow that any action or choice has mental states (or their neural realizers) as causes. However, they may insist that reasons explanations of action are irreducibly teleological rather than causal, and it is teleological and not causal explanations that bear on whether a choice or action is free and whether its agent is morally responsible for it (Sehon 1997; n.d.). It is open to a teleologist to argue that since it is teleological explanations that are pivotal to free choice or action, whether an action is deterministically or indeterministically caused has little, if anything, to do with such choice or action, or with responsibility (Sehon n.d., sec. 8.1.).

However, teleologists may embrace *Kant's Law* and *Equivalence* (the latter is the principle that the proposition that one ought not to do something is equivalent to the proposition that it is impermissible for one to do that thing). If they accept these principles, they will be committed to the view that impermissibility requires alternatives. Teleologists may also opt for either the objective view (one is blameworthy for something only if it is impermissible for one to do it) or some variant of subjective views (one is blameworthy for something only if one does it while nonculpably believing that it is impermissible for one to do it). Independently of whether they regard determinism or indeterminism as a threat to free action or responsibility, teleologists, then, have to take seriously the thesis that luck affects the range of our moral obligations and things for which we are morally responsible.

NOTES

1. Persson (2013, 226–27, 239) rejects the objective view. Others who endorse the view that an agent can be blameworthy despite doing no wrong include Moore 1912, 101; Parfit 1984, 25; Thomson 1991, 295; and Zimmerman 1997.

2. Insightful discussion concerning this issue is to be found in Zimmerman 1993.

3. For a near identical view, see McKenna 2012, 19–20, 58–59.

4. Zimmerman (2008; 2014) argues for roughly, though not quite, the view that Jill ought to maximize expected value. He critically discusses Persson's solution in 2014, 48–57.

5. Of course, if as Zimmerman (2008; 2014) argues, Jill ought to give A, then (with innocuous assumptions) she will not be blameworthy for giving A.

6. "Plain ought" is a term Fred Feldman introduces in his discussion of over-ridingness. See Feldman 1986, 212–15.

7. There is a complication, however. In his 2014, 142, it appears that Pereboom rejects the objective view.

8. See, also, Foot 1978; Stocker 1990; Williams 1976; and Wolf 1982.

9. See Haji 1998, 140–67 for a defense of this view.

10. Here, we ignore worries of determinism.

11. If one is averse to the category of the amoral, this principle can be modified in this way: Other things equal, one is more blameworthy for doing something it is impermissible for one to do (if one does it while nonculpably believing that it is impermissible for one to do it) than for doing something it is not impermissible for one to do (while nonculpably believing that it is impermissible for one to do it).

12. Persson (2013) holds this combination of views: there is only forward-looking responsibility in our world (but no desert-entailing responsibility), and our world accommodates moral obligation.

13. More exactly, Widerker (2003) thinks that Frankfurt-type examples are unsuccessful but what he calls "IRR scenarios" (which are relevantly like Frankfurt examples) impugn the principle of alternate possibilities. See, for example, Widerker 2006; 2009.

14. On this luck objection, see, e.g., Waller 1988; Mele 1999a; 1999b; Berofsky 2000; Haji 2009a.

15. Franklin (2011) has recently advanced a powerful criticism of the luck objection. See Haji 2012b for a response to Franklin. More on the luck objection can be found in Hume (1739) 2000, 261–62; Van Inwagen 2000; 2011; Clarke 2003; 2011; Fischer 2011a; 2011b; Mele 2006; 2007; 2013b; Nelkin 2007; O'Connor 2007; 2011; Almeida and Bernstein 2011; Ekstrom 2011; Kane 2011; and Tognazzini 2011. I give an outline of my version of the luck objection in ch. 7.

16. Here, I am assuming that other necessary conditions of blameworthiness do not require that one could have done otherwise.

Chapter 6

Ramifications

In this chapter, I examine some ramifications of the dual primary conclusions of the preceding two chapters: Because of luck, the range of things it is obligatory for us to do and for which we are morally blameworthy is narrow. I first say something about the impact of these views on "strong character," being disposed to fulfill one's moral obligations and to avoid wrongdoing, and "weak character," being disposed to wrongdoing. Then I discuss the influence of these conclusions on some putative moral aims of education.

6.1 CHARACTER, OBLIGATION, AND BLAMEWORTHINESS

With his typical wit and moral insight, in a passage (laced with irony) Mark Twain pronounces, "I am morally superior to George Washington. He couldn't tell a lie. I can and don't."[1] When Luther broke with the Church of Rome in the sixteenth century, he reportedly made the now famous declaration: "Here I stand. I can do no other." With no reservation and pronounced emphasis, a mentally healthy and loving mother declares, "I couldn't but rescue my child from the monstrous waves." Whether someone can in fact be constitutionally or psychologically incapable of performing various actions is controversial. Far less contentious is that the sort of person one is, or broadly, one's character, influences the types of action one can or cannot perform. The *extent* of this influence is debatable. Suppose it was literally true of Washington that he could not bring himself to lie, given his disposition to be honest. Then since obligation requires avoidability, and he could not have prevented himself from telling the truth, it is false that on the relevant occasion it was obligatory for him to tell the truth on that occasion. As I invited the reader to envision in chapter 1, picture again a George Washington endowed with sundry virtues—generosity, loyalty, kindness, and so forth. Assume that the influence of these virtues on his conduct precluded him from doing certain things on certain occasions. For example, he could not tell a lie nor betray a friend (unless compelled to choose between dishonesty and disloyalty). Then the range of things it is morally obligatory for Washington to do diminishes considerably. As one becomes more "virtuous" insofar as one cannot refrain from doing what it is seemingly obligatory for one to do, this thing that is ostensibly obligatory for one will not in fact be obligatory for one. Furthermore, what is relevantly true of our hypothetical paragon of virtue is true of many others as well. The devoted mother, Ann, finds it unthinkable not to rescue her child from the violent waters. If she could not have refrained from saving (or attempting to save) her child, then, again, it is false that on the relevant occasion it was obligatory for her to save (or attempt to save) her child then.

In certain theological traditions the divine properties, such as omnibenevolence, that God exemplifies, prevent God from performing various actions or bringing about various states of affairs. Ponder this conception of omnibenevolence. Some parts of possible worlds are creatable, other parts are not. Assume that each creatable part is a contingent state of affairs whose actualization

the past does not render impossible so that it is open to an omnibenevolent being to bring about such a state of affairs. Such a being
strives to bring about all the creatable states of affairs it (correctly)
believes obtain in the best possible world. (A world is a best world
if no other world is better than it is.) Perhaps there is no best world
but there are only optimal worlds. Possible world, w, is optimal if
and only if w is at least as intrinsically good as any other possible
world. If there are only optimal worlds, an omnibenevolent being
strives to bring about the creatable states of affairs it (correctly)
believes obtain in an optimal world. The omnibenevolent being's
preferences, in turn, are shaped by the states of affairs that obtain
in the best world, if there is one, or in an optimal world, if there
is no best world. Keeping in mind the principle that one ought,
as of some time, t, to see to the occurrence of a state of affairs,
p, if and only if (simplifying) one brings about p in all the best
worlds accessible to one as of t, we may now provisionally define
"Consequential-omnibenevolence" in this way:

> C-Omnibenevolence: x is C-omnibenevolent = df. for any creat-
> able state of affairs, p, x prefers to bring about p if and only if x
> has a true belief that either p obtains in the world that x ought to
> bring about, if there is a best, or that p obtains in a world that it is
> permissible for x to bring about, if there are only optimal worlds;
> and if x prefers to bring about p, then x attempts to bring about p
> if x believes x can.[2]

Understanding the concept of omnibenevolence in this way, roughly
an omnibenevolent being cannot prefer to bring about a state of
affairs that is intrinsically worse than some alternative. If this is true,
then just like the hypothetical Washington, there are several contingent and "nonfully past" states of affairs this sort of God (assuming

there is one) won't be able to refrain from bringing about because of its divine nature—its goodness. Restricted in its activities in this way, the range of things that are obligatory for such a being will be pretty constrained.

Second, turning from good to evil, imagine a villain, Villiana, who performs vile deeds that she cannot avoid performing. We are stricken with a result seemingly just as paradoxical as the result we obtain with stalwart Washington: It is not true that it is impermissible for Villiana to perform any of these deeds. What's more, if moral blameworthiness requires moral impermissibility, and moral impermissibility requires avoidability, then Villiana would not be blameworthy for the deeds that she cannot avoid performing. If blameworthiness requires nonculpable belief in what it is impermissible for one to do, then if not deluded about the moral statuses of her vile deeds—they fail to be morally impermissible for her because she cannot but perform them—then yet again she would not be blameworthy for them.

Some people (e.g., Anscombe 1958) have proposed that we should stop thinking about obligation or impermissibility and return to a sort of Aristotelian ethics of virtue. We should assess conduct not by invoking deontic categories such as being obligatory or impermissible but by appeal to suitable virtue concepts such as being fair, generous, or compassionate, or being unjust, intemperate, or cowardly. Maybe, if one is drawn to defend something like Anscombe's view, one could help oneself to the two primary conclusions regarding the scope of obligation and blameworthiness to support partially this sort of revision to an ethics of virtue. Needless to say, the undertaking would be unfruitful if the pertinent virtue concepts could not be analyzed independently of the deontic ones of obligatoriness, permissibility, or impermissibility.

6.2 ON THE MORAL AIMS OF EDUCATION

Education is "teleological": It has aims or goals. It is also value-directed or "normative": Its aims are deemed worthy of pursuit. It is commonplace to distinguish between relatively specific and relatively general educational aims. As examples of the former, children should have reading, writing, and effective oratory skills, as well as knowledge of cultural history, literature, elementary natural science, mathematics, art, and music. As examples of the latter, it has been proposed that children should develop into critical thinkers and autonomous agents. Education's relatively general aims have frequently been thought of as its *ultimate aims*. This is apparently because although relatively specific educational aims may vary considerably depending upon contingences such as economic or cultural ones, the ultimate aims seem more basic, stable, and universal.[3] These aims play a pivotal role in regulating and structuring moral and other types of normative education.

Which candidates reasonably qualify as education's ultimate aims, and how is their putative privileged status of being ultimate to be justified? Addressing these challenging questions, Harvey Siegel proposes that "critical thinking is, at a minimum, 'first among equals' in the pantheon of educational ideals. . . . [and] is rightfully seen . . . more dramatically, as the ultimate educational ideal" (1988, 137). He advances the following argument for this interesting proposal:

> Consider a case in which . . . [some ideal, such as critical thinking] conflicts with some legitimate other. In such a case, one might argue that the other should override critical thinking in this instance. And perhaps so it should. But it requires rational argument, and appeal to reason, in order to make the case for the preferability of the rival ideal to that of critical thinking.

And such appeal is, of course, an appeal to, and an honoring of, the latter ideal itself. Consequently, an overriding of critical thinking by a rival educational ideal at one level requires acknowledgment of the reign of critical thinking at the next highest level. In this way critical thinking must preside over and authorize the force of its rivals.[4] (1988, 137)

Contrast Seigel's favored candidate of education's ultimate aim and its proposed defense for being ultimate with John White's approach.[5] According to White:

Personal autonomy is a central liberal value. It rests on an even more fundamental value in human life—personal well-being. Autonomous well-being is only one variant of the more general concept, given that people can flourish or not flourish in non-liberal—for example, traditional-tribal—as well as liberal societies. (1999, 193)

White's strategy traces its ancestry to Aristotle. In Book I of the *Nicomachean Ethics* Aristotle advances what seem to be "bedrock" or foundational values or aims that supposedly carry their justification on their sleeves. The bedrock aims identified concern what is good for both individuals and society at large, and are closely tied to what it is to flourish as private persons and as public citizens. In the early sections of the *Nicomachean Ethics* Aristotle says that the good life is the life of flourishing and virtue. To achieve a state of well-being, proper social institutions are necessary. The political setting must enable people to cultivate the peculiarly human excellences, the moral and the intellectual virtues, which are necessary for the good life. Indeed, Aristotle proposes that the state should actively encourage people to inculcate the virtues in order for its citizens to flourish. Their flourishing, in turn, ensures that the political order flourishes as well.[6]

White's Aristotelian approach assumes that education's rock bottom aim is to raise our children in such a fashion that, of the many different ways in which their lives could turn out, each child gets a life that is good in itself—intrinsically valuable—for him or her. On this approach, identifying and justifying what we may call education's "specific, substantive, and ultimate aims," such as ensuring that our children develop into autonomous agents, or virtuous agents, or critical thinkers, requires exposing how these aims are essentially associated with personal well-being.

I want to contribute modestly to the literature on ultimate aims by casting doubt on whether we can hope to achieve what may reasonably be taken to be various specific, substantive, and ultimate aims. An outline of the primary reasoning for this skeptical position reduces to this: Achieving these aims requires that we be free in the sense of having the ability and opportunity to do otherwise. Drawing on the preceding arguments of this book, factors beyond our control (or luck) ensure that we are frequently not free in this sense. Hence, achieving these aims is largely beyond our reach.

Taking my cue initially from White's insightful ruminations on the Aristotelian approach, I assume that among the specific, substantive, and ultimate aims of education are: (a) *Uprightness.* Children should develop into morally upright agents disposed to fulfill their moral obligations and to avoid wrongdoing. (b) *Virtuosity.* Children should develop into morally virtuous agents disposed to perform actions that manifest virtue. (c) *Appraisability.* Children should develop into morally responsible agents disposed, minimally, to perform actions for which they are not morally blameworthy and, desirably, to perform actions for which they are morally praiseworthy.

To stave off a preliminary worry, the pronouncements of *uprightness*—what it is obligatory for agents to do—need not conflict with those of *virtuosity*. Consider, for instance, the following strategy to develop a sort of Aristotelian ethics of virtue that confirms compatibility. In this view, the primary normative status of an act (whether it is morally permissible, impermissible, or obligatory) is a function of the net amount of virtue its agent manifests in performing it. Assume that we have a list of all the virtues and the vices. Assume, moreover, that for any possible action, there is a number that represents its "virtue value": Take the total amount of virtue its agent would manifest if this agent performed it and subtract from it the total amount of vice its agent would manifest if this agent performed it. This sort of virtue ethical theory would then say: An act is permissible if and only if no alternative has a higher virtue value than it has.

6.3 IMPERILED AIMS

The conclusion that many acts which one initially may plausibly take to be obligatory (impermissible or permissible) for one are not in fact obligatory (impermissible or permissible) for one has disturbing implications for child education. Let's consider some of them.

6.3.1 *The Defeat of Uprightness*

Suppose Ann, the devoted mother, received a fairly conventional education. During the course of her upbringing, she acquired several moral beliefs and values. Assume that over time she developed dispositions to perform actions she deemed to be obligatory for her and to avoid performing actions she nonculpably regarded to be impermissible for her. Still, given our previous discussion on obligation and freedom to do otherwise, on several occasions on which she performed actions that she took to be obligatory for her, she fulfilled no obligation at all (because she could not have avoided doing what she did on those occasions). A sobering thought is that educators, whether parents, teachers, or friends, could have done nothing to see to it that she did end up fulfilling obligations: As obligation requires avoidability, and, on many occasions, she could not have done otherwise because of factors beyond her control, and, moreover, nothing anyone else could have done would have made it the case that she could have done otherwise on those occasions, what is seemingly obligatory for her on those occasions is not obligatory for her no matter what education she received.

6.3.2 *The Defeat of Appraisability*

I also assumed that another of education's goals is *appraisability*: Children should develop into agents who are disposed, minimally, to perform actions for which they are not morally blameworthy and, desirably, to perform actions for which they are morally praiseworthy. Restricting discussion to moral blameworthiness, I have argued that impermissibility, just like obligation, requires alternative possibilities. Due to factors beyond our control, on many occasions we cannot do otherwise. Hence, on many occasions it is not impermissible for us to do what we do on these occasions. I have also argued that the changeability of obligations over time (partially because of luck) strongly suggests that frequently what we nonculpably take to be impermissible for us is not impermissible for us. To introduce another character, imagine that Sally always does what it is prudentially best for her to do even if doing so requires that she do what it is morally impermissible or what she nonculpably deems it is morally impermissible for her to do. Consider an occasion on which she does what appears to be in her long-term self-interest but is seemingly morally impermissible for her—she A-s. Assume this time around that, relevantly like Ann, she cannot refrain from A-ing on this occasion because she cannot, during the pertinent time span, acquire motivation to refrain from A-ing. We obtain skeptical results concerning her being to blame for A-ing by the now familiar pattern of reasoning. If blameworthiness requires impermissibility, and impermissibility requires avoidability, Sally, who cannot refrain from doing what is seemingly impermissible will not be blameworthy for such deeds. If blameworthiness requires nonculpable belief in what is impermissible, then Sally may erroneously but nonculpably believe that many actions that she cannot refrain from doing are impermissible for her to do, and so may be blameworthy for doing them (or at least, so assume). Or, she may nonculpably believe that she is doing wrong when she is doing nothing of this sort because of the changeability of obligations. However, if rational and enlightened about her mistake concerning the moral statuses of her actions, her enlightenment would diminish blameworthiness; she would not be blameworthy for pertinent seeming wrongdoings.

One may remark that if one of our aims is to see to it that children develop into agents who are *not* blameworthy for their actions, education is not needed to attain this end; for the most part, left to their own devices children *will* turn into agents who are frequently not to blame for their conduct. If the germane arguments of the previous chapters are cogent, this is indeed so. However, the relevant moral is that no matter what educators do, children will mature into agents who are neither praiseworthy nor blameworthy for perhaps much of their behavior, and this should give us reason to pause about whether it is rational to privilege *appraisability* as an ultimate end of education.

In sum, reduction in what is obligatory or impermissible for a person, ultimately because of our frequently not being able to do otherwise, together with requirements of blameworthiness that link this species of agent-appraisal and impermissibility, markedly constrains the range of what we are blameworthy for or would constrain this range if we were not deluded about whether our actions were obligatory, permissible, or impermissible. A similar sort of argument, which I will not develop here, that appeals to the principle that praiseworthiness is essentially tied to obligation or permissibility or nonculpable belief in obligation or permissibility, establishes that the range of things for which we are praiseworthy is considerably narrow as well.

We may conclude that the educational goals of *uprightness* and *appraisability* are for the most part unachievable. Alternatively, if these goals are largely beyond our reach, we should reconsider whether these proposed goals should indeed be *bona fide* goals of education.

6.3.3 Spreading the Net: More Is at Stake

As we remarked, Siegel takes critical thinking to be education's ultimate aim. As there is no obvious association between our capacity to think critically and freedom to do otherwise, the sort of argument marshaled to show that *uprightness* and *appraisability* are endangered will not threaten critical thinking. Similarly, one may believe that educating for *virtuosity* should remain squarely in our sights; we should strive to ensure that our children develop into virtuous agents. Despite its being true that frequently we cannot do otherwise, if we are appropriately trained and nature cooperates, seemingly nothing precludes our acting from generosity, kindness, loyalty, and so forth. Indeed, one may think that most of education's putative ultimate goals remain unaffected by the argument in the two antecedent sections. Regarding moral education, Nel Noddings and Michael Slote write:

> There seem to be three main philosophical theories of morality (or four, if we separate virtue ethics and communitarianism) that could potentially influence current understanding of moral education. Virtue ethics and mainstream communitarianism would naturally encourage a form of moral education in which schools and parents would seek to inculcate good character in the form of specific (labeled) habitual virtues. Kantian/Rawlsian rationalism/liberalism would seemingly encourage moral education to take the form of developing certain capacities for moral reasoning and certain very general principles [derived from a general duty of respect for the autonomy and dignity of every person] that can be applied to different moral dilemmas or decisions. Finally, an ethic of care would most naturally see moral education as a matter of children's coming to an intelligent emotional understanding of the good or harmful effects of their actions on the lives of other people as well as deepening understanding of defensible ways to live their own lives. Care involves caring for oneself as well as others. (Noddings and Slote 2003, 349)

Simplifying somewhat, Noddings and Slote suggest that the aims central to the "liberal paradigm" of education are tied to personal autonomy, moral reasoning, and critical thinking, whereas those at the heart of the "nonliberal" paradigm are affiliated with good character, moral sentiment, and caring relationships involving benevolence and kindness. Aims of the first sort are concerned with encouraging self-conscious and conscientious attention to one's own goals, values and choices, and promoting obedience to universal moral rules and principles. Aims of the second sort are associated with enforcing spontaneous other-directed reactive attitudes and feelings, and inculcating particular acts of caring.

White, who builds on the liberal position that R. S. Peters, P. H. Hirst, and R. F. Dearden enunciate in the 1960s, depicts liberal education and its goal as follows:

> Education aims at promoting pupils' personal well-being. In a liberal-democratic society . . . this will include personal autonomy. (White 1990, 36)

Here is another revealing passage:

> Autonomy depends on the existence of options. Education cannot supply these, but it can make students aware of them. Its job is partly to open up horizons on different conceptions of how one should live—ways of life, forms of relationship, vocational and nonvocational activities. But a broad understanding of options is not enough. Autonomous agents also need to understand themselves. They need to interpret their major goals and establish priorities among them, and to discern possible psychological obstacles arising to their self-directness.... They need also to be equipped with qualities of character. They have, for instance, to be able to withstand pressures to conform to what authority or public opinion want them to do. For this they require the critical independence of thought to asses others' arguments, as well as the moral courage to stand up for their own views. Exercise from as early an age as practicable in making choices and reflecting on these is a further requirement—as is a whole-heartedness of commitment to activities of their own choosing. (Callan and White 2003, 97)[7]

In contrast to emphasizing values of individual choice and personal well-being, nonliberal educational theorists call attention to community values, traditions, and good habits and they underscore the desirability to care for other people and to act out of immediate concern for the welfare of others.

It would seem that even if frequently we cannot do otherwise ultimately because of factors beyond our control, and so *uprightness* and *appraisability* as goals of education are imperiled, surely, the components of an ethics of care, for example, or some of the goals White underscores—autonomy—for instance, can and should remain fundamental educational goals. For these other goals, allegedly, remain unaffected by the sort of argument that throws suspicion on *uprightness* and *appraisability*. However, this is overly optimistic, as I now argue.

White plausibly suggests that although education cannot supply the options that autonomy—a putative ultimate goal of education—demands, education can make students aware of such options. If nurtured to become autonomous agents, when the time comes our children can make intelligent choices among these options; they can select among "different ways of life, forms of relationship, [and] vocational and nonvocational activities." Depending upon one's view of autonomy, if, in virtue of factors beyond one's control, one cannot on many occasions do other than what one does on those occasions, one may judge that one's autonomy concerning one's pertinent choices on those occasions is severely compromised. Elaborating, when we make choices or decisions we perform mental actions. The argument developed in the fourth chapter for the view that, usually, we cannot do otherwise does not discriminate between mental actions and overt ones. Hence, even if we have the option to choose among different ways of life or vocational activities, we will normally not be able to make *choices* regarding these ways of life or activities other than the ones we make as a result of factors beyond our control. Supposedly, the picture White has in mind when he addresses pertinent options is not merely that education makes us aware of these options. Also envisioned is that if we are fortunate to have such options, under mundane circumstances our natures would not preclude us from making a choice other than the one we made. But this image is distorted. For example, how Sally turns out to be will depend partly but vitally on her childhood upbringing and her genetic constitution. As I hitherto explained, such factors play a substantial role in curtailing choice. Or suppose, as Noddings and Slote propose, an ethics of care sees moral education (partly) as a matter of deepening children's understanding of defensible ways to live their own lives. We have an analogous concern here as the one just discussed in selecting among, for example, different vocational activities. Contrary to what would presumably be desirable, one would frequently be unable to make a choice about caring for others or oneself different from the one that one actually made.

It should be stressed, however, that whether lack of freedom to do otherwise per se undermines autonomy is controversial. Many semicompatibilists, for example, who believe that determinism is incompatible with freedom to do otherwise have defended the position that determinism is, nonetheless, compatible with autonomy or moral responsibility.[8] The problem regarding educational aims I wish to raise is a somewhat different one.

One of education's objectives is to channel decisions in various directions. Presumably, we hope that a person like Sally would develop the disposition to do what is morally required of her (assuming it was possible for her to fulfill her obligations) rather than to develop the disposition (she has) always to do what is prudentially required of her. An ethics of care would, again, discourage our children from making decisions regarding others that are in conflict with central edicts of such an ethics. White would want our children to mature into agents who make decisions consonant with withstanding "pressures to conform to what authority or public opinion want them to do." Briefly, even if they cannot refrain from doing or choosing as they do or choose, it is desirable that as they acquire various cognitive and other psychological capacities, children make certain sorts of decision; abbreviating, it is desirable that they make "apt" decisions. But how do we get maturing children to make *such* decisions? The answer that readily comes to mind, of course, is to *educate* them: We "open up horizons on different conceptions of how one should live"; we get them to appreciate the advantages and pitfalls of the alternatives; we strive to convince them of the virtues of autonomy, and so forth. Presenting them with such options should, hopefully, influence the choices they make even if, frequently, they cannot refrain from making the choices they do. The *extent* of this influence, however, is difficult to discern. It is not contentious that factors beyond their control affect the choices they make. But how much control do *others*—especially *educators*—have over these factors when practices such as indoctrination are ruled out? It seems none at all or very little over some of them, such as genetic constitution; presumably more over others. It is, then, controversial just how much influence educators have in channeling children's decisions in certain directions. Perhaps it is minimal, and the rest is simply up to luck—to factors beyond one's control.

One may press the following objection.[9] Suppose the skeptical arguments developed in this book are sound and, for example, uprightness is generally unattainable since most people most of the time are not able to do otherwise. How much in the end should this affect education's aims? Isn't there room here for a kind of innocuous illusionism of the following sort? For practical purposes, let those of us charting the course of education assess its ultimate aims under the (illusory) belief that uprightness for most people is attainable.

Admittedly it really is not attainable, but if we teach and aim as if it were, we would be more likely to generate educated adults who, although they are not able to act otherwise, on many occasions act as if they are seeking to do what they morally ought to do. More so, in those situations in which they are able to act otherwise, they would be disposed to believe for good reasons that what they ought to do is what morality requires of them. Why would not an aim so specified be enough for counting among education's ultimate aims?

I prefix the reply to this objection with the following remarks. First, I have assumed that lack of freedom to do otherwise is no hindrance to acquiring the capacity for critical thinking. Presuming we educate for critical thinking, we would hope or maybe it should be an aim of education that as they mature into critical thinkers children come to realize that, roughly, given their natures, frequently they will not be able to do or choose other than what they do or choose; and so, frequently, they will not do anything it is morally permissible, impermissible, or obligatory for them to do. Moreover, more often than not they will be neither morally praiseworthy nor blameworthy for much of their conduct. Remember, White proposes that autonomous agents need to *understand themselves*: "They need to interpret their major goals and to establish priorities among them, and to discern possible psychological obstacles arising to their self-directedness." In striving to understand themselves, children who become critical thinkers should come to appreciate that in certain respects the moral playing field is fairly level: No matter what one's religious outlook, cultural background, racial denomination, or economic standing—no matter what one's endowments or fruits of a Rawlsian natural lottery—regarding moral *appraisability* (being praiseworthy or blameworthy for conduct) and moral *uprightness*, we are all much more alike than different.

This should have some fairly radical consequences for social arrangements such as the distribution of benefits and burdens when the desert bases are impermissibility, praiseworthiness, or blameworthiness. For example, other things equal, we may reasonably suppose that a person who has done no wrong or avoided wrongdoing deserves more of a share of a benefit than one who has done intentional wrong. Should we all be alike in that much of what we do is not impermissible for us to do, then this sort of distribution would be largely improper in our world. For another example, assuming that at least in the criminal law, legal culpability coincides (or should coincide) more or less with moral culpability, enlightened about the paucity of guilt, we would have to do some serious rethinking about the structure of our institution of criminal law.

Educating in the liberal tradition underscores minimizing morally irrelevant differences. It seems that our efforts in many parts of the world to do so have been less than successful to say the least. Country of birth, especially when one is indigent, which in many cases has profound effects on one's life prospects, is regarded to be a pertinent basis for "keeping one out." This is so even though place of birth is as morally irrelevant as skin color. Should our skepticism concerning moral responsibility and impermissibility have secure foundations, there is a sense in which these things are morally irrelevant as well: Being blameworthy or praiseworthy for one's conduct should not be a basis for "keeping one out" because we are largely *not* morally responsible for any of our conduct.

Returning to the option of mild illusionism and skepticism about purported educational aims, my second remark is that the relatively specific aims of education, such as acquiring reading, writing, and oratory skills, and having knowledge of elementary natural science, literature, art, and so forth, remain unaffected by my skeptical arguments.

The third remark is that should virtue appraisals (or at least some of them) remain intact even if we are unfree to do otherwise, we should be mindful of the rationale for educating for virtue.[10]

Particularly, the rationale should not be that the person who acts out of kindness, generosity, and so forth, will be disposed to fulfill her moral obligations and perform actions for which she is not blameworthy. Nor is it transparent that, necessarily, the virtuous agent will live a life that is good in itself for her. For example, if a form of hedonism as an account of personal well-being is true—if, roughly, the good life is the pleasant life—then a "successful" criminal may live a life that is highly good in itself for her. Regarding educating for virtue, perhaps one will be able to develop the rationale that it is (intrinsically) good that one be virtuous, or the *world* will be better if, generally, people acted from virtue. But then this would affect what are taken to be the ultimate aims of education. Maybe the aim of something like social or world betterment would replace the proposed aim of *personal* well-being.

This last remark points the way to responding to the proponents of mild illusionism. We value truth; we desire to believe the truth (or so we hope). Perhaps educators are not doing anything morally objectionable by attempting (if they do) to turn children into morally upright agents. But if the preceding skeptical arguments are sound (as the objection grants), then if they value truth, educators should stare the facts in their face. More often than not, those they are guiding into adulthood are not going to fulfill their obligations (or do wrong) because, more often than not, they will have no obligations to fulfill (or violate). As the objection queries, what would be amiss if we adopted mild illusionism; we simply carried on *as if* (roughly) our natures did not preclude us from having obligations? We continued to educate for uprightness, appraisability, and so forth, full well knowing that these goals remain largely unattainable. This sort of pretense, though, would usher in this problem: What exactly would be the rationale for educating for, say, uprightness? One could not, of course, duly propose that the fulfillment of obligation is intrinsically good, and this supplies us with a powerful incentive to go along with the pretense. More often than not, there would be no obligations for us to fulfill (or to violate). In the previous paragraph, I alluded to other rationales. One concerned the personal well-being of agents. If we educated for uprightness even realizing that this goal is largely beyond our reach, our children would end up living lives that were overall intrinsically good for them. However, as noted, it is not obvious that living as if one had moral obligations, and conducting oneself in a way in which one would if one were morally conscientious, is conducive to personal well-being. It is not pellucid that morality contributes to personal well-being in way in which, for instance, enlightened self-interest does not. A second rationale is that were we to behave in ways in which we would if we were morally upright agents, the world would be better off. Perhaps there might be something to this claim. But then we should be honest with ourselves: We should educate for world betterment. What educators would do if they were aiming, generally, for world betterment might diverge considerably from what they would do if they were aspiring to turn children into, for example, morally upright agents. In addition, should world betterment be the goal educators are aiming for, then they should own up to another challenge: It is far from clear that the world would in fact be better if, acquiescing in mild illusionism, educators aimed at turning our children into morally upright agents.

Reflecting on this objection from mild illusionism, maybe some will suggest that obligation is not what we really we care about. We just want people to do certain things in certain situations, whether or not these things are rightly regarded as obligations. This objection raises two important and complex issues. Here, I simply expose pathways to be explored to respond to pressing questions these issues generate.

The first intricate issue concerns, roughly, the "value" or importance of various normative assessments, such as morally deontic assessments of permissibility, impermissibility, and obligation, and responsibility assessments of praiseworthiness and blameworthiness. Remember, assessments of obligation are "act-focused"; they are concerned primarily (though not exclusively) with appraisals of actions (omissions, or states of affairs). In contrast, assessments of responsibility are "agent-focused"; in the first instance they are appraisals of agents, and are only derivatively appraisals of the conduct for which agents are praiseworthy or blameworthy.

Regarding obligation, if someone were to claim that we want Augustine not to steal the pears, and we want him to aid the needy, one important justification for the desired conduct is the presumption that it is morally impermissible for Augustine to steal, and it is morally obligatory or permissible for him help those in need. This sort of justification would have no place in a world in which no judgments of obligation, permissibility, or impermissibility were true. If the sort of skeptical argument previously developed concerning morally deontic assessments is sound, we could not rightly counsel our children not to steal on the basis that it is impermissible for them to steal in all those instances in which it turns out that it is not impermissible for them to steal. This "deontic rationale" to refrain from stealing would have to be replaced with some other rationale, perhaps some of the ones discussed in the previous response to the objection from mild illusionism, rationales having to do with, for instance, personal well-being or social betterment.

Like assessments of obligation, evaluations of praiseworthiness and blameworthiness have several dimensions of importance. An intelligent discussion of these dimensions merits an independent book-length investigation. Here, however, we have the benefit of drawing from elements of the lengthy, pertinent literature in the free will debate: What would life be like if no one were ever morally responsible for any of one's conduct? In intriguing work, Pereboom, an optimist of sorts, develops the position that a conception of life without the freedom that responsibility requires would not be devastating to morality or to our sense of meaning in life, and in certain respects it may even be beneficial (see, e.g., his 1995; 2001; 2014).[11] Others are less sanguine (e.g., Kane 1996; Haji and Cuypers 2008; Haji 2012a; Vargas 2013). Needless to say, this is not the place to adjudicate this debate.

The second knotty issue is whether different moral concepts could pick up the slack if we were indeed (largely) bereft of responsibility or obligation. This is, again, an enormously difficult issue that should properly be discussed elsewhere. Here, I limit myself to the following comments.

First, education should equip children with skills and dispositions that enable them to build or participate in deeply valued interpersonal relationships. To do so, it is important to nurture the attitudinal life of children. For example, children need to learn when it is appropriate to feel resentment, guilt, gratitude, sympathy, indignation, or anger, and when to forgive. Such sentiments, reactive attitudes, or emotions play highly complex roles in interpersonal exchanges and relationships. A number of them are either directly in various respects or somewhat less directly in other respects associated with responsibility.

As an example of relatively direct association, forgiveness—something central to healthy, interpersonal relationships—presupposes that the person who is forgiven is forgiven for something she was morally blameworthy for doing. If no assessments of responsibility were true at our world, then it would seem that forgiveness would be endangered. We would then have to rethink what might (if anything) take the place of forgiveness. Pereboom (1995, 40), for instance, has proposed that an *analogue* of forgiveness would survive in a world bereft of blameworthiness. More or less, the analogue is a decision to continue the relationship despite something bad having befallen the forgiven party, and recognizing that the relationship has been impaired as a result of the relevant actions of the forgiven.[12] Even if no agent is morally blameworthy for any of her conduct, the agent can still choose to restore a previously impaired relationship with moral resolve, and the willingness to apologize for her untoward behavior.

My objective is not to evaluate whether Pereboom's moral analogue of forgiveness can suitably replace forgiveness. Rather, I wish to underscore the fact that with blameworthiness imperiled, it seems that forgiveness proper cannot duly be on the mentor's list of moral education. Instead, forgiveness might be replaced by something like Pereboom's "relationship restoration." The way we go about educating for the skills or dispositions for relationship restoration may depart significantly from the way we go about educating for the skills or dispositions required for forgiveness.

A number of the relevant sentiments, reactive attitudes, or emotions are also associated with responsibility somewhat circuitously because of their relationship, conceptual or otherwise, with moral impermissibility. To illustrate, it is widely accepted that one feels appropriate (as opposed to misplaced or ill-founded) guilt for having done something only if one is blameworthy for having done it. In this respect, the association between guilt and responsibility—blameworthiness—is quite direct. But blameworthiness has ties with impermissibility. Hence, if the latter is imperiled so is the former, and if blameworthiness is endangered, so is well-founded guilt. Elaborating somewhat, if well-founded guilt presupposes being blameworthy, and blameworthiness requires impermissibility, then guilt will not be appropriate in a world with no alternatives. If well-founded guilt presupposes being blameworthy, and, alternatively, blameworthiness requires nonculpable belief in what is impermissible, then if enlightened about the moral statuses of one's actions in a world in which one generally cannot do otherwise with the consequence that nothing (or almost nothing) would be impermissible for one to do, guilt will once again not be appropriate.

In the steps of Pereboom's strategy one might look for suitable moral replacements (if any) for guilt. Even assuming there are such candidates, this would once again shift what is on the mentor's list for moral education; guilt will be stricken off and replaced by its analogue (if any).

To collect results, whether we merely want people to do various things in various situations, independently of whether these things are appropriately regarded as obligations or whether people are morally responsible for them masks complex issues. My own inclination (supported by preliminary argument) is that much of value in our lives would be lost if we were indeed deprived of obligation or responsibility (see, e.g., Haji 1998; 2002; 2012a).

NOTES

1. As quoted by Peter van Inwagen in 1983, 63–64.
2. See Haji 2009b for refinements.
3. A useful collection of essays on educational aims is Marples 1999.
4. See Haji and Cuypers 2011 for critical discussion of this argument.
5. Siegel continues to endorse the view "that the fostering of rationality and critical thinking is the central aim, and the overriding ideal, of education" in his 1997, 2. He writes, "this ideal is by far the one most widely advocated in the history of philosophy of education, from Plato to Dewey and beyond" (1997, 189, n. 1).
6. Toward the end of the *Nicomachean Ethics*, Aristotle says that the best life is the life of *theoria* or philosophical contemplation.
7. See also White, 1982; 1990; and Callan and White 2003. Standish (1999, 35–40) advances a summary of Peters's, Hirst's, and Dearden's liberal position. Christopher Winch's distinction between "weak" and "strong autonomy" is also relevant to the debate regarding the liberal conception of personal autonomy; see Winch, 1999 and 2002.

8. See, e.g., Fischer and Ravizza 1998. In his 1995, Mele discusses both compatibilist and incompatibilist accounts of autonomy.
9. I thank Michael McKenna for this objection.
10. See Haji 2012a, sec. 4.6., on lack of freedom to do otherwise and the truth of judgments of virtue.
11. Also, see Waller 2011.
12. Also, see Pereboom 2001, 201.

Chapter 7

Some Thoughts on the
Metaphysics of Free Will

7.1 CONSTRAINED SKEPTICISM

Some people have concluded that we are neither morally blameworthy nor praiseworthy for any of our conduct. Their skepticism
regarding responsibility is propelled primarily by the thought that
what may broadly be characterized as various control requirements
of moral responsibility are not, or cannot, be satisfied in our world.
For instance, it has been argued that responsibility requires that
we be the ultimate originators of our actions, but both determinism and indeterminism preclude ultimate origination. Others have
claimed that a precondition of responsibility is that agents have the
power voluntarily and intentionally to perform and to refrain from
performing actions but have argued that determinism or its falsity
preclude us from having this sort of dual power. This book places me
in the skeptics' arena. My skepticism, however, is fueled by different considerations. What we can or cannot do is frequently a matter
of luck. Owing to luck, oftentimes we cannot refrain from making
the choices we make or performing the overt actions we perform.
But since moral obligation presupposes that we are able to do otherwise, much of what we do will not be obligatory, permissible, or

impermissible for us. If we are rational in that we are aware of this fact when we make choices or do various things in everyday life, given plausible principles that link blameworthiness with obligation or impermissibility, frequently we will not be blameworthy for our conduct. So it is the moral requirement of responsibility (and not its control requirement), together with luck's recurrently precluding us from doing otherwise, that fundamentally undergirds my skepticism about both obligation and blameworthiness.

Some readers may insist that all told, it is lack of freedom to do otherwise that, in the end, is the scaffold for my skepticism. But as these readers may see it, freedom to do otherwise is part of the control that both obligation and blameworthiness presuppose. Here, I would caution that several compatibilists (e.g., Fischer and McKenna), agnostics (e.g., Mele), and skeptics (e.g., Pereboom), appealing to Frankfurt examples, have championed the position that at least responsibility does not require freedom to do otherwise. Suppose they are right about this. Still, given the moral requirement of responsibility—and here one may pick one's favorite candidate, either some version of the subjective view or the objective view—we will yet be saddled with the problem of constrained skepticism to which I have called attention.

I have focused my efforts on arguing for a reduced scope of blameworthiness and have largely ignored praiseworthiness. But with suitable amendments, modifications to pertinent arguments I have advanced should sustain the view that luck also narrows the range of things for which we are praiseworthy. To give just a flavor of the arguments, suppose, first, that a precondition of praiseworthiness is obligation or permissibility: One is morally praiseworthy for doing something only if it is morally obligatory or permissible for one to do this thing (*Praiseworthiness/Obligation*). However, since nothing can be obligatory or permissible for one unless one could have done otherwise, and luck frequently precludes our being able to do otherwise, habitually it will not be obligatory nor permissible for us to do what we do. Given *Praiseworthiness/Obligation*, it would follow that more often than not, we are not praiseworthy for what we do. Suppose, second, that *Praiseworthiness/Obligation* is to be rejected in favor of a "belief" replacement of this sort: One is praiseworthy for doing something only if one does it in the nonculpable belief that one is doing right for right's sake (e.g., Zimmerman 1988). Then if one is not mistaken about the primary moral statuses of one's actions, it would again appear that one would frequently not be praiseworthy for one's actions.

It should be expected that some will challenge my claim about the extent of the reduction in obligation and blameworthiness: Just how sweeping is the decline? The honest answer is that I cannot pretend to know. But I believe we can be confident that there are many occasions in life when persons make choices or perform overt actions for which it is prima facie plausible (barring philosophical reflection) that they are morally responsible but for which our appraisal of responsibility would be mistaken. The appraisal would be erroneous for reasons of the sort I have advanced: The pertinent agents could not have done otherwise because of luck.

7.2 FRANKFURT EXAMPLES AND GUIDANCE CONTROL

The guarded skepticism I have argued for is not grandiose in that I have not given reasons to believe that no one has done, or ever will do anything it is obligatory or impermissible for one to do, or no one is, or ever will be blameworthy for anything one does. In particular, it is important to recognize that I have not argued that determinism usurps the control that moral blameworthiness, and more generally, moral responsibility requires. Indeed, I have (so far) remained largely neutral over the debate concerning whether determinism or indeterminism can accommodate the sort of control or freedom that responsibility demands.

However, some will disagree. They might propose that my skepticism is much more far reaching than I have made it out to be. To explain, very many theorists who believe that at least some persons are morally responsible for at least some of their actions, who however otherwise divided on their views regarding the merits (or shortcomings) of libertarianism or compatibilism concur that the following view—the "Guidance View"—is on sure footing—they agree that responsibility requires that one have the ability to grasp and be guided by good reasons. A prominent elucidation of one component of the Guidance View appeals to the concept of responsiveness to reasons—responsibility presupposes the capacity to recognize and react to reasons. In my 1998 book, I defended an agent-based reasons-responsiveness account. The account is agent-based, as opposed to mechanism-based, because it implies that agents, and not mechanisms or processes involving agents, such as the process of ordinary practical deliberation, are sensitive to reasons.[1]

The details of the account I proposed are of no moment, but some may think that my overall, sympathetic stance toward Frankfurt examples I have deployed, for instance, to motivate the view that obligation is susceptible to luck, is detrimental to the sort of reasons-responsiveness account I favor. It is, thus, *not* true that various commitments I have made in this work leave unscathed my view of the control (or a central element of this view) that moral responsibility requires. Consequently, it is false that my skepticism regarding responsibility is not grandiose. It may not be overtly grandiose, but it is covertly so because these very commitments call into question a vital control requirement of responsibility (reasons-responsiveness). Without the requisite sort of control, no one is ever morally responsible for anything.

What precisely is the concern? Why is it thought that agent-based reasons-responsiveness does not sit well with Frankfurt cases? Let's start with a pair of examples that helps to illustrate the underlying idea of this sort of responsiveness. The first member of the pair is simply Augustine's case (*Theft*) minus the counterfactual intervener or Augustine's Stage 1 case. We may suppose that in this stage, a number of instantiations of the following counterfactual schema are true. If there were sufficient reason for Augustine to do otherwise, and he recognized these reasons, he would do otherwise for these reasons. So, for instance, if his close friend had asked him to aid in an emergency involving her grandson, Augustine would have done so instead of stealing the pears; if he had been commissioned by the emperor to appease some monks, he would have done so, and so forth. In other words, there is a relatively wide range of scenarios where Augustine would have refrained from stealing in virtue of recognizing and acting on the basis of sufficient reasons not to steal or to do something other than steal.

In the second member of the pair, as a result of complex and effective manipulation of which she is totally in the dark, Augusta steals some apples. Her decision to steal and her subsequent stealing causally issue partly from engineered-in irresistible desires. Details of the case can be supplied to make it clear that she is not responsible for the theft. Some may be tempted to propose that in a case of this sort, responsibility is undermined precisely in virtue of its being true that Augusta could not have done otherwise; given the manipulation, she could not have refrained from making the decision to steal and then steal. A reasons-responsiveness theorist, convinced that alternative possibilities are not required for responsibility, possibly on the basis of Frankfurt examples, will offer an alternative explanation for nonresponsibility: Augusta is not aptly responsive to reasons in that even if she were aware of sufficient reasons to do other than steal the apples, she could not do otherwise on the basis of those reasons. Perhaps under certain extreme conditions—she realizes, for instance, that if she does not refrain from stealing the apples, her son will be killed—she would act on sufficient reasons to do otherwise. But the range of scenarios where she would have recognized sufficient reasons to refrain from stealing the apples and would have acted on those reasons is relatively constrained in comparison, for example, to the range of scenarios where Augustine (in Stage 1) would have recognized sufficient reasons to refrain from stealing the pears.

In sum, assuming satisfaction of all other requirements of blameworthiness, the element of the Guidance View of interest has it that because Augustine is aptly responsive to a sufficiently wide range of reasons, he is morally responsible—blameworthy—for stealing the pears, but in virtue of not being so responsive, Augusta is not responsible for stealing the apples. This element of the Guidance View has the following core.

> *Reasons-Responsiveness (The Core)*: Regarding an action (mental or otherwise) of hers, an agent is aptly responsive to reasons only if in a suitably wide range of scenarios where she would have recognized sufficient reasons to refrain from performing that action or to have done otherwise, she would have refrained from performing that action or would have done otherwise on the basis of those reasons.

The Core dovetails well with proposed lessons of Frankfurt examples—that responsibility depends on the actual sequence of events that culminates in action, and the control responsibility requires is one-way control. A fully developed reasons-responsiveness account will work out pertinent details of the Core, such as the appropriate range of reasons to which one must be responsive if one is to be aptly reasons-responsive. However, these details, with the exception of one to be introduced, are of no import to the general problem that Frankfurt examples supposedly highlight for this core.

It should be relatively straightforward to discern this problem. Revert to Augustine's Stage 2 scenario in which Ernie is on the scene. Imagine that Augustine comes to appreciate that he has sufficient reason to do other than steal the pears; he has sound reason to aid his friend who calls on him. However, owing to Ernie's presence, Augustine cannot translate this reason into action; his reasons-responsiveness, as specified in the Core has been hijacked. Since the condition in the Core has apparently not been met, and this condition is necessary for responsibility because its nonsatisfaction would reveal that Augustine's action is not relevantly free, contrary to partisans of Frankfurt examples who also accept the Core, Augustine is not morally responsible for stealing the pears in Stage 2. In brief, the gist of the problem is that assuming reasons-responsiveness is necessary for responsibility, Frankfurt examples are ineffective counterexamples to PAP because they undermine reasons-responsiveness.

Prima facie, there is something suspect about this putative objection. Why? The fundamental issue it raises is whether an agent, such as Augustine in our example, is sufficiently sensitive to reasons when there is a Frankfurt-type counterfactual intervener on the scene. But if Augustine acts no differently in Stage 2 than he does in Stage 1, and there is no interference in Stage 2, why believe he is not reasons-responsive in Stage 2 when he is so in Stage 1? We can profitably examine this issue by reminding ourselves of pertinent features of the two stages.

In Stage 1 there is no counterfactual intervener in the wings. Mentally healthy Augustine decides to steal the pears, and on the basis of this decision, steals the pears. Apt reason states of his appropriately cause his decision. Furthermore, we may safely assume that he is suitably reasons-responsive. Specifically, he is reasons-reactive in that he would have reacted to a suitable range of reasons to do otherwise. Had he had sufficient reasons to do otherwise, he would have recognized these sufficient reasons and would have acted on the basis of them. In this respect, Augustine is different from manipulated Augusta.

In Stage 2, careful not to introduce any *other* changes in Stage 1, Ernie the counterfactual intervener makes his debut. With his mind-reading capacities (or some other mechanism that enables him reliably to predict what Augustine is about to decide to do), his presence in Stage 2 ensures that Augustine could not have done otherwise or so we are granting. Unaware of Ernie's presence, Augustine conducts himself in Stage 2 in just the way in which he does in Stage 1. We are supposing that in Stage 1 Augustine is aptly reasons-responsive (particularly, he is appropriately reactive to a pertinent range of reasons), and his choice is suitably caused. By design, Ernie does not intervene at all; he does not finagle with Augustine in any way. But then, it seems, he does not in any way affect Augustine's capacity to respond to a range of reasons. Furthermore, no additional factors affect these capacities. It is not that Augustine's desire to steal the pears magically crystallizes into an irresistible one; Augustine acts from weakness of will; a crazy neuroscientist alters his brain, or so forth. So why believe that Augustine is no longer reasons-responsive in Stage 2?

One might object that I am simply missing a crucial fact. In Stage 2, Ernie guarantees that Augustine cannot do otherwise. Hence, there is *ample* reason to believe that his reasons-reactive capacity—his capacity to react to sufficient reasons to do otherwise—is detrimentally impacted.

However, the vital point still remains: Ernie does *not* intervene. If one thinks nonintervention does affect Augustine's capacity to react to sufficient reasons to do otherwise, one ought to provide an apt rationale. Why precisely is this so? What does Ernie do in virtue of which it is reasonable to suppose that this capacity *is* adversely affected?

One may oblige with the following. Nonintervention from but the mere presence of Ernie makes it the case that Augustine cannot do otherwise. As this is so, nonintervention affects Augustine's capacity to do otherwise then and there—in his Frankfurt situation. If this is true, in turn, there *is* sound reason to believe that nonintervention also negatively affects his reasons-reactive capacities that he has in Stage 1; specifically, in Stage 2 he is no longer reasons-reactive.

However, this rationale is problematic. We understand how a Frankfurt case works; we comprehend how the intervener blocks alternatives. The explanation of why Augustine cannot do otherwise in Stage 2 does not in any way appeal to the intervener's affecting any intrinsic agential properties that presumably are the basis or grounds of the relevant reasons-responsive capacities. Contrary to what unfolds in Stage 2, *should* these properties be tinkered with, there may well be a problem with the capacities that are grounded in these properties.

Still not assuaged, one might rejoin with the following. Suppose an agent is reasons-reactive. Then, as entrenched in the Core, in any scenario, if there were a sufficient reason for her to do otherwise, she would do otherwise for those reasons. Augustine (by stipulation) *is* reasons-reactive. In Stage 2 of his Frankfurt scenario, there may well be sufficient reason for him to do otherwise. But he cannot do otherwise in this scenario. Isn't this a *big* problem for the Core?

Well, is it? The condition in the Core entails that with respect to an action, if an agent is reasons-responsive, there is a suitably wide range of scenarios where she recognizes sufficient reasons to do otherwise and does otherwise for those reasons. The suggestion implicit in the last few paragraphs in response to the allegedly *big* problem is that the suitably wide range of scenarios in which an agent does otherwise on the basis of apt and sufficient reasons to meet the condition the Core demands exclude Frankfurt-type scenarios, and, moreover, this exclusion not be arbitrary or ad hoc. Frankfurt scenarios may nonarbitrarily be excluded because the relevant agential properties pertinent to reasons-responsiveness—the intrinsic properties that ground the agent's capacities to recognize and react to sufficient reasons to do otherwise—remain wholly intact in these scenarios, in contrast, for example, to scenarios (such as Augusta's) that involve responsibility-undermining manipulation.

Here is a partial but nonetheless revealing first stab to test for reasons-responsiveness. We may initially broadly differentiate scenarios in which the agent is not reasons-responsive from those in which she is. Regarding the former, with certain exceptions, if there is *no* suitably wide range of scenarios where the agent has sufficient reason to do otherwise and fails to do otherwise for those reasons, she is not reasons-responsive. An exception, for example, would be global Frankfurt cases in which whatever an agent does, she does "on her own" but in which coincidentally she could not have done otherwise because of an ever-watchful counterfactual intervener. We may, next, have a mixed bag of cases, some in which the agent has sufficient reasons to do otherwise and does otherwise for those reasons, and others in which the agent has sufficient reason to do otherwise but fails to do otherwise on their basis. Confine attention to the latter and examine why the agent cannot do otherwise in these scenarios. There are a number of possibilities, including: (a) Frankfurt-type scenarios or scenarios relevantly like them in that the intrinsic properties that ground the agent's reasons-responsive capacities are intact or unaffected. It is, roughly, "extraneous" factors that prevent the agent from doing otherwise in these scenarios, factors that do not have any effect on the intrinsic grounding properties of these capacities, factors that do not relevantly physically incapacitate the agent or alter her mental constitution, and so on. There is no good reason to believe that the existence of such scenarios precludes reasons-responsiveness. (b) Scenarios in which at the time of or at some time prior to action, the intrinsic properties that ground the agent's capacities to do otherwise have been finagled with so that the agent is unable to react to sufficient reasons to do otherwise. Manipulation scenarios (such as Augusta's) are scenarios of this sort. Presumably, the agent would not be responsible for what she does in these scenarios. (c) Scenarios in which the intrinsic properties that ground the agent's supposedly reasons-responsiveness capacities have not been finagled with, etc. Still, she is not reasons-reactive. Even if there were sufficient reasons to do otherwise, she could not do otherwise for those reasons. In these scenarios, again, she is not reasons-responsive; she lacks the relevant capacities to react to apt sufficient reasons to do otherwise. There may yet be other sorts of scenario in which the agent cannot do otherwise. Some person may have (freely) fashioned her character so that she would not be reactive to reasons to do otherwise in relevant scenarios. Whether such a person would be reasons-responsive is something that need not be dealt with here.

To summarize, Frankfurt examples do not undermine the condition for reasons-responsiveness in the Core. The germane part of that condition entails that to be aptly reasons-responsive, the agent must be reasons-reactive in a suitably wide range of nonactual scenarios. The apparent problem for the Core under the microscope is that the pertinent agent (like Augustine) in a Frankfurt scenario cannot react to sufficient reasons to do otherwise, and so contrary to partisans of such examples, Frankfurt examples are not effective counterexamples to PAP; they are not examples in which despite not being able to do otherwise, the agent is morally responsible for what she does. I have argued that there is no reason to deny that the pertinent agent in a Frankfurt scenario is reasons-responsive. The intrinsic properties that ground her reasons-responsive capacities remain intact, unaffected by anything in the scenario. So, such an agent does not violate the condition of reasons-responsiveness embedded in the Core. Briefly put, Frankfurt examples motivate rejection of PAP without opposing a proposed central element of the Guidance View that responsibility requires being suitably responsive to reasons.

7.3 FROM THE FRYING PAN INTO THE FIRE: FRANKFURT EXAMPLES YET AGAIN

Appealing to intrinsic "grounding" properties to meet the objection that Frankfurt examples unseat reasons-responsiveness accounts of the Guidance View may seem to expel me from the frying pan only to land me into the flames: The appeal threatens Frankfurt examples themselves. Elaborating, in Stage 1 Ernie is not on the scene, and Augustine decides to steal the pears. Assume that he could have decided to do something else instead; for example, he could have decided to refrain from stealing. Next Ernie is introduced, but he is on the sidelines. Although he has the power to interfere, he does not exercise this power in Stage 2. The intrinsic properties of Augustine that ground his relevant powers (abilities or capacities), including his powers to deliberate or reason, remain unaffected. Whatever powers supervene on these intrinsic properties, Stage 1 Augustine and Stage 2 Augustine share these very powers because in each stage they retain these properties. Call these powers "IN-powers." Since Augustine in either stage has the relevant IN-powers, it is false that in Stage 2, he lacks the power or ability to decide to refrain from stealing (Vihvelin 2013, 102–14).

Regarding Frankfurt examples, with Jones assuming the role of Augustine and Black the role of counterfactual intervener Ernie, Kadri Vihvelin writes:

> What makes someone a Preemptor is the fact that his intervention is causally triggered, *not* by the subject's beginning to act or try to act contrary to the Preemptor's plan, but by some *earlier event* that is a reliable indicator of the fact that the subject will, in the absence of intervention, perform some action (overt or mental) contrary to the Preemptor's wishes. This earlier event might be a blush, twitch, or other involuntary sign that occurs just before the subject begins to make an unwanted decision or perform an unwanted action. (2013, 98)

So, for instance, Ernie in our Frankfurt example is a Preemptor. Vihvelin explains:

> So long as a Preemptor Black [or Ernie] does not intervene, Jones is able to choose to do what he likes. It so happens, thanks to the peculiar setup of the case, that Jones is able to choose otherwise only if he chooses what Black wants him to choose. So long as Black does not interfere, Jones is able to choose otherwise, even though he doesn't. He has alternatives even though he does not take them. (2013, 105)

To be clear, Vihvelin's position is the following:

> Insofar as Black is a Preemptor, he has the *power* to make a difference to the facts about what Jones is able to choose. But since Black does not exercise his power, these facts remain unchanged and Jones remains as free to choose as he was before Black came on the scene. (2013, 106)

However, Stage 1 Augustine has a power (or some sort of ability or capacity) that Stage 2 Augustine lacks: In his situation, Stage 1 Augustine can *bring it about* that he decides to do something other than steal the pears whereas in his Frankfurt situation Stage 2 Augustine cannot bring it about that he so decides; for example, he cannot bring it about that he decides to refrain from stealing the pears. Barring other problems with Frankfurt examples—or if there are any, assuming they are irrelevant to the objection under scrutiny—there is no scenario in which Ernie is on the scene, he is alert, and Augustine decides to do something other than steal the pears. Should this be disputed, the onus is on one to describe, in relevant detail, such a scenario. Here, we may remind ourselves of some of Nelkin's germane thoughts on Frankfurt cases. In *Villain*—a Frankfurt example—Joe cannot refrain from pushing the child off the pier (in one sense of "cannot") because of counterfactual intervener Max. Nelkin concedes that Joe's pushing the child off the pier is "inevitable." She says that in "this sense, having an ability to do X is precluded when it is inevitable that the agent will not do X (call this the 'inevitability-undermining' sense)." (As documented, she also believes that in the interference-free capacity sense of "can," Joe can do otherwise; Joe has "nonstandard" alternatives.)

Call the additional power Stage 1 Augustine has to bring it about that he decides to do something other than steal but which Stage 2 Augustine lacks the "bringing about" power. What we should conclude is that the presence of Ernie (and his mind reading machinery should he use such machinery), affects Augustine's bringing about powers. Lest this still appears mysterious, maybe we should say that in Stage 2, Augustine cannot exercise his relevant IN-powers because of the presence of Ernie and his mind-reading equipment.

When they insist that responsibility requires freedom to do otherwise, partisans of the principle of alternate possibilities seem to have something like the following in mind. Return, again, to some of Kane's views on alternatives. Kane calls choices or actions by which we may form and reform our existing wills (our characters, motives, and purposes) "self-forming actions." He elaborates:

> They are the actions, I argue, that are required at *some* times in their lifetimes, if agents are to have libertarian free will; and they are the actions that cause the Core Problem for FSEs [Frankfurt-style examples]. For it can be shown that if vicious regresses are to be avoided, two conditions must be satisfied by such will-setting or self-forming actions (SFAs): They must be undetermined by the agent's pre-existing will and the agents must have what I call *plural voluntary control* (PVC) over them. That is, agents must have the power to voluntarily and purposefully perform them and the power to voluntarily and purposefully do otherwise (where "voluntarily" here means that actions are not coerced or compelled and "purposefully" that they are not done merely by accident or mistake, inadvertently or unintentionally). . . . It would not suffice, for example—if these actions are to be "will-setting" and not already "will-settled"— that the agents could voluntarily and purposefully perform them, but could only do otherwise by accident or mistake, inadvertently, involuntarily or unintentionally. If that were the case, agents could never form or *reform* their own wills, for they would always be acting *from a will already formed* and set one way. And having the power to form and reform one's own will is a precondition on my view for having freedom of *will* of the kind required for moral responsibility in a genuine libertarian sense, rather than merely freedom of *action*. (2013, 61, notes omitted)

Taking their cue from this passage, defenders of PAP should concur that, minimally, it must be that if one is to have the control responsibility requires in performing a certain bodily action or making a choice, *A*, in one's circumstances, in those circumstances both one can *bring about* and one can refrain from *bringing about A*. Such a defender would insist that if Augustine is responsible for his decision to steal, assuming all other conditions of responsibility are satisfied, it is not merely because he has the IN-powers to decide to do otherwise; he must also have the relevant bringing about powers. Or, if one wants, Augustine must also be able to exercise his IN-powers in "both directions": He must be able to so act that he brings about his decision to steal (if he brings about this decision) and he brings about some alternative decision (if he brings about this alternative). I doubt, then, whether PAP is to be understood as entailing that an agent is morally responsible for doing *A* (or deciding to *A*) only if she can bring about *A* and she has the IN-powers to refrain from *A*-ing, when it is borne in mind that one's having the IN-powers to refrain from *A*-ing does not entail that (in my terminology) one can bring it about that one refrains from *A*-ing. Vihvelin says that so "long as Black does not interfere, Jones is able to choose otherwise, even though he doesn't. He has alternatives even though he does not take them" (2013, 105). However, again, it is not simply that Augustine does not "take" the alternatives he has in his Frankfurt situation; it is also true that he cannot bring it about that he makes some decision other than the decision Ernie wants him to make. PAP presumably is not to be deciphered as a principle that entails that an agent is morally responsible for making some decision only if she voluntarily and intentionally makes that decision, and she has alternatives to this decision, albeit ones she cannot bring about.

There are, of course, other readings of PAP. Mele (2003b; 2013a) distinguishes between what he calls "simple ability" to A (*S-ability*) from an ability to A intentionally (*I-ability*). He explains:

> My friend Joe has no special powers over dice. A minute ago, he tossed a three with a fair die. He was able to do that, in a straight-forward sense of "able," one in which it is a truism that we never do anything at any time t that we are not able to do at t. In short, Joe was S-able to toss a three. Although Joe was not able to toss a three intentionally, he is able now to tie his shoes intentionally now. That is, he is I-able now to tie them now. (2013a, 81)

Where A is a directly free action, consider the following versions of PAP.

> PAPs: A person is morally responsible for doing A at t only if at
> t he was S-able to refrain from doing A at t.
> PAPi: A person is morally responsible for doing A at t only if at
> t he was I-able to refrain from doing A at t.

Presumably, Kane believes that PAPs is too weak; agents need more than the simple ability to do otherwise to be responsible for what they have done (assuming all other conditions of responsibility are satisfied). They require at least the ability intentionally to do otherwise. Somewhat analogously, regarding a directly free action A, to be responsible for doing A at t an agent needs at t the I-ability to do A, and at t, the I-ability to refrain from doing A, and not merely some ability at t to refrain from doing A which is such that she can have this ability without being able to bring it about that she refrains from doing A at t.

In Stage 2 it is false that Augustine can bring it about that he decides to do something other than steal the pears even though he retains the IN-powers he has in Stage 1. But it looks as though he is still responsible for making the decision that he does in Stage 2. If this is indeed so, then PAP is in trouble.[2]

There is an additional concern with Vihvelin's strategy to undermine Frankfurt examples. Some Frankfurt examples have no Preemptors. The example I developed in the second chapter features two independent causal pathways to Pemba's decision to kill Reubens, one deterministic (process p) and the other indeterministic (Pemba's own practical reasoning). As Preemptors are conspicuously absent in a Frankfurt example of this sort, it seems that this type of example escapes Vihvelin's concerns. Mele and Robb (1998; 2003) also develop a dual pathway example in which deterministic process p will cause the relevant agent (like Pemba) to make the apt decision under all conditions save the one in which Pemba makes this decision on his own. This sort of example that involves "trumping" is also free of Preemptors.

7.4 THE TRADITIONAL DILEMMA

The constrained skepticism about responsibility for which I have argued teaches us something about the traditional dilemma concerning determinism and responsibility (or free will). The dilemma, capsulized, is this. If determinism is true, no one is ever morally responsible for anything (or no one has free will); if determinism is false no one is ever morally responsible for anything (or no one has free will). Either determinism is true or it is not. So no one is ever morally responsible for anything (or no one has free will).

7.4.1 *Determinism, Obligation, and Blameworthiness*

Assume that determinism is true and it precludes any agent from being able to refrain from choosing as she did or from doing otherwise. Assume, further, that the dual control moral obligation requires is of the sort no agent can have if determinism is true. Then nothing will ever be obligatory, permissible, or impermissible for any agent. It would then follow that any one of the three candidates for the moral requirement of blameworthiness (the objective view, the simple subjective view, or the complex subjective view), in conjunction with the assumption that we can never to otherwise, encumbers us with the sort of skeptical conclusions I argued for but writ large. For example, if blameworthiness requires impermissibility, and impermissibility requires that we could have done otherwise in a sense of "could have done otherwise" determinism precludes, then determinism expunges blameworthiness. If some version of the subjective view is true, then if we were not deluded about the primary moral statuses of our choices or actions, again, no one would be morally blameworthy for these things.

One of the most prominent compatibilist views in the current free will literature is semicompatibilism. Semicompatibilism concerning blameworthiness is the doctrine that even if determinism is incompatible with freedom to do otherwise, determinism is compatible with blameworthiness. Semicompatibilists should face up to some sobering facts. If moral blameworthiness requires moral impermissibility, and moral impermissibility requires avoidability, then semicompatibilism concerning blameworthiness is not viable. Favoring semicompatibilism, I have rejected objective views in favor of subjective views. If we have no alternatives, whether strong incompatibilist or weak compatibilist ones, we may still be morally blameworthy but only if we are mistaken about the moral statuses of our relevant choices or actions; blameworthiness would yet again hang on a thread. For if we aware that none of our actions is morally impermissible, then, if rational, we would not act in light of the belief that we were doing something that it was impermissible for us to do.

So, even presupposing subjective views, we would not be blameworthy for our conduct.[3]

One avenue of escape would be to argue against the assumption that obligation requires that one could have done otherwise in a sense determinism rules out. In other words, one might attempt to sustain the view that there are compatibilist-friendly accounts of our being able to do otherwise, and it is one of these accounts that underpins the truth of judgments of moral obligation. (I say something in support of such a view below.) This would not be music to the ears of semicompatibilists.

7.4.2 Indeterminism, Obligation, and Blameworthiness

What would follow if determinism were false and if our reason states nondeterministically caused some of our choices or overt actions? This is a difficult issue. Here I limit discussion primarily though not exclusively to what should be expected if, in the estimation of many, the most promising version of libertarianism, modest action-centered libertarianism (hereafter "modest libertarianism") were true.

7.4.2.1 MODEST LIBERTARIANISM AND THE LUCK OBJECTION

Modest libertarian accounts require that to choose or act freely an agent must have the capacity to engage in practical reasoning and to guide her behavior in light of the reasons she has.[4] Such accounts are *modest* because they avoid appeal to agent causation, or to Kantian noumenal selves, Cartesian minds, or the like in explaining free action, and they dictate that free behavior for which an agent is morally responsible is the outcome of causal processes. This sort of libertarianism requires that a free action be made for reasons, and its being made for reasons consists, partially, in its being nondeviantly and nondeterministically caused by the agent's having those reasons.

Libertarian views allow that an indirectly free action whose freedom derives from the freedom of other actions to which it is suitably related may be determined by its immediate causal precursors. A directly free action is free independently of inheriting its freedom from the freedom of other events. Modest libertarian theories differ from compatibilist ones in that they imply that even the immediate causal antecedents of a directly free action do not determine that action. Given these antecedents, and the natural laws, there is some chance that action will not occur.[5] With *action-centered* modest libertarianism the event that is directly free and nondeterministically caused is the making of a decision, a mental action (Clarke 2000, 23).

Accounts of acting for a reason generally require that the connection between an agent's having some reason for performing an action and that action's occurring consists, partly, in the exercise of a certain degree of control by the agent. The minimal template for constructing modest libertarianism starts with our best compatibilist view of freedom, to which "host" is added the libertarian constraint that germane reason states nondeterministically cause free decisions. The resulting libertarianism specifies that an agent's "active" control—the sort of control free action or responsibility requires—in making a decision consists in apt agent-involving events causing nondeviantly that decision. In such a libertarian view, the factors that constitute an agent's active control in making a free decision are the very ones shared by this view and its compatibilist host: Deliberative processes with appropriate causal histories causing nondeviantly the decision. Refer to this thesis about control as the thesis that *control is causal*.[6]

Unlike its compatibilist rivals, modest libertarianism (seemingly) gives us dual control; with directly free actions, given exactly the same past and the laws, one could have done otherwise.

As Kane insists, any modest libertarian account of free action or responsibility worth its salt should give us dual *intentional* control. He explains, as formerly noted, that an agent's decision is free only if she exercises plural voluntary control in making it (Kane 2005, 138; 2011, 384–85, 389).

The problem of libertarian luck—frequently referred to as the problem of present luck (Mele 2006, 66)—which attempts to show that modest libertarianism is incompatible with a nondeterministically caused action's being free or with an agent's being morally responsible for such an action, may be energized in different ways. I focus primarily on two such ways and then outline a third involving contrastive explanation.

7.4.2.2 THE NO EXPLANATION VERSION
Standardly conceived, akratic or incontinent action (whether the action is a bodily action or a mental action, such as a decision) is free, intentional action contrary to the agent's better or best judgment. Continent action is, roughly, action in accordance with one's better judgment. Imagine that in the actual world, W, Peg has reasons at t to decide to A at some later time and competing reasons to decide to B at that later time. After some deliberation she forms the all-things-considered judgment that it is best for her to decide to A, and she continently decides to A. Assume that the reasons she has to so decide nondeviantly and nondeterministically cause this decision. To introduce a term of art, the causal trajectory, or a segment of such a trajectory, of an agent's decision (or action) is *smooth* provided it is free of responsibility-undermining (or responsibility-diminishing) factors, such as, for instance, the impact of manipulation of the sort that vitiates responsibility or a breakdown in agency; the agent does not succumb to akratic or other irrational influences in making the decision she makes; and barring unusual circumstances, such as the occurrence of events

over which she lacks any control and which would prevent her from deciding consistently with her best judgment, and in the absence of new information, further deliberation, or reconsideration, she decides in accordance with such a judgment.

Now consider two variations of Peg's initial scenario. In the first, the segment of the causal trajectory that "commences," roughly, with Peg's deliberations about whether to decide to A and extends to her making at t the decision to A in W, is smooth. We may suppose that Peg exercises self-control in deciding to A, and at t she indeterministically decides to A. We may assume, furthermore, that there is an apt reasons explanation of Peg's deciding at t to A in W: Her reason states nondeviantly cause her decision. It is vitally important that there be such a causal explanation because modest libertarians agree that active control is necessary for responsibility-level control, and active control just consists in one's reason states appropriately causing one's actions. Since at t Peg indeterministically decides to A in W, there is a world, W^*, that has the same natural laws as W, and is past-wise indiscernible from W, right up to t in which at t Peg does not decide to A; suppose, instead, that she decides at t to B in this world. Dub such a world with the same pre-t past—t is the time of decision—and laws as the actual world—a "contrast world." Is there an appropriate connection between her reason states and her deciding at t to B in W^*, as modest libertarianism requires, if Peg is to exercise active control in deciding at t to B in W^*? In short, is there what we may call a "*detailed reasons explanation*" of her deciding to B in W^*?

Consider three possibilities concerning Peg's deciding at t to B in W^*. First, Peg's reasons to B causally generate her continent decision to B. This option, however, is inconsistent with the assumption that the past is fixed. Recall, Peg in W judged that it is best for her to A, so she must have judged similarly in W^*, and furthermore, the relevant segment of the causal trajectory to her deciding to A in W

is smooth. If Peg decides to B in W^*, then her so deciding seems to be akratic: Her deciding to B is a (putatively) free, mental action that is contrary to what we may assume is a consciously held best judgment of hers.

Second, Peg's decision to B in W^* is akratic. If so, there is a problem in understanding the etiology of Peg's deciding to B, assuming that the relevant segment of the causal trajectory to her deciding to A in W is smooth. In customary accounts of akratic action, when an agent performs a strict akratic action, the motivational strength of the desire from which her act causally derives (the motivationally strongest desire) is misaligned with her consciously held best judgment (see, e.g., Watson 1975; Mele 1995, ch. 2). If we accept these typical accounts, Peg's best judgment that she ought to A should stand opposed to her, assume, stronger desire to B. With Peg's supposedly libertarian free decision in W^*, however, there is no such misalignment because the past in this world right up to t is indiscernible from what it is in W. So, the motivational strength of Peg's desire to B in W^* does not differ from its motivational strength in W. However, we may safely suppose that because she continently decides to A in W, her desire to A has greater motivational clout than her competing desire to B and, moreover, there is no misalignment between this stronger desire and her judgment that it is better for her to A. So how is Peg*'s akratic decision to B in W^* to be explained?

Elsewhere (e.g., Haji 2000b; 2009a; 2012c), I have argued that without some change in the etiology of her action, such as, for instance, unlike what actually transpires in W, Peg fails to exercise self-control and selectively focuses on the immediate short-term pleasures of B-ing, and downplays the long-term benefits of A-ing prior to deciding at t, there is no detailed reasons explanation of her deciding at t to B in W^*.

Some libertarians might object that akratic misalignment does not preexist the pertinent choice but is created by the akratic agents themselves when they choose (see Kane 1999a, 114, n. 17). I return to this suggestion shortly.

Regarding the second option that Peg akratically decides to B in W^*, it is implausible that a modest libertarian be committed to the view that in Peg-like cases in which Peg acts continently in W, Peg could have freely decided to do otherwise in some contrast world only if she had akratically decided to do otherwise. This sort of commitment would violate the standard modest libertarian's proposal that in garden variety cases of free action, the agent has the power to do otherwise intentionally and rationally.

On the third option, if Peg decides to B in W^* in opposition to her consciously held best judgment, she has suffered a breakdown in agency.[7] If so her decision to B, even supposing that in this case she *decides* to B, is presumably not free.

In sum, we have been entertaining the first variation of Peg's case in which Peg indeterministically decides at t to A in W, and the relevant segment of the causal trajectory to her so deciding is smooth. Stipulating that W and W^* have the same laws of nature and pre-t history, it appears that there are no appropriate causal connections between her deciding to B and her reason states to account for Peg's deciding as she does in W^*. With no such connections, Peg does not exercise active control in deciding to B in W^*. Since modest libertarians concede that active control is essential for responsibility, it would appear that she is not responsible for deciding to B in W^* (Haji 2012a, sec. 6.3). Some may prefer to claim that it is a matter of luck that Peg decides to B in W^*. If Peg does indeed make the decision to B in W^*— she performs a mental action—then one may more aptly claim that it is *partly* a matter of luck that Peg decides to B in W^* when it is implicitly understood that a decision's being partly a matter of luck (in the pertinent way) is apparently incompatible with its being free or one's being morally responsible for it. (I will, henceforth, frequently omit this qualification in discussing the luck objection.)

SOME THOUGHTS ON THE METAPHYSICS OF FREE WILL

To introduce the second variation of Peg's case, assume again, that in the actual world W, Peg decides at t to A, and the relevant segment of the causal trajectory to her deciding to A is smooth. In the contrast world W^*, however, Peg supposedly exercises an extra measure of control than the control she exercises in W, in making the decision that she does, at the very moment when she makes that decision. (Remember, W^*—the contrast world—or one of such worlds has the same past up to the time of Peg's decision and the same laws as W.) The suggestion to be considered is that akratic misalignment need not precede choice but can be created by libertarian free agents at the moment of choice. I address the more general, former case in which a libertarian free agent exerts control in deciding as she does at the very time of decision-making. If this control is causal, as the libertarian insists, it is presumably not antecedents of action, but causal elements of action that are among the causes of the agent's, such as Peg's, decision to B in the germane contrast world, W^*, *at the moment, t,* that Peg makes this decision, that differentiates this case from the variation in which W^* is no different than W at times preceding t or at t save for the decision that Peg makes at t in each of these worlds.

To describe an apt contrast world in the second variation, assume that in W^* something—a belief—comes to Peg's mind at the very time, t, that she makes the decision to B, and the event of the belief's coming to mind is a cause of her decision to B (but not one that precedes her decision to B). Adding one more vital detail, it is indeterministic whether this belief comes to her mind at t. Assume that, consistent with the past and the natural laws being what they are, while this belief comes to her mind in W^*, it does not in W. More carefully, there are worlds in which the belief comes to her mind at the time she decides to B, and other worlds in which it fails to come to her mind at this time when she decides to B. To assume otherwise—that W and W^* do not differ at all from each other (given the past and the laws) at all times right up to the time of decision—would simply result in this second variation of Peg's case not being relevantly different from the first. As we have seen, the first does not serve the libertarian's cause.

Focusing on such a contrast world, W^*, dub the event that is the belief's indeterministically coming to Peg's mind at the time she decides to B, and that is a cause of her deciding to B, "E." It may be pronounced that we now have a perfectly cogent causal explanation of Peg's deciding to B in W^*: Event E is the difference maker. At the time of choice, no such event comes to Peg's mind in W; recall, the relevant segment of the causal pathway to Peg's deciding at t to A in W is smooth. However, because E does come to her mind at the time she makes the decision at t to B in W^*, and E is a cause of her deciding to B, there is, in principle, no mystery about the appropriate causal history of her deciding at t to B in W^*.

This explanation of why Peg decides at t to B in W^* is problematic. It is indeterministic whether the pertinent belief comes to Peg's mind in W^*. In some W^*-like worlds, the belief at t comes to Peg's mind, and Peg decides at t to B; in other such worlds, this belief fails to come to Peg's mind at t, and she still decides at t to B.[8] But because these latter W^*-like worlds do not differ in any respect from W right up to the time, t, of decision, Peg decides at t to A in W, and the relevant segment of the causal pathway to her deciding at t to A in W is smooth, yet again there appears to be no causal explanation of Peg's deciding at t to B in these W^*-like worlds. In these worlds her reason states seem not to be appropriately connected to her deciding to B because they favor her deciding to A, and there is no difference maker, such as event E, that distinguishes these worlds from W.

If we grant that there is a problem concerning an explanation, in terms of her apt reason states, of why Peg decides at t to B in W^*, and so, given relevantly analogous reasoning, there is such a problem concerning such an explanation of why Peg decides at t to A in W, and we accept the thesis that *control is causal*, the problem of libertarian luck seems pressing.[9]

A few cautionary remarks are in order to stave off misunderstanding of the *No Explanation* version of the luck problem. First, some may propose that it is lack of a contrastive explanation in terms of prior elements in an action's trajectory—in our example, why Peg decides to A in the actual world rather than decides to B—that fuels the luck objection. This is no part of the *No Explanation* version. Second, nor does this version rely on the premise that if an outcome of practical deliberation, such as a decision, is not guaranteed by antecedent factors, specifically, the agent's reasons or reason states, then that outcome is a matter of responsibility-undermining luck.

7.4.2.3 THE PURE LUCK VERSION

The *Pure Luck* version takes it for granted that there is a detailed reasons explanation of whatever decision Peg makes in the relevant worlds or remains agnostic about this issue. It focuses our attention on luck in a different way. Here is one: With an indeterministic agent such as Peg, it is false that the agent has some *further* power to influence causally which of her alternatives she realizes, a power over and above the mere chance of acting differently, and a power over and above the power to exercise proximal control in making whatever decision she makes (e.g., Clarke 2003, 96; Pereboom 2014, 31–39). A second way, perhaps a variation of the first, is that if one agent does one thing and another refrains from doing that thing, "and there is nothing about the agents' powers, capacities, states of mind, moral character and the like that explains this difference in outcome, then the difference really just is a matter of luck" (Mele 1999a, 280). Maybe some might propose that a central feature of yet another variation of the *Pure Luck* version, or some third independent version, is the following. Modest libertarianism faces the problem of luck because for any undetermined action there is no contrastive explanation of why the agent performed that action rather than another that the agent could have performed at the time.

As modest libertarians might see it, the *Pure Luck* version places an unfair burden on them that their compatibilist rivals do not bear. An insightful underlying thought of proponents of the *Pure Luck* version, succinctly summarized by Mele, is that it is no more up to Peg at *t* whether she decides to *A* or instead decides to *B* than it is up to a genuinely random generator whether the number it outputs at *t* is 7 or 11 in a scenario in which it has only a few possible outputs at the time (Mele 2013b, 244). A libertarian may remind us about the thesis that the control free action requires is essentially causal. As I understand his elegant construction of the luck objection, Mele has never contended that the problem of present luck for libertarians arises partly because there is no account of some salient contrastive fact, such as, in our working example, why at *t* Peg decides to *A* rather than *B* (2006, 73).[10] In this respect, the *Pure Luck* version does not differ from the *No Explanation* version. This is all for the good. For libertarians may contend that the following scenario is coherent: There is a reasons explanation of why at *t* Peg decides to *A* in world *W*, there is such an explanation of why at *t* Peg decides to *B* in world *W** that has the same pre-*t* past and the laws as *W*, but there is no account of why, at *t*, Peg decides to *A* rather than *B* in *W*. However, if there is such a reasons explanation of each of the things that Peg decides at *t* to do in each of these worlds, and we accept the thesis that control is causal, no matter what she does at *t*, Peg exercises no less control at *t* in deciding to do what she does than she would if determinism were true.

It appears that what fundamentally drives the *Pure Luck* version, which Mele's thought concerning the randomizing machine nicely captures, is not what at rock bottom energizes the *No Explanation* version. As I have explained in several places (e.g., Haji 2000b;

2009a; 2012c), what fuels the *No Explanation* version is the idea that the alleged outcome in W^*—Peg's deciding at t to B—is not appropriately connected to her reason states or her deliberation, all of which favor her deciding to A. The issue that merits careful scrutiny concerns a detailed reason-explanation of why the agent—Peg in our example—akratically decides to B in W^*. I concur that if Peg, for instance, were to fix her attention vividly on various salient factors during the time she deliberates about what it is best for her to do, this may raise significantly the probability that she decides at t to A (rather than B) in the actual world. To focus the enigma, imagine that in the actual world Peg successfully does whatever she can do prior to t to raise considerably the probability that she will decide at t to A, and goes on at t to A. Then in W^* in which at t Peg decides to B, it is also true that prior to t, Peg's relevant activities have raised appreciably the probability that at t she will decide to A. Yet at t, she decides to B in W^*. Doesn't this simply compound the conundrum: What *is* the detailed reasons explanation of her deciding at t to B when this decision is akratic? All her pre-t reasoning supports her deciding to A in W^*, but holding constant this reasoning she still decides at t to B in W^*. Needless to say, it will not do simply to claim that Peg's reasons that favor her deciding to B "prevail" in W^* (but not in the actual world). Why do they "prevail," given that W^*'s relevant pre-t history mirrors the relevant pre-t history of the actual world?[11]

Some may wonder why they should agree that Peg does not freely do A in the actual world W even though they may agree that Peg may not freely do B in the contrast world W^*. It's possible that Peg may intentionally but not freely do B in W^*. In these sorts of case, we presume that there are apt connections between Peg's reason states and her B-ing in W^*, and there is a suitable detailed reasons explanation of why she B-s in W^*. Aptly amplified, the explanation should shed light on why her B-ing in W^*, although intentional, is not free. The doubt concerning Peg's not, at t, freely doing A in W if it is assumed that at t she does not freely do B in W^* may be dispelled if we reflect on the following. Why should it make a difference regarding whether or not Peg *freely* A-s in W that the initial focus is on what she does in W rather than on what she does in the contrast world W^*? Elucidating, imagine that we had spun the tale about Peg by describing, *first*, the contrast world and what she decided in that world. In this world at t, Peg B-s. Assume that her B-ing in W^* is intentional but not free. Next, we switch to the actual world, W, in which, given the same past and the laws of W^*, at t, Peg A-s. If it is conceded that in the *initial* development of the story—the version in which it is presumed that there is a detailed reasons explanation of Peg's A-ing in W—it looks as though it is a matter of luck that Peg B-s in W^*, then it should be conceded too, that starting with the relevant goings on in W^* in which Peg supposedly intentionally but not freely B-s, it looks as though it is a matter of luck that Peg A-s in W.

One might not be convinced. Fischer gives us an insightful way to think about why, despite Peg's indeterministically doing A at t in W, there is no element of responsibility-threatening luck that taints her A-ing at this time in W, and so her A-ing in W may well be free.

> Suppose causal determinism obtains and I choose (for my own reasons, in the "ordinary way") at t_2 to raise my hand at t_3, and I do in fact raise my hand at t_3. Imagine, further, that whatever is required for the responsibility-grounding relationship between my prior states at t_1 and my choice at t_2 to raise my hand at t_3 is present; that is, let us say that the requisite glue that connects my prior states with my choice at t_2 is present. . . . Now imagine another possible world W_2 in which everything is the same as W_1 in respect of the way the causal sequence that actually leads to my choice at t_2 to raise my hand at t_3

(everything, that is, apart from causal determination). In W_2 as in W_1, I choose for my own reasons, in the "normal way," at t_2 to raise my hand at t_3 (and I do indeed raise my hand at t_3). . . . But we now add that there is a genuinely random machine in W_2, but not in W_1. Let's say that I begin my deliberations at t_1 about whether to raise my hand; my last moment of deliberation is $t_{1.9}$ and I make my choice at t_2. The random machine "operates" in W_2 between times t_1 and t_2. (By "operating" I simply mean that the machine goes through a series of internal states culminating in either M_1 or some other state at $t_{1.9}$.) For our purposes, we can focus on state M_1. That is, if the machine is in state M_1 at $t_{1.9}$, there are two possibilities, each with a fifty-percent objective probability attached to it. The first possibility is that the machine does nothing—it "goes to sleep," as it were, and does not trigger any causal interaction with the world . . . The second possibility is that it will initiate a causal sequence that would *preempt* my choice at t_2 to raise my hand at t_3. . . . It is assumed that the process involving the machine in W_2 is genuinely random. . . . Further, let us suppose that, as things actually go in W_2, the machine's state at $t_{1.9}$ is indeed M_1, and, further, the machine simply "goes to sleep" and never triggers any causal interference in the sequence flowing through me to my choice at t_2 to raise my hand at t_3. . . . In both worlds W_1 and W_2, I choose and do exactly the same thing (type-identical choices and actions), as a result of relevantly similar processes. More specifically, we have assumed that the causal process linking my prior states and my choice is the same in relevant respects in both worlds; thus, if the requisite glue connecting the prior states with the choice obtains in W_1, it also obtains in W_2. Presumably, the mere existence and operation of the machine in W_2 should not in any way threaten these claims about the responsibility-grounding relationship. . . . Notice, however, that W_2 is causally indeterministic during the relevant interval. Indeed, W_2 is causally indeterministic in the relationship between my prior states at $t_{1.9}$ and my choice at t_2. (2014, 60–62)

According to Fischer, the machine example shows that indeterministic choice per se does not threaten the "requisite glue"—whatever is required for the responsibility-grounding relationship—that connects the agent's prior states with his later pertinent choice or action.

However, it's not pellucid whether Fischer's innovative thought experiment involving the randomizing machine lays the problem of luck to rest. First, I introduce a friendly but important amendment to Fischer's case. In the passage quoted, Fischer says that "my last moment of deliberation is $t1.9$ and I make my choice at $t2$" (2014, 60). The problem of luck for modest (and other) libertarians arises pivotally (though not solely) because if the choice (or decision) of interest in $W2$ is directly free at $t2$, then there is a possible world with the same past *right up to $t2$*, and the same laws as $W2$, in which the agent refrains from making this choice. There is no obvious problem of luck (of the sort under scrutiny) if, for example, my deliberation or events involving my deliberation at $t1.9$ in $W2$ deterministically issues in my choice at $t2$. Now for a preliminary worry, imagine "that the requisite glue that connects my prior states with my choice at $t2$ is present" in $W2$. That is, a responsibility-conferring process causally results in my decision (a directly free action) at $t2$ to raise my hand at this time in $W2$. Fischer and Ravizza argue that "an agent is morally responsible for an action [or choice] insofar as it issues from his own, moderately reasons-responsive mechanism" (1998, 86). An agent makes a mechanism his own by taking responsibility for it (241): "Moderate reasons-responsiveness consists in regular reasons-receptivity, and at least weak reasons-reactivity, of the actual-sequence mechanism that leads to the action" (89). Elaborating,

> A mechanism of kind K is moderately responsive to reason to the extent that, holding fixed the operation of a K-type mechanism, the agent would *recognize* reasons (some of which are moral) in such a way as to give rise to an understandable pattern (from the viewpoint of a third party who understands the agent's values and beliefs), and would *react* to at least one sufficient reason to do otherwise (in some possible scenario). That is, a mechanism is moderately responsive to reason insofar as it is "regularly" receptive to reasons (some of which are moral), and at least weakly reactive to reasons. (243–44)

Assume that the "requisite glue" between my prior relevant states and my decision at $t2$ is the operation of this sort of reasons-responsive mechanism. Suppose there is some chance that this mechanism not produce this decision; there is a contrast world, $W3$, with the same pre-$t2$ past and laws as $W2$ in which at $t2$ I refrain from raising my hand at $t2$. But the same sort of reason-responsive process that issues in my decision at $t2$ to raise my hand in $W2$ also issues in my decision at $t2$ to refrain from raising my hand at $t2$ in $W3$. Add to this story that the randomizing machine is present and "asleep" in apt places in both worlds. Compare this story with a standard sort of tale that attempts to capture a problem about libertarian luck: In $W2$, a process modest libertarians regard as responsibility-conferring indeterministically gives rise to my decision at $t2$ to raise my hand at $t2$. If this decision is directly free, there is world, $W3$, with the same past and laws as $W2$ in which at $t2$ I decide to refrain from raising my hand at $t2$. Assume that the same sort of indeterministic process that causally results in the decision that I make at $t2$ in $W2$ also results in the decision that

I make at this time in *W3*. In this second version of the tale, the problem of present luck is not allayed simply by supposing that the decisions in both worlds result from the same sort of allegedly responsibility-conferring processes that event-causal libertarians favor. Indeed, the tale both seeks to expose the problem of luck and invites solutions. Analogously, we should be wary that the luck problem has been laid to rest in virtue of the stipulation that, in the first version of the tale, a compatibilist-friendly supposedly responsibility-conferring process or mechanism gives rise to the decisions in both worlds.

The problem with the randomizing machine example I wish to underscore is that it seems not to show that, reverting to a previous case involving Peg, even if one concurs that Peg does not freely do *B* in the contrast world *W**, one may well agree that Peg freely does *A* in the actual world *W*.[12]

Imagine, this time, that the machine in some nonactual world, *CW*, with the same past and laws as the actual world, is triggered, and I fail to raise my hand at *t*; in *CW* I *B* at *t* and not, as I do in the actual world, raise my hand at *t*. (One may elect to focus on the relevant decision instead—in *CW* I *decide* at *t* not to raise my hand. This won't affect the ensuing reasoning.) Assume that my *B*-ing at *t* in *CW* is an intentional action that is appropriately connected to my apt mental states—assumption AS. Assume, further, that the actual world *W* has the same pre-*t* history and laws as *CW*, and at *t* I raise my hand in *W*—I do *A* in *W*. Then I do not see how we get the apt causal connections that presumably, Fischer believes we do between my *A*-ing (at *t*) and my reason states in *W*. We don't get these connections for reasons I have already attempted to explain. There appears to be no detailed reasons explanation of my *A*-ing at *t* in *W* given that (i) *W* and *CW* share the same pre-*t* history and the laws, and (ii) my *B*-ing at *t* in *CW* is an intentional action that is aptly connected to my pertinent reason states in *CW*. In other words, there is a tension between assumption AS and the view that in W there is a suitable connection between my A-ing at t and my reason states. Without this suitable connection, what reason is there to believe that my A-ing at t in W is free?

To explain the problem somewhat differently, no matter what one's view about the nature of actions—whether one endorses, for instance, a causal theory, a teleological theory, or a noncausal theory—an event is an intentional action only if it is suitably *connected* to one's reason states. We are imagining that there is this sort of connection between my B-ing at t in the contrast world, CW, and my reason states. It may be that I continently B, akratically B, or intentionally but not freely B in CW. Call the "actional" pathway or the salient segment of this pathway to my B-ing "Path 1." Suppose that if there were an apt actional pathway to my A-ing at t in the actual world, W, it would be a different pathway, "Path 2." I can't see how it *can* be Path 2 if at t, I intentionally do B at t in CW and B issues from Path 1. As long as we assume that the relevant worlds—for instance, W and CW—are, as the event-causal libertarian supposes, worlds in which the agent does or can intentionally perform actions, and in the contrast world there is an appropriate connection between the action that is indeterministically performed in that world and the agent's reason-states, it appears that in the actual world the apt action of the agent is not free.

It seems that the luck objection applies, as it were, in both directions if it is assumed that the libertarian agent's directly free action, at t, is appropriately, or assumed to be appropriately, connected to her reason states in the actual and the contrast world (or worlds). Given this assumption, the luck objection appears to show that neither Peg's doing A at t in W, nor her doing B at t in W is free or is an action for which she is morally responsible.

Typical event-causal libertarians, such as Kane, embrace the following "plural intentional" condition on directly free action.

LFA: At t, S freely does A in world, W, only if A is an intentional action, and there is a world W^* with the same pre-t history and the same laws as W in which at t S does something other than A (perhaps S refrains from A-ing or performs some other action B instead), and this alternative action (or refraining) is intentional.

If S's A-ing at t is an intentional action, there are appropriate connections between S's reason states and S's A-ing without which there is no detailed reasons explanation of S's intentionally A-ing. Here is a way in which a libertarian may rationalize the claim that Peg may, at t, freely do A in the actual world W consistently with not A-ing at t in some contrast world, CW. Suppose Peg indeterministically A-s at t in the actual world, W, and, as in Fischer's story, we assume that there is a suitable connection between Peg's reason states and her A-ing at t in virtue of which her A-ing at t is free. We may conclude, for reasons that should now be familiar, that in the contrast world, CW, there are no appropriate connections between her reason states and whatever it is that Peg does, if she does indeed do anything, at t. Why the qualification concerning whether Peg does anything at t in CW? Suppose Peg B-s at t in CW, and B is a bona fide *action* but neither intentional nor free. Consider these two theses:

Thesis-1: S performs an action B at t only if there are apt connections (whatever these precisely are) between S's pertinent reason states and the event that is S's B-ing.

Thesis-2: The denial of Thesis-1.

An endorser of Thesis-2 may propose that a person may perform action B for no reason at all, where "no reason at all" is to be interpreted in a way that allows for the possibility that B is an action that S performs despite there being no connections between S's reason states (such as S's beliefs and desires) and S's B-ing. If there are such actions, call them "strange-actions."[13]

Revert to the assumption that Peg A-s at t in the actual world, W, and there is a suitable connection between Peg's reason states and her indeterministically A-ing at t in virtue of which her A-ing at t in W is free. Then in the contrast world, CW, there are no appropriate connections between her reason states and whatever it is that Peg does, if she does anything, at t. If Thesis-1 is true—if an event is an action only if there are apt connections between that event and the agent's reason states—let alone not performing an intentional action, Peg does not, at t, perform any action at all in CW. The event-causal libertarian may consequently, consistently endorse these claims: At t, Peg indeterministically and freely does A in W, and there is a possible world, CW, that has the same past and laws as W in which, at t, that agent does not do A. This sort of libertarianism would be one-way libertarianism.

If Thesis-2 is true, then, at t, Peg performs a strange-action in CW. Provided Thesis-2 is true, an event-causal libertarian may consistently adopt these views: At t, Peg indeterministically and freely does A in W, and there is a possible world, CW, that has the same past and laws as W in which, at t, Peg does something other than A that is a strange-action. (Here, I overlook the distinction between a strange-action and a strange-omission. Presumably, if there are strange-actions, there are strange-omissions too.) Refer to this sort of libertarianism as "liberal libertarianism."

Both one-way and liberal-libertarians accept the view that S's action at t in world W is directly free only if there is a possible world, CW, with the same past and laws as W in which at t S does not do A. One-way libertarians claim that the relevant activity—if there is such activity and whatever it is—that S engages in at t in CW is not an action. Liberal libertarians claim that whatever activity S engages in at t in CW is a strange-action (or a strange-omission). Either sort of libertarian—one-way or liberal—is committed to rejecting the plural intentional condition on free action (LFA) which typical event-causal libertarians accept.

Why favor, or plump for, either one-way or liberal libertarianism? Fischer's motivation is clear. He wants to show that semicompatibilism concerning moral responsibility is secure even if it were to turn out that indeterminism is true:

> The problem [of luck] is not just a challenge for the libertarian; it is also an issue of interest to a semicompatibilist who believes that our moral responsibility should not be conceptualized so that it "hangs on a thread." I have indeed contended that our status as persons and morally responsible agents should not hinge on the falsity of causal determinism. To suppose that we would need to adjust such basic views of ourselves in light of the discovery of the truth of the doctrine of causal determinism is, in my view, implausible. And I think it is equally implausible to suppose that we would have to give up these central views of ourselves—as free and morally responsible agents—if we were to become convinced that causal indeterminism obtains. (2014, 52)

Still, one may wonder what, *unlike* typical compatibilist views, either variety of libertarianism—one-way or liberal—would give us and that some may value. Mele suggests the following (although, in the relevant context, he is addressing neither of these varieties of libertarianism). So called "soft libertarians" leave it open that freedom of choice and action and moral responsibility are compatible with determinism. But they maintain that the falsity of determinism "is required for a more desirable species of these freedoms and for a more desirable brand of moral responsibility" (1996, 123). Why "more desirable" from their perspective? Here is Mele's thoughtful suggestion:

> What some libertarians want may be the possession of an explanatory bearing on some of their actions that they would lack at any deterministic world. They may desire to make an explanatory contribution to some of their actions, the making of which cannot be fully explained by the laws of nature and the state of their world at some time prior to their having any sense of the apparent options. In short, they may want, as I shall put it, the power of indeterministic initiation. (1996, 131)

One-way or liberal libertarians, like soft libertarians, may propose that their variety of libertarianism is to be preferred to an otherwise similar compatibilist view without the indeterminism because their brand of libertarianism can accommodate the ability of agents to make contributions to their directly free choices or actions they are not causally determined to make—they value the ability to be indeterministic initiators. Determinism precludes agents from having such an ability.

I have no qualms about whether one would find more *desirable* either one-way or liberal libertarianism than a relevantly similar compatibilist view absent the indeterminism. Rather, the pressing issue is whether indeterministic initiation is *required* for free choice, free action, or moral responsibility. Why is the relevantly similar compatibilist view—RS-compatibilism—that we may stipulate is the "host" theory for these varieties of liberal libertarianism defective?

It is not to the credit of one-way or liberal libertarianism that either allows for dual intentional control; in this respect, these sorts of libertarianism do not differ from RS-compatibilism. Nor do they have an edge over RS-compatibilism in that they have resources not available to the RS-compatibilist to respond to various pertinent worries concerning free action or moral responsibility, such as how to differentiate deviant causal chains culminating in choices from nondeviant ones.

Interestingly, Pereboom has argued that determinism and varieties of covert manipulation that supposedly undermine responsibility do so in virtue of violating a putative necessary condition of moral responsibility: Being the ultimate sources or initiators of our choices. Pereboom encodes this condition in principle (O):

(O): If an agent is morally responsible for deciding to perform an action, then the production of this decision must be something over which the agent has control, and an agent is not morally responsible for the decision if it is produced by a source over which she has no control. (2001, 4)

(O) lends itself to different readings depending on how "control" is unpacked. Setting aside for now this complication, Pereboom argues that no compatibilist account of moral responsibility is true because, contrary to what these accounts entail, determinism *undermines* responsibility in virtue of depriving us of ultimate sourcehood; principle (O) can't be satisfied in a deterministic world. If this argument against compatibilism is sound, then (as Pereboom himself maintains) no libertarian account (aside from agent-causal accounts he believes) is true either because such accounts also violate principle (O). At least it would appear that in Pereboom's assessment, both one-way and liberal libertarianism have no advantage over RS-compatibilism.

I have argued that principle (O) or variations of (O) that result from disambiguating the notion of control in formulations of (O) won't sustain an argument against compatibilism (2009a, 136–38). I underscore a point similar to one I have made previously (2009a, 137–38). Suppose "control" in principle (O) denotes "indeterministic ultimate control," the sort of control that soft libertarians favor. Understanding "control" in this way yields this sort of variation of principle (O): An agent's decision is free and she is morally responsible for it only if she is an indeterministic initiator of this decision. In the absence of a cogent rationale for this condition on free decision, an RS-compatibilist may reject it on the basis that it begs the question against compatibilism.

These reflections on one-way and liberal libertarian views shed light on the following issue: If, as I have argued, at t, one has a direct obligation to do something only if, at t, both one can intentionally do and refrain from doing that thing, why should the refraining be intentional? Alternatively, why does obligation require two-way *intentional* control? Why not, instead, a two-way control requirement, but only one of these ways be intentional? It may be helpful here to think yet again of one-way libertarianism or liberal libertarianism. The former entails that at t, S performs a directly free action, A, only if at t S does A, and there is a possible world with the same past and the laws in which at t S does not to A. Such a world may be a world in which at t S fails to do anything at all. Similarly, regarding obligation, the query is why this analogous condition is suspect: At t, S has a direct obligation to do A only if at t S intentionally does A, and there is a possible world with the same past and the laws in which at t S does not to A. Again, such a world may be one in which at t S doesn't do anything at all. In response, in a case of this sort, we don't get *two-way control*. Without dual control of this sort, why does obligation call for our being able to do otherwise? Why the alternative possibilities requirement in the first place? The suggestion that one directly ought to do A only if one is the ultimate originator of A, and having alternative possibilities is a logical requirement of being such an originator is fishy because ultimate origination seems not to be required for direct obligation.

Reflect on Mele's famous Ann/Beth scenario. Ann and Beth are both philosophy professors but Ann is far more dedicated to the discipline. Wanting more production out of Beth and not scrupulous about how he gets it, the dean of the University enlists the help of new-wave neurologists who "implant" in easygoing Beth Ann's values. These implanted values (elements of which may be desires) are unsheddable for Beth: Given her psychological constitution, ridding herself of these values is not a "psychologically genuine option" under any but extraordinary circumstances (Mele 1995, 172). The manipulation results in Beth's being, in relevant respects, the psychological twin of Ann. Such manipulation leaves personal identity intact: Premanipulated Beth is identical to her postmanipulated later self. The first few engineered-in desires of victimized Beth cause her to exercise fourteen hours of intellectual muscle on her first day of work after psychosurgery; in brief, Beth A-s. (One may take her A-ing to be her making the decision to A if one insists that directly free actions are mental acts of decision-making.)

In a scenario of this sort it may be morally obligatory for manipulated Beth to donate to UNICEF even though it is only because of engineered in apt values, desires, beliefs, and so forth that she donates to this charity. Unlike responsibility appraisals, obligation appraisals are not agent-focused; they are primarily act-focused, and this, I hypothesize, lies at the crux of why we should not believe that there is an ultimate origination requirement for moral obligation even though some may be inclined to the view that there is such a requirement for moral responsibility.

A libertarian, perhaps influenced by some of Steward's view on action, who believes that an event is an action of some agent only if he can make it occur (or bring it about) and he can refrain from making it occur runs up against the luck problem if such a libertarian accepts the following proviso.

> *Proviso P*: At t, S performs an action A in world W only if (i) there is an apt connection between S's reasons states and A in W, (ii) there is some world, W^*, with the same pre-t past and the same laws as W in which at t S refrains from doing A, and (iii) there is an apt connection between S's reasons states and what S does or refrains from doing in W^*.

Assume that objective *pro tanto* reasons move us to action by causing us to acquire apt desires (or other suitable pro-attitudes) and perhaps beliefs. These desires or desire/belief pairs, on their own or together with other agent-involving elements, then causally generate the pertinent action. Imagine that Peg has a moral obligation to give medicine A to Jim. Her having this obligation (or her being aware that she has it) is an objective *pro tanto* reason for her to give A to Jim. Assume that in the actual world, this reason or her knowing that she has it, gives rise to a desire to give A that, in conjunction with other antecedents of action, including her best judgment that she ought to give A, nondeterministically causes her to give A. Assume, furthermore, that this action is *not* akratic. Consider the relevant nonactual contrast worlds in which Peg supposedly indeterministically does something other than give A to Jim. If she indeterministically and akratically gives B rather than A in these worlds, then for the reasons previously explained, it seems not to be true that her giving B nondeviantly arises from apt reason states. Some may suggest that in these worlds, perhaps Peg has a prudential obligation to give B, her having this obligation is an objective *pro tanto* reason for her to give B, and this reason causes her to acquire a desire to give B that, in turn, with other antecedents of action, nondeterministically causes her to give B. However, with the past and the laws fixed, if Peg gives B in some nonactual contrast world, she does so akratically. I have yet to see a plausible account of a detailed reasons explanation of such an action, given *Proviso P*. If there is no detailed reasons explanation of Peg's administering B in the contrast worlds, then as I argued before, provided one endorses *Proviso P*, there is no reason to accept the assumption that there is such an explanation of Peg's giving A in the actual world.

Remove the supposition from the scenario involving Peg above that objective reasons give rise to her giving A to Jim. Assume, simply, that Peg has a desire to cure Jim, this desire together with apt beliefs constitute her normative Davidsonian reason for giving A, and these reasons nondeterministically cause her continent action of giving A. This modification of the scenario should do nothing to dispel the concern that there is no suitable detailed reasons explanation of Peg's *akratically* giving B in the relevant nonactual worlds in which she gives B.

7.4.2.4 GRIFFITH ON THE LUCK OBJECTION
Megan Griffith proposes that

> LH: Something is a matter of luck for A only if it happens to A. (2010, 45)

She further submits that the following principle, the principle of "Responsibility Undermining Luck" is true:

> RUL: In the free will context, something is a matter of luck for A if and only if it happens to A. (2010, 46)

She explains that if something happens to a person, it is not something he does (2010, 46). Elaborating, she says:

> RUL cashes in on the distinction between doing and happening. What happens to someone is not something she does. In the free will context, that something happens to A is sufficient for its being a matter of luck, since it rules out her having done it. Since this is ruled out, her responsibility for it is undermined. (2010, 46)

In a footnote, she underscores the following:

> The claim is not that what one does does not happen, in the sense of "occurring." After all, many (if not most) actions are also events. The claim is, instead, that doing and happening are mutually exclusive in the sense that if one does something in the sense meant here, this something does not happen to her (2010, 53, n. 11).

As an illustration of how RUL bears on the luck objection, Griffith revisits a version of the objection according to which the difference between the world in which Peg A-s and those in which, holding fixed the past and the laws, Peg B-s, is just a matter of luck. Since nothing explains this cross-world difference, it is concluded that Peg's A-ing (or B-ing) is also just a matter of luck. Griffith remarks:

> Because the possible-worlds argument removes the emphasis from the action, it initially appears to avoid violating RUL. But perhaps not. Emphasizing that luck resides in the cross-world difference (or the unavailability of an explanation for this difference) creates a problem for the argument. Cross-world differences (and the unavailability of explanations) do not happen to anyone. (2010, 48)

If principles LH and RUL are true, it would be a mistake to claim that it is a matter of Luck (for Peg) that Peg A-s or that she decides to A. Peg's deciding to A, for example, is not something that *happens* to her; it's something she *does*. However, there are concerns with these principles. Regarding RUL, suppose that you have promised to obey my every instruction. I give you a loaded pistol. You are standing a few inches away from me. I ask you to take aim at my foot and pull the trigger. You do so. It is farfetched that *my foot's being injured* (as a result of being struck by the bullet)— something that happens to me—is a matter of luck (for me). RUL rules otherwise. In another case, mischievous psychosurgeons have developed a fascinating machine. If its red button is pressed, one of two things will happen. Either process p or process q will be initiated in your brain. It is indeterminate which of these processes will occur on pressing the button. Imagine that there is a 50% probability that either will occur. If p is initiated, it will cause you to acquire various beliefs and desires, and produce other pertinent changes in your brain, with the result that you will intentionally A on the basis of your acquiring the germane desires, beliefs, and so forth. If q is initiated, another set of events will occur in your brain with the result that you will intentionally B. The button is pressed and process p unfolds; you intentionally A. Had you been left to your own devices, you would not have A-ed nor would you have B-ed. It seems that this is true: (L1) it is a matter of luck for you that p is initiated in your brain. It also seems to be true that, (L2), it is a matter of luck for you that if p is initiated in your brain, then you intentionally A. It appears to follow from L1 and L2 that (L3) it is a matter of luck for you that you intentionally A. Even if one rejects the implicit "rule of inference" that if it is a matter of luck for you that p, and if it is a matter of luck for you that if p, then q, then it is a matter of luck for you that q (or some apt version of this principle), each of L1, L2, and L3 seems highly plausible although your intentionally A-ing is not something that happens to you. Some of Griffith's remarks suggest that in a case of this sort, we may grant that L1 is a matter of luck for you (as p's being initiated in your brain is something that happens to you), but your intentionally A-ing is *not* a matter of luck for you because your A-ing is something you do. I don't find this credible. Indeed, as I explain below, in what strikes me as being a relevantly similar case, Griffith also seems to concede that an event, pertinently like the event that is your intentionally A-ing, is a matter of luck for some agent.

For a third counterexample, to RUL, reconsider *Theft*. It is a matter of luck for Augustine that it is not impermissible for him to steal the pears in Stage 2. But that it is not impermissible for him to steal the pears is not something that happens to Augustine.

Griffith advances another interesting set of claims about the luck objection. She writes:

> Explanation brings in other issues—issues that are "extraneous to the causal story. . . . And it is fair to say that agents who cause, for reasons, have a strong *prima facie* claim to control. Both sides can agree on this point. Undermining the *prima facie* claim requires more than an appeal to one's intuitions in these cases. There is no additional story of why unavailable explanations ought to amount to a lack of control (i.e., the decision's happening to the agent). (2010, 49)

The *No Explanation Version* of the luck objection questions whether there is an explanation of why Peg decides to B (in W^*). If there is no plausible explanation in terms of her reason states—if there is no detailed reasons explanation—of her deciding to B, then she lacks the control modest libertarians claim is necessary for responsibility for one's actions. Perhaps some will be inclined to the view that since Peg *decides* to B in W^* there must be an explanation for this decision on the basis of her reasons but this explanation is simply not accessible to us. Even if one goes along with this mystery position, there is still this well-recognized alleged problem (that Griffith thinks is plausible) with modest libertarianism: Having contributed all she can to her deciding to A (in the actual world), it appears that Peg has no further causal involvement in the decision that is made. So it seems that the decision that Peg makes is a matter of luck for Peg.

Significantly, reflecting on this sort of concern, Griffith says:

> This problem is not constituted by the unavailability of an explanation. It is constituted by a lack of control. It just happens to the agent that A occurs instead of B, since the agent has no involvement beyond those states or events that leave it causally open. So in the end, the event-causal libertarian cannot give the agent the control she needs. (2010, 51)

I reemphasize the following. If there is no detailed reasons explanation of why Peg decides to B in W^*, then it seems that unless we are drawn to the mystery position above, we have good ground to conclude that Peg's decision to B is not appropriately caused by her reason states. If this decision is not so caused, then she lacks the (causal control) that modest libertarians deem essential for responsibility. In addition, Griffith claims that *it just happens to the agent—Peg in our example—that A occurs instead of B.* Focus on the relevantly similar claim that *it just happens to Peg that decision B occurs in W^*.* But since decision B is Peg's decision, it is a decision she makes. Presumably, this decision of Peg's is an intentional mental action, and in virtue of being such an action, assume (contrary to what I have argued) that it is aptly associated with Peg's germane reason states. I cannot see how it could be otherwise. If one grants that Peg *decides* to B in W^*, then Peg intentionally *does* something—she makes the decision to B—in W*. But now there's a problem: It would seem that Griffith has to concede that one and the same event—*Peg's making the decision to B in W*—*can both happen to a person and it can be something that this person does; it just happens to Peg that B occurs, *and* Peg *decides* to B.[14]

7.4.2.5 STEWARD ON THE LUCK OBJECTION

Let's now look at another criticism of the luck objection. Steward believes that her agent-centered libertarianism, Agency Incompatibilism, has the resources to escape this objection. She proposes that the concept of agency includes the dual theses of matters being up to an agent, and an agent's settling some matters (how she moves her body) by acting. An agent can settle some matter at a time only if that matter is not already then settled. But if determinism were true, every matter would be settled. Steward concludes that agency is possible only if determinism is false. In one of her examples relevantly similar to the example featuring Peg, Joe's reasons in the actual world, W, favor his moving in with his girlfriend. At t, he decides to move in. In one of the pertinent contrast worlds, W*, which is law-wise and past-wise indiscernible from W right up to t, Joe decides to refrain from moving in. Don't we have a problem of luck in this example too? Not according to Steward. She explains:

> In the original case, we had to allow for Joe's performing a positive action [such as deciding to move in with his parents] that he has no reason or motivation whatever to perform and every reason and motivation not to perform. But in the present case, we simply have to allow for the possibility that he might *not* have done something at a given time t that in fact he *did* do at

that given time. That the world should have gone forward in this way instead of the way in which it in fact went forward, is not something that would have been rationally unintelligible or which we have trouble understanding as anything other than the operation of an alien force, operating counter to Joe's wishes and reasons and hopes. Though he had many reasons, we are supposing, to decide to move in with his girlfriend, Joe need not have had any particular reasons for making the decision *then*. If he had decided at *t* that he ought to put off the decision about moving in with his girlfriend until a later date just in case there were any drawbacks he might not have thought of and notwithstanding his sense that the decision ought to be clear-cut, that would not have been irrational or unintelligible or in the least at odds with our conception of how it is that human beings operate under the influence of ordinary sorts of human motivation. It is arguable . . . that anything that counts as an action has to be someone's doing something for a reason. However even if this is conceded, it is not at all obvious that we also have to have reasons for doing the things we do *at the times* at which we do them as opposed to the numerous other things we might have done at the times in question. (2012, 170)

In this passage Steward underscores two things that bear on the luck objection. First, in W^*, at t, Joe fails to make any pertinent decision as opposed to making some decision that differs from the one at t that he makes in the actual world. W^* concerns an omission of Joe whereas the actual world (W) concerns a "positive" action. Second, it is not irrational or unintelligible that, given the same past and the laws, Joe fails to make any decision at this time in W^*. But whether Joe's failing to make any decision is not irrational or unintelligible depends on pertinent details and not on whether the relevant event at issue is an omission or a commission. Suppose that in the actual world, Joe has no reasons whatsoever to hesitate about making his decision at *t*. He has weighed the relevant facts carefully, deliberated judiciously, and is resolved to move in with his girlfriend. If the scenario remains otherwise unchanged—for example, if nothing new comes to his mind at the moment of decision—then, given this background, one might well wonder why he failed to make any decision at *t* in W^*. Again, it is not that in the actual world, Joe is on the fence about what to do, is waiting for some further information, or is pondering some long-term consequences of the proposed move, and so forth. Under such conditions, his omission at *t* in the contrast world (W^*)—whether this omission is intentional or not—is no less puzzling than, for instance, his making some alternative decision at *t* in this world. Again, there seems to be no plausible causal explanation, in terms of his reasons states, of why at *t* he refrains from making any decision in the contrast world, when allowing for exactly the same pre-*t* history and the same laws, he is resolved to move in with his girlfriend in the actual world, and, at *t*, he decides to move in.

Steward reflects on a slightly modified scenario in which Joe must decide at a given moment "if an opportunity is not to be lost" (171). For example, if at *t* Joe does not make a decision then, the offer from his friend will be retracted. In this version of the case, Joe did have a reason to move in with his girlfriend at a specific time. Assuming no other changes in the case, what is the detailed reasons explanation for Joe's omission in W^*? Isn't luck just as much of a problem in this case? Steward thinks not:

> The scenario we are trying to imagine is one in which Joe simply does *not* make that decision at the time in question. We are concerned with an omission, a failure to act, not with an action. It may be that it would have been irrational for Joe not to have made the decision then, but there is simply no issue, as

there was in the original case [in which Joe makes a different decision], about whether Joe really counts as the agent of an action in the counterfactual scenario in which he fails to decide at *t* to move in with his girlfriend. For we are not, in general, agents of all our non-actions (though we can sometimes be responsible for them). There is no question of its having been possible for Joe not to have made the decision at *t* seeming to entail the possibility that an event beyond his control should have occurred. (172)

We have already dealt with the point about omissions. If Joe's reasons do favor his making his decision at *t*, and all the other pertinent details of the case remain otherwise unchanged, what accounts for his not making, at *t*, any decision in the contrast world W^*? Steward suggests a rationale:

Though not deciding at *t* to move in with his girlfriend would have been irrational in one way (because it prevents Joe from doing something he very much wants to do), it is not at all irrational in another. We have a general tendency, if we are prudent, not to rush into irrevocable decisions without careful thought and there therefore *are* reasons speaking for refrainment from deciding in the case imagined, because there are always general reasons speaking for caution and further thought (though of course, they can be outweighed by the need for urgency in a given case). This helps to make sense for us of what might have gone on in a situation in which Joe dithers too long and loses his opportunity. We understand perfectly how faint-heartedness and lack of resolve can enter into situations in which we are robbed of the time to think properly about what we should do. So it seems to me that it is unproblematic to insist that even in situations like this, where time is of the essence, there is no difficulty attaching to the assumption that the agent could have *not* made the wanted decision at the time in question. (172)

Even if we concur that there are always general reasons for caution and further thought, assume that Joe has taken these reasons into account in his deliberations about whether to move in. Why, then, does he fail to make any decision at t in W^*? Similarly, we may simply take it for granted that in the actual world, Joe does not dither because of faint-heartedness or lack of resolve. It may also be worth reemphasizing a point Kane and other libertarians have made about control. In typical cases of free action, the control that libertarian agents are meant to enjoy is two-way or plural rational control. It would be an undesirable consequence of a libertarian view if it entailed that in every instance of free action, in the apt contrast world or worlds (like W^*), agents always acted akratically or otherwise irrationally.

Finally, reminding us of her conception of an action being the settling of matters, Steward proposes the following:

> For unless the alternative possibility of refrainment at t exists, Joe's *actual* act of decision-making is not properly representable as the active intervention into the world that the Agency Incompatibilist insists all actions must be. The crucial thing is that the *actual act* be something that did not have to happen, for otherwise, in the Agency Incompatibilist's opinion, it simply cannot be an act. But it does not matter a bit if the various *alternative* scenarios do not involve any activity on the part of Joe, for they are simply the foils in the light of which we know that his actually deciding something at t was a real intervention in the world on his part. The crucial point so far as the Agency Incompatibilist is concerned is that it does not follow from the fact that there is no reason-giving explanation of

why Joe decides as he does *at t* that his actual decision was not an intervention in the world by him. On the contrary things are, precisely, settled by *Joe*, who, possessed at *t* of the two-way power to decide or not to decide to move in with his girlfriend, goes ahead and exercises his power to decide, thereby settling the matter. (174)

We have, however, already seen reason to question Steward's view that nothing can be an action unless its agent could have done otherwise. Furthermore, Steward's following claims raise concerns about her dismissal of Frankfurt examples: "The crucial thing is that the *actual act* be something that did not have to happen, for otherwise, in the Agency Incompatibilist's opinion, it simply cannot be an act. But it does not matter a bit if the various *alternative scenarios do not involve any activity on the part of Joe*" (emphasis added). Think of the alternative sequence (in which the agent does not act on his own) in a typical "prior sign" Frankfurt case that features a counterfactual intervener. Suppose that in Stage 1 of this example (where the counterfactual intervener is absent), Joe decides at *t* to move in with his girlfriend. In Stage 2, he behaves no differently even though, unbeknownst to him, he could not have done otherwise. Had he displayed an involuntary sign that he was about, at *t*, to decide differently, the counterfactual intervener would have killed him. If, in the case Steward discusses in the last quoted passage, "it does not matter a bit if the various alternative scenarios do not involve any activity on the part of Joe," it shouldn't matter that in the alternative sequence of the Frankfurt case at issue, there is no activity on the part of Joe. It shouldn't matter in the sense that despite no activity in the alternative sequence, it appears that what Joe does in the actual sequence seems to be a (mental) action even though he could not have done otherwise. One may be concerned that if it is true that Joe *could* have displayed some alternative involuntary sign, this is sufficient for its being the case that he could have moved his body in a different way than the way in which he did. If this is a legitimate worry, simply switch from a prior sign Frankfurt case to one that features no such sign (such as the two-pathway case I previously outlined).

I conclude that Steward has not blunted the force of the luck objection.

7.4.2.6 LUCK AND OBLIGATION

Take the outline of the *No Explanation* version of the luck objection as background for the following argument schema to support the view that modest libertarianism undercuts the truth of judgments of objective *pro tanto* reasons. (1) There is an alternative possibilities requirement for the truth of judgments of objective *pro tanto* reasons: No one, for example, can have such a reason to do something unless one can do otherwise. (2) Just as moral obligation (or moral responsibility) requires control, so does reasons-wise obligation. (3) The control reasons-wise obligation demands is "two-way": One must have control in doing and in refraining from doing what reason requires. (4) This control is largely causal; it consists in apt reason states appropriately causing one's germane options. (5) Given that modest libertarianism precludes such control (as previously argued), it precludes the truth of judgments of objective *pro tanto* reasons. I focus on the last two steps since the first three have already been addressed.

What sort of control over and above the ability to do otherwise does reasons-wise obligation require? Suppose, from the perspective of objective *pro tanto* reasons, Peg reasons-wise ought to give medicine A to a patient. Imagine that Peg does indeed give A, and her reason states (supposedly) nondeterministically cause the event that is her giving A. Her appreciation of the objective *pro tanto* reason to give A causally gives rise to an apt desire, and this desire along with suitable beliefs nondeviantly and nondeterministically cause her to give A. If she indeterministically gives A, there is a contrast world (a world with the same past and the laws as the actual world) in which she refrains from giving A. In this world, either Peg gives no medicine to the patient, or she gives some medicine other than A. Assume, furthermore, that partly on the basis of the objective reason she has for giving A, she forms the best judgment that she give A, and actional members of the segment of the causal trajectory culminating in her giving A, including apt desires and beliefs, and her best judgment smoothly give rise to her giving A: No new information comes to her mind prior to her giving A, she does not succumb to akratic influences, and so forth. Then, for the reasons adumbrated above in addressing indeterminism, luck, and responsibility, Peg's refraining from giving A in the contrast world, contrary to what has been assumed, is not an action that properly and causally derives from her reason states.

Consequently, it is hard to see how Peg's not giving A, and let us suppose, her giving B instead in the contrast world in which she fails to give A is an intentional action that derives from Peg's reasons, objective or otherwise, not to give A. Elucidating, in the contrast world, it appears that Peg does not act on the basis of reasons. She does not do so because acting on the basis of reasons requires that suitable reason states appropriately cause her action or choice, something that is *not* so in the contrast world as, again, reflection on the previous discussion involving indeterminism and luck should confirm.[15] This is not a decisive consideration for the view that obligations of reason require a certain variety of control. But it is a consideration that seems to shore up the intuition that just as responsibility requires control, so do obligations of (objective) reasons.

As for the sort of control, I have argued that if one reasons-wise ought to do something, give medicine A for instance, then one can do and one can refrain from doing that thing. But if one is to execute one's reasons-wise obligation to do something, such as giving A (or not giving A and giving B instead), one must have control both in giving A and in giving B. It is implausible to hold that although reasons-wise "ought" requires our having alternatives, it only requires control with respect to one of the alternatives but not the other (or others); for example, regarding Peg, reasons-wise "ought" only requires that Peg have control in giving A, but not in giving B if she were to give B (or vice versa).

It should now be straightforward to see that modest libertarianism endangers the truth of judgments of objective *pro tanto* reasons. The scenario in which Peg gives medicine A to the patient suggests that when she indeterministically gives A, she lacks the sort of control in refraining from giving A in the contrast world in which she does not give A that obligations of reason require.

In sum, if Peg has an objective reason to give A, then she can give and refrain from giving A. Whichever of these options she elects, she has control in doing what she does if she gives A on the basis of this reason. This control is largely causal: Apt reason states (or neural realizers of these states) nondeviantly cause her relevant action. But whether an agent can have this sort of two-way control if her action is nondeterministically caused, as modest libertarianism requires, is suspect.

Typical libertarians accept LFA—roughly, the requirement that to perform a directly free or to be responsible for a directly free action, one have dual intentional control concerning that action: Minimally, one intentionally performs the action and in contrast worlds, one intentionally fails to perform that action or one intentionally performs some other action instead. Modest libertarians who embrace LFA will run afoul of its requirement of dual control even if they reject the assumption that our having objective reasons presupposes that we have alternatives, or believe that reason-wise obligation (or moral obligation) is tied not to objective reasons but to Davidsonian ones. For I remind the reader of the following. Assume that objective *pro tanto* reasons move us to action by causing us to acquire suitable pro-attitudes that nondeviantly cause the relevant action. Assume that Peg morally ought to give medicine A to Jim. This obligation (or her knowing that she has it) is an objective *pro tanto* reason for her to give A to Jim that in the actual world nondeterministically causes her to give A, a continent action. In nonactual contrast worlds Peg allegedly indeterministically and akratically gives B to Jim (or does not give A). It is not true that her giving B in these contrast worlds nondeviantly arises from apt reason states.

Drop the supposition that Peg's having objective reasons cause the event that is her giving A to Jim. Assume, instead, that her having normative Davidsonian reasons to give A nondeterministically cause her continent action of giving A. As I proposed above, even in this version of the scenario, there is no detailed reasons explanation of Peg's akratically giving B in the contrast worlds in which she gives B.

If modest libertarianism cannot accommodate our acting on the basis of objective reasons, then it undermines the truth of any normative assessment essentially associated, logically or conceptually, with such reasons, such as morally deontic assessments of obligation, permissibility, and impermissibility. If this in turn is true, once again we may invoke the template of reasoning previously called upon to generate skepticism regarding moral obligation and blameworthiness. To repeat only one element of this template, suppose modest libertarianism cannot accommodate obligation because it cannot accommodate the truth of judgments of objective *pro tanto* reasons. Then if blameworthiness requires impermissibility, it seems that modest libertarians will have to concede that no one is ever morally blameworthy for any of one's conduct.

We may briefly revert to a matter of some urgency. A precondition of moral obligation is that one have alternatives: One morally ought to do something only if both one can and one can refrain from doing it. Direct obligations, as we previously noted, are restricted to intentional actions one can perform, and, we may now add, to actions one can intentionally refrain from performing as well. In other words, if one morally ought to do something one is directly obligated to do, then both one can intentionally do and refrain from doing that thing. Are the alternatives that direct obligations require "strong" incompatibilist alternatives? Are they of the sort that, given the past and the laws, one could have done otherwise? Or are they a species of weak compatibilist alternatives?

If A is a direct obligation for some agent, then she intentionally can do A and intentionally can refrain from doing A. Again, if one *intentionally* does or omits to do something—performs an overt action, makes a decision, or refrains from making some choice—then this overt action, decision, or omission must be suitably connected to one's apt reason states (or their neural realizers). Causal theorists of action regard this association as causal: One performs an intentional action only if one's suitable reason states nondeviantly cause this action. In addition, if A is a direct obligation for an agent, then it is not the case that A is fluky in the sense of "fluky" that versions of the luck objection highlight. Suppose one submits that, necessarily, one has a direct obligation to do A only if one can refrain from doing A, and the notion of "can" here is the strong incompatibilist one. In other words, assume that, necessarily, one has a direct obligation to do A only if A is a libertarian directly free action. Then no one in a suitably indeterministic world (and, needless to say, in a deterministic world) would have a direct obligation to do anything. (A world is suitably indeterministic only if the etiology of agents' actions in that world feature indeterminism at the right junctures; roughly, at the time of decision, the agent could have refrained from making that decision.) For either putatively libertarian directly free actions are too fluky (as the *Pure Luck Version* suggests). Or if one has reservations about this charge of flukiness, none of the libertarian views of interest—standard event-causal modest libertarianism, one-way libertarianism, or liberal libertarianism—gives us two-way intentional control. But why accept the thesis that obligation requires a sort of control—"incompatibilist two-way intentional control"—that has this feature: No action is such that one can have this sort of control in performing it? Alternatively, why accept the thesis that it is obligatory for one to perform an action only if, necessarily, in performing this action, one will fail to exercise the putative control—incompatibilist two-way intentional control—that obligation requires? Without good reason to support this thesis, it seems reasonable to conclude that the control obligation requires is not strong incompatibilist control. Direct obligation does not presuppose that we have strong incompatibilist alternatives; rather, it presupposes that we have weak compatibilist alternatives.

It should be cautioned that one can have such weak alternatives even if there is indeterminacy at some juncture in the pathway to choice or action. For instance, it may be that Peg indeterministically acquires certain beliefs; these beliefs may then, together with other apt mental items, such as desires and a judgment about what it is best for her to do, deterministically give rise to her decision to *A* in the actual world. It appears that a nonaction-centered libertarianism of this sort won't undermine direct obligation.

Ponder these claims:

> R1: If impermissibility requires avoidability, and if blameworthiness requires impermissibility, then determinism is incompatible both with impermissibility (or, more generally, obligation) and blameworthiness unless obligation

and blameworthiness require only weak compatibilist alternatives.

R2: If impermissibility requires that one's actions not be fluky, and blameworthiness requires impermissibility, then the falsity of determinism is incompatible both with impermissibility (or, more generally, obligation) and blameworthiness. The "falsity of determinism" is shorthand for "worlds in which determinism is false and the etiology of agents" actions in these worlds feature indeterminism at the time agents make decisions or perform overt actions.

R1 is true if "avoidability" denotes "strong" avoidability: Consistent with the past and the laws remaining fixed, one could have done otherwise. For if impermissibility calls for one being able to do otherwise, and assuming determinism effaces alternatives, nothing is impermissible for any agent in a deterministic world. However, regarding impermissibility, if the "can" associated with one's being able to do otherwise when it is impermissible for one to do something is some weak compatibilist "can," then determinism does not preclude impermissibility (barring independent problems for the compatibility of obligation and determinism). As for R2, if obligation and impermissibility are incompatible with the sort of flukiness displayed in appropriate scenarios in which Peg's indeterministically A-s, then R2 is true if the luck objection is sound; suitably indeterministic worlds will be devoid of moral impermissibility, and if blameworthiness presupposes impermissibility, devoid of blameworthiness too.

Entertain another pair of claims.

R3: If impermissibility requires strong avoidability, then determinism is incompatible with impermissibility (or, more generally, obligation) unless obligation requires weak compatibilist alternatives.

R4: If impermissibility and blameworthiness require that one's actions not be fluky, then the falsity of determinism is incompatible both with impermissibility (or, more generally, obligation) and blameworthiness.

R3 like R1 is true if determinism expunges strong alternatives, and R4 like R2 is true if the luck objection is sound.

7.4.2.7 DETERMINISM AND STRONG ALTERNATIVES

Vihvelin has argued that determinism does not preclude us from having free will. She says:

> We are entitled to believe, and should believe, that free will is not only possible and compossible with determinism but that we actually have the free will that common sense says we have. (2013, 168)

Vihvelin argues for this thesis largely (though not exclusively) by showing that arguments for incompatibilism regarding free will all fail. Assume that this intriguing thesis—free will is compossible with determinism—is true. Then just like the modest libertarian, a person who endorses determinism would be entitled to the view that, given exactly the same past and the laws, one could have done otherwise. But then it would seem the argument I developed for the view that modest libertarianism undermines the truth of judgments of objective *pro tanto* reasons, with appropriate and minor adjustments, would also show that determinism undermines the truth of judgments of objective *pro tanto* reasons. In brief, if modest libertarianism runs up against the luck objection, then any compatibilist view, wedded to the thesis that determinism is compossible with free will—any appropriate "two-way compatibilist view"—would do so as well. This would not bode well for either moral obligation or moral blameworthiness.

Previously, I deliberated briefly on Mele's suggestion that soft libertarians may prefer their variety of libertarianism to an otherwise parallel compatibilist view without indeterminism because they value being indeterministic initiators—they value freedom from control by the past—and their brand of libertarianism can accommodate indeterministic initiation. It is not open to a two-way compatibilist to propose, similarly, that she values this sort of compatibilism for reasons analogous to the reasons soft libertarians value their brand of libertarianism. A two-way compatibilist view is incompatible with agents being indeterministic initiators of their actions or choices if it is assumed that determinism precludes this sort of agency.

7.4.3 A Slight Digression: Compatibilism and Luck

I have defended the view that modest libertarianism seems to succumb to a problem of luck. Recently, Neil Levy (2011, ch. 4) and Mirja Perez de Calleja (2014) have argued that compatibilist accounts, which unlike libertarian ones maintain that free action and determinism are compatible, are susceptible to a similar problem. In this section, I argue for a twofold thesis: The problem of compatibilist luck, at least on one interpretation of this problem, is not novel insofar as it is a manifestation of a more general concern to which compatibilists and libertarians have responded or can mine resources to respond; and this response is *not* an effective response to the problem of libertarian luck.

Above, I offered different ways to think about this problem. The *No Explanation Version* assumes initially that there is an explanation in terms of her reason states of why Peg decides at t to A in the actual world. Given this explanation, and the libertarian constraint that an action A performed at t is directly free only if there is another possible world with the same past and laws in which, at t, the agent does not do A, there seems to be no detailed reasons explanation of why Peg at t decides to B in the contrast world. Her deciding to B in the contrast world (and by comparable reasoning, her deciding to A in the actual world), hence, appear to be a matter of luck. In the *Pure Luck Version* whereas Peg decides at t to A in the actual world, assuming that her decision to A is a libertarian free decision, there is some world with the same past and the laws as the actual world in which she decides at t to B. Even assuming the thesis that the control free action and moral responsibility require is causal, and assuming there is a plausible and detailed reasons explanation of why at t Peg decides as she does in the pertinent worlds, it appears that it is matter of luck that she decides as she does in these worlds, or the cross-world difference, her deciding in one way in the actual world and deciding differently in the contrast world, is a matter of luck.

Entertain the thesis that the problem of luck (for typical libertarians) is generated by (i) the requirement that an action A performed at t is directly free only if there is another possible world with the same past and laws in which, at t, the agent does not do A, and (ii) there seems to be no detailed reasons explanation of why, in relevant worlds, the agent does what she does. (Proponents of the *Pure Luck Version* will, of course, not invoke (ii) in their development of the problem.) Compatibilists accept neither (i) nor (ii). So why should it be thought that they also face an analogous problem of luck?

Ponder the following from Perez de Calleja 2014:

A decision performed at a time at which the agent is psychologically able (and suitably skilled and placed) to refrain from deciding that way in the circumstance is subject to cross-world luck, whether the world is deterministic or indeterministic. Bob, in particular, is lucky that he decides as he does rather than otherwise because in a nearby possible world where the salient causes and background conditions which are relevant to his deciding one way or the other in the circumstances are the same (including his reasons, his character traits and even his way of deliberating), he decides otherwise instead. If we make Bob's world deterministic, we don't thereby eliminate the nearby possible worlds where Bob's counterpart does otherwise in conditions which don't *significantly* differ from Bob's. (Though, of course, since the worlds at issue are deterministic, either the past or the laws must differ *in some way* to produce different outcomes.) (114–15)

In this passage, Perez de Calleja's recommends that the problem of luck for compatibilists may be exposed if we pay attention to deterministic worlds (i) that are similar in relevant respects—we are to hold fixed in these worlds a host of factors that are, roughly, pertinent to the agent's, such as Peg's or Bob's, deliberations; (ii) that differ with respect to certain extraneous factors—as a first stab, factors over which the agent has no control; and (iii) in which it is in virtue of the presence or absence of these factors, that the agent decides to do one thing in some of these worlds but decides differently in some of the other worlds.

Regarding (i), Perez de Calleja proposes that we hold fixed "the salient causes and background conditions ... relevant to [the agent's] deciding one way or the other in the circumstances," where these things include the agent's reasons, character traits, and deliberation. Also, hold fixed "the attitudes, tendencies, skills and features of the circumstance ... relevant to what [the agent] is motivated and disposed to do in the circumstance" and "relevant motivations" (2014, 115).

With respect to (ii)—the extraneous factors that are allowed to vary across the (pertinent) deterministic worlds—I am unsure what sorts of thing Perez de Calleja has in mind. Consider Levy's gloss on such factors.

> Present luck is luck at or near the time of (putatively) directly free action, which significantly influences that action. Prima facie, there are many ways in which compatibilist agents are subject to present luck. Agents' decisions are significantly influenced by all kinds of chance factors over which they did not exercise control. Mele (2006) emphasizes one (though he does not seem to conceive of it as an instance of present luck): Which considerations come to mind is—apparently—a matter of luck for an agent (we cannot control which considerations come to mind, because we do not satisfy the epistemic conditions on control over considerations; to satisfy these conditions, with regard to any consideration, that consideration would need already to have come to mind) . . . Our moods may influence what occurs to us, and what weight we give to considerations that do cross our minds (indeed, the force with which considerations strike us can itself vary from time to time, by chance). Our attention may wander at just the wrong—or just the right—moment, or our deliberation may be primed by chance features of our environment, and so on. All these factors are genuinely chancy, and we lack control over them. They thereby make our decisions subject to present luck, regardless of the causal structure of the universe. (2011, 90–91)

Suppose some consideration—some belief, for instance—nondeterministically comes to mind during one's deliberations. Attending to it may well affect one's "relevant motivations." Careful or even cursory attention to such a belief could, for example, affect desire strength. Similarly, one's mood may make salient, or dim from attention, various other considerations that may figure in deliberations about one's choices. So it will not do to characterize the external factors merely as factors that are beyond our control; we have, after all, granted that the coming to mind of some belief, or being beset by some mood, may be beyond our control. I fail to see how this concession would generate a problem of luck in any significant way analogous to the problem of luck that seemingly afflicts libertarianism. I propose instead that to motivate a problem of luck for compatibilism, it would help to conceive of the external factors in contexts in which the agent deliberates about what to do in the following fashion:

Luck Inducing Extraneous Factor (Lief): Some factor F is a luck inducing extraneous factor in deliberative contexts if, roughly, F affects what a mentally healthy agent, S, decides to do by bypassing S's capacities of deliberative control.[16]

Mele (1995, 166–72, 183–84) gives an illuminating summary of the sorts of capacity I have in mind. He says that most normal, healthy human agents have the following capacities in some measure: the capacity to modify the strengths of their desires in the service of their normative judgments, align their emotions with relevant judgments, master motivation that threatens to produce or sustain biased beliefs that would violate their principles of belief acquisition and belief retention, assess rationally their values and principles, identify with their values and principles on the basis of informed critical reflection, and modify their values should they judge that this is called for.

Some may think that the bypassing condition is too strong. Wouldn't it be sufficient that the "difference maker" is some factor that comes to mind, fails in *any* way to exert *any* sort of influence upon the agent's deliberations, what she desires or values, her pertinent beliefs, and so on, but *does* affect the outcome of deliberation: the agent's decision? Well, this might be so, but then the factor does *not* differ from a factor that bypasses the agent's capacities of deliberative control in respects required to motivate the alleged problem of compatibilist luck (and a possible response to this problem). It is a factor regarding which an agent has no control and that does not affect her deliberation although it can have a pronounced influence on the outcome of deliberation. If one prefers a suitably amended conception of a Lief that includes these features, one may conscript this conception.

The story about compatibilist luck to be told may now seem plausible. Perez de Calleja writes:

> There is in Bob*'s deterministic world some fact about the past or the laws which could in principle be adduced in a contrastive explanation of Bob*'s deciding as he does rather than otherwise: the laws of nature and whole history of Bob*'s world, up to the moment he decides to cheat, are compatible only with that decision to cheat (indeed, with that very one, down to all its microphysical details). Similarly, in the case of Bob** (the deterministic counterpart who does the right thing instead), there is a contrastive explanation of his deciding *not* to cheat instead of deciding otherwise (in that very circumstance and with those very reasons and dispositions . . .): the whole history of the world up to that instant plus the deterministic laws of nature are compatible only with Bob**'s deciding not to cheat, exactly as he does. But I cannot see what good it does to Bob* and Bob**, regarding the freedom or rational control they have, that there is a contrastive explanation of their decisions, since these contrastive explanations do not feature causes which distinctively rationalize, or even saliently cause, their deciding as they do rather than otherwise. (2014, 116)

We are to imagine that in each of Bob*'s and Bob**'s deterministic worlds, factors to be held fixed in Perez de Calleja's estimation of what these are—reasons, character traits, relevant motivations (however precisely "relevant" is to be construed), and so forth—and their necessary prerequisites (if any) are indeed fixed, and what makes the difference in the agent's outcome is some Lief. Maybe some neurological factor affects which decision Bob* makes *without* affecting any of the fixed factors. It would then seem that the relevant cross-world difference that Bob* decides to cheat whereas Bob** does not is a matter of luck.

Understanding the problem of compatibilist luck in the manner I have suggested brings us to the proposal in the first paragraph of this section that compatibilists (and, indeed, libertarians) have resources to address *this* problem of luck that cannot be used to deflate the problem of libertarian luck.

A slight detour will be helpful. Libertarians and compatibilists concur that varieties of manipulation can sabotage moral responsibility. Furthermore, they may help themselves to similar explanations of why the particular sort of manipulation usurps responsibility. In Mele's Ann/Beth case, Beth's first postsurgery action—her A-ing—causally derives from engineered in springs of action. One may reasonably judge that Beth is not responsible for doing A, and one may so judge regardless of whether Beth deterministically or indeterministically A-s. The obvious first-pass rationalization of Beth's nonresponsibility is that Beth's A-ing is a result of responsibility-undermining manipulation. A more revealing explanation advanced independently by Mele (1995, 66–72, 183–84) and myself (Haji and Cuypers 2008; Haji 2009a) is that among the proximate causes of Beth's A-ing are springs of action that Beth acquires via processes that completely bypass her capacities of deliberative control.

If this explanation of why manipulation in an Ann/Beth sort of case undercuts responsibility is in the right ballpark, it seems it can easily be co-opted to account for why, for instance, Bob* cheats in scenarios of the following sorts. In *Manipulated Bob**, morally conscientious Bob* is manipulated in a manner analogous to the manner in which Beth is. The covert value engineering results in his deciding to cheat. In *Unlucky Bob**, but for some Lief, some neurological factor that "vetoes" what would have been Bob*'s decision not to cheat without affecting any of the fixed factors—Bob*'s character traits, motivations, deliberation, and so forth—Bob* decides to cheat. In either of these cases, the diagnosis for nonresponsibility may plausibly appeal to bypassing. It is noteworthy that in *Unlucky Bob**, no desires, values, or the like are implanted in Bob*; in this respect, the case differs from *Manipulated Bob**. However, the cases are also relevantly similar. In either, there is some factor (or cluster of factors) with respect to which an agent has no control, it bypasses the agent's capacity of deliberative control, and even if it does not affect the agent's deliberation, it can radically affect the outcome of that deliberation. If such a factor can undermine responsibility in manipulation cases, such as *Manipulated Bob**, compatibilists and libertarians have no reason to deny that this sort of factor may also undermine responsibility in cases like *Unlucky Bob**.

No such appeal would appease the problem of libertarian luck. Liefs play no part whatsoever in generating the luck problem in either the *No Explanation* or the *Pure Luck* versions of this problem.

Some may object that I have simply misunderstood the problem of compatibilist luck. They may support this allegation in this way: (a) Modest libertarians face the problem of present luck because for any undetermined action there is no contrastive explanation of why the agent performed that action rather than another that was causally possible at the time. Perez de Calleja does not affirm that compatibilists encounter *all* the same problems of luck

SOME THOUGHTS ON THE METAPHYSICS OF FREE WILL

that libertarians do, but only *this* one. (b) Any appeal to Liefs will not mitigate the problem of compatibilist luck as, once again, I have misconceived this problem. Perez de Calleja's main idea, it may be elaborated, can be captured in this tale. Suppose Kim is torn about what to do. Should she call in sick or go to work? Suppose the motivational strength of her reasons favoring each decision is about equal. Suppose she decides to call in sick and her decision is a libertarian directly free decision. In a contrast world with the same past and laws as the actual world, she decides to go to work. Given that the actual world and the contrast world (or worlds) do not differ with respect to the relevant past and the laws, it seems there is nothing that can explain why Kim decides one way (rather than another) in the actual world and a different way (rather than another) in the contrast world. It may be proposed that Perez de Calleja contends (or should be understood to contend) that what gives rise to this problem is not indeterminism per se but the fact that Kim is motivationally torn (e.g., 2014, 112, 117). To show this the objector may continue, assume, once again, that Kim is torn about what to do and decides to call in sick, but this time her decision is causally determined. Imagine a different possible deterministic world in which Kim is psychologically identical but some other factors are different and in which Kim decides to go to work. While there *is* a difference in these deterministic worlds that explains the divergence in decisions, there is no *psychological* difference—no difference, for example, in Kim's reason states—that accounts for the divergence. This is enough to show that if there is a worry about luck for libertarians in the prior case involving indeterminism, there is also a worry for compatibilists in the subsequent case involving determinism.[17]

In reply, attending first to (a), neither Mele nor I believe that a concern about *contrastive* explanation is required to motivate the problem of libertarian present luck. One may generate the problem, as the *No Explanation Version* seems to show, simply by asking about relevant detailed reasons explanations of the pertinent decisions in the actual world and the contrast world.[18] Furthermore, limiting attention to the contrast world in which Kim decides to go to work, if there is a problem about an explanation of why she makes the decision that she does in this world, wouldn't there *ipso facto* be a problem about a contrastive explanation too? In that world why did she decide to go to work rather than decide to call in sick? It's worth emphasizing that I have decidedly *not* attributed to Perez de Calleja the view that "compatibilists encounter *all* the same problems of luck that libertarians do." One of my aims is simply to appreciate what Perez de Calleja takes to be a problem of compatibilist luck that she finds analogous to the problem of libertarian present luck.

This brings me to (b). I focus on the charge that Liefs won't appease the problem of compatibilist luck. Perhaps the concern is the following. I claimed above that, regarding features of the contrast world that are supposed to be different from the actual world, "I am unsure what sorts of thing Perez de Calleja has in mind." It may further be claimed that what I say about Liefs suggests that the contrast world includes factors that bypass Kim's agential capacities. But if this is so, then libertarians and compatibilists can easily explain why Kim is responsible in the actual world but not in the possible world where her agential capacities are bypassed. But this is *not* the kind of difference that Perez de Calleja has in mind. After all, she contends that the worlds will be identical with respect to "the salient causes and background conditions which are relevant to [Kim's] deciding one way or the other in the circumstances" (Perez de Calleja 2014, 115). Surely if the (deterministic) contrast world includes features that bypass Kim's agential capacities but no such bypassing occurs in the actual world, then the deterministic worlds are not the same with respect to the salient causes. Take two determined worlds in which Kim makes different decisions and yet she is psychologically identical. While there are physical differences in these worlds that will allow us to explain why Kim makes different decisions in each of the worlds, there will be no explanation of why she so decides in terms of the causes that rationalize Kim's different decisions. That is, we will only be able to explain contrastively the difference by appealing to physical differences in the worlds, and Perez de Calleja suggests that this won't disparage the problem of compatibilist luck.

In response, suppose that a highly sophisticated psychosurgeon, Psyo, specializes in Liefs. Psyo discovers a certain class of Liefs—MLiefs—that work in this way: They do not affect desire strength, what an agent desires, what beliefs an agent has about values, or, more generally, they have no influence on any factors that affect deliberation. Although MLiefs bypass the agent's capacities of deliberative control, they affect the outcome of an agent's deliberations. To illustrate, imagine that in Kim's case the psychological or "deliberative" factors in the actual world and the contrast world (or worlds) leading to the decisions Kim makes in each world are identical. Save for an MLief, MLief-1 (perhaps some neural factor, such as a neural event or process), Kim would have decided to go to work in the actual world. The difference in the decisions Kim makes in the actual and contrast worlds is *not* to be accounted for in terms of the causes that rationalize Kim's different decisions but by appeal to MLiefs. Fully cognizant of this fact, Psyo wants Kim to decide to go to work. He sees to it that MLief-1 does indeed exert its influence on which decision Kim makes: Without his "engineering in" MLief-1 or initiating a process involving this Lief, Kim would have decided to call in sick. Presumably, if compatibilists (and libertarians) of a certain bent are willing to grant that the sort of manipulative engineering in the Ann/Beth case undermines free action or responsibility, they would also grant that the manipulative engineering involving MLief-1 in Kim's case undercuts these things too. Furthermore, their explanation of why manipulation undermines responsibility in the former case would be of the same sort that explains why manipulation undermines responsibility in the latter—a sort of explanation that essentially appeals to Liefs. Notice, in addition, that manipulator Psyo could be left out of the story entirely without affecting its moral. Just as flying through a certain region may, for some reason, turn Beth into the psychological twin of Ann, but for some naturally occurring physical factor—MLief-1—Kim would have decided to call in sick.[19] In sum, regarding Kim's case, compatibilists could propose that there is a vital causal factor, an MLief-1 type of factor, that influences the *outcome* of Kim's deliberations. Its influence completely bypasses Kim's capacities of deliberative (or agential control). So Kim's pertinent decision is not free.

To gather results, in what many will take to be a case featuring manipulation that undermines free action or responsibility, the Ann/Beth case, manipulated Beth is not responsible for her apt postsurgery choices or actions. Refer to the cluster of the desires, values, and so forth covertly implanted in her as "Factor F." Compatibilists and libertarians may agree that it is in virtue of Beth's having no control over how she acquires F—the acquisition of F bypasses her capacities of deliberative control—and the fact that F affects the outcome of her deliberation—the decision she makes—that she is not responsible for her relevant postsurgery decision. Transitioning, next, to cases such as *Unlucky Bob** or cases involving MLiefs, it is open to compatibilists (and libertarians), again, to draw on a similar explanation for nonresponsibility in these cases: The affected agents have no control regarding the pertinent Liefs, and although these Liefs do not affect their deliberation, they decidedly affect the outcome of their deliberation. But then if Factor F undermines responsibility, Leifs (or MLiefs) should do so as well.

I end with this final remark. The bypassing view may not curry favor among some compatibilists (or libertarians for that matter).

But compatibilists (and libertarians) who believe that manipulation of the sort featured in the Ann/Beth case and in Psyo's scenario undermines free action or responsibility will respond with the appropriate tools in their compatibilist (or libertarian) arsenals. These tools, whatever they are, that speak to manipulation, presumably won't help them to resolve the problem of libertarian present luck (if this is indeed a problem).

I've attempted to render plausible the view that the problem of compatibilist luck is not new in that it is an instance of a more general sort of problem to which both compatibilists and libertarians have attended. In broad strokes, the sort of problem is this. There are various factors regarding which an agent has no control and, generally, of which the agent is unaware that may undermine the responsibility-level freedom for an action she performs or usurp responsibility for that action. For instance, in various stories of manipulation against which compatibilist and libertarian contenders are (partially) tested, we find such factors. Causal theorists of action who claim that an event is an action only if it is nondeviantly caused by appropriate springs of action inherit the burden of distinguishing genuine action-producing causal chains from deviant motion-producing chains. One may roughly regard the latter sorts of chain as being infected by the kinds of factor in question—Liefs. Proposed solutions to these sorts of concern are *not* solutions to the problem of libertarian luck because this latter problem is different altogether. The problem of libertarian luck has essentially nothing to do with Liefs but much to do with the libertarian thesis that to perform directly free actions, the future must be open in a certain way: Given exactly the same past and the laws up to the time of action, we can make actual several different pathways that are extensions of the fixed past. Standard compatibilists have resources to respond to the problem of compatibilist luck that typical libertarians cannot exploit to respond to the problem of libertarian luck.

7.5 OUR MORALLY MESSY WORLD

I conclude on this note. Not being grandiose but limited, the skepticism concerning the scope of obligation and blameworthiness I have argued for shows that our world is morally messy in the following respect. Oftentimes (or maybe I should be more circumspect and say that it appears that oftentimes), we will not act in a morally upright fashion—we won't do anything it is morally obligatory or permissible for us to do—nor will we do what it is impermissible for us to do; and oftentimes, we will not be to blame for what we do. But if we do have access to alternatives on some occasions, barring other barriers, this will open up room for obligation and blameworthiness on those occasions (assuming incompatibilism regarding obligation or blameworthiness is off the table). It is unclear how we would go about figuring out whether in some instance some person did not in fact do something that it was morally impermissible for her to do. This would be a problem not merely because we would fail to, or it would be difficult for us, to know what sort of world she was bringing about in so acting. It would be a problem also because we would not know whether she did not have alternatives on the pertinent occasion or we would not know that she did no moral wrong because of the changeability of obligations over time. If the objective view is true, we would then be burdened with the unhappy consequence that frequently (if not always) we would remain in the dark about whether such persons were in fact morally blameworthy for much of their behavior.

I suppose if we were concerned with whether some person acted in the belief that she was doing wrong, irrespective of whether she did in fact do wrong, we would proceed in the usual sorts of way in which we proceed, whatever these sorts of way are, to uncover what her relevant beliefs were. Again, however, if it were be become common knowledge that more often than not, we do not do anything it is morally obligatory, permissible, or impermissible for us to do, then, presumably, people would infrequently act in the belief that they were doing wrong. This, in turn, *would* constrain the range of blameworthiness.

How we would negotiate our way through this moral mess—how, for example, we would go about treating people who have violated the law, or react to people who have done what it is seemingly impermissible for them to do, or what agenda we would set for the moral education of our children—invites careful thought.

NOTES

1. Fischer and Ravizza develop and defend a mechanism-based account in their 1998.
2. See Mele 2006, 82–87, for an insightful discussion on different versions of PAP.
3. I ignore complex subjective views according to which one is morally blameworthy for something only if one acts in light of the nonculpable belief that one is doing something it is morally amiss for one to do because, as I have declared, I do not have an analysis of moral amissness.
4. Such accounts have been defended or discussed by Dennett 1978; Fischer 1995; 2011b; Mele 1995; Kane 1996; 1999a; 1999b; Clarke 2000; 2003; 2011.
5. A recent defense of this sort of view is to be found in Kane 1996.
6. Endorsers of teleological and noncausal accounts of action won't accept the view that freedom—or responsibility-level control is essentially causal.
7. On breakdowns of agency, see Mele 2006, 60–61, 125–29; and 2008, 268–71.
8. One may attempt to argue that there can be no worlds in which this belief fails to come to Peg's mind at t, and she still decides at t to B. I have no idea what this argument would be.
9. Mele develops a solution to this problem in his 2006, 105–36.
10. In his 2013b, Mele formulates the problem of (present) luck independently of appealing to any concerns of explanation.
11. Chris Franklin (2014) has attempted to circumvent the luck problem by enriching modest libertarianism with a mental item that can play the functional role of a self-determining agent. I discuss his views in a forthcoming paper (Haji n.d.).
12. To be fair to Fischer, in an earlier paper Fischer says that the machine example "does not vindicate indeterminism in a context in which the agent has . . .

moral-responsibility conferring control in both the actual sequence and the alternative sequence" (2011b, 58).

13. Teleological theorists may deny that these actions are strange-actions.
14. Griffith proposes that agent-causal views of free action circumvent the luck objection. I have doubts about whether this is so (Haji 2012a, 41–43).
15. Here, I set aside noncausal or teleological accounts of action.
16. Needless to say, I assume that Liefs are not susceptible to our influencing or shaping them by, for instance, our past actions.
17. I thank an anonymous referee for this objection.
18. See note 8.
19. I need take no stance here on whether (i) Liefs (of any sort) always influence what actions an agent performs, or (ii) it's possible for agents to shape Liefs or exert control on how Liefs affect outcomes.

BIBLIOGRAPHY

Almeida, Michael and Mark Bernstein. 2011. "Rollbacks, Endorsements, and Indeterminism." In Robert Kane, ed., *The Oxford Handbook of Free Will Second Edition*. New York: Oxford University Press, 484–95.

Anscombe, G. E. M. 1958. "Modern Moral Philosophy." *Philosophy* 33: 1–19.

Aristotle. 1941. *Nicomachean Ethics*. In Richard McKeon, ed., *The Basic Works of Aristotle*. New York: Random House.

Arpaly, Nomy. 2006. *Merit, Meaning, and Human Bondage: An Essay on Free Will*. Princeton, NJ: Princeton University Press.

Audi, Robert. 1997. "Acting for Reasons." In A. Mele, ed., *The Philosophy of Action*. Oxford: Oxford University Press, 75–105.

Berofsky, Bernard. 2000. "Ultimate Responsibility in a Deterministic World." *Philosophy and Phenomenological Research* 60: 135–40.

Bishop, J. 1989. *Natural Agency*. Cambridge: Cambridge University Press.

Brand, Miles. 1984. *Intending and Acting*. Cambridge, MA: MIT Press.

Brandt, R. 1959. *Ethical Theory*. Englewood Cliffs, NJ: Prentice Hall.

Callan, E. and White, J. 2003. "Liberalism and Communitarianism." In N. Blake, P. Smeyers, R. Smith, and P. Standish, eds., *The Blackwell Guide to the Philosophy of Education*. Oxford: Blackwell, 95–109.

Campbell, J. K. 2011. *Free Will*. Oxford: Polity Press.

Camus, Albert. 1946. *The Stranger*. Translated by Stuart Gilbert. New York: Knopf.

Capes, Justin. 2012. "Blameworthiness without Wrongdoing." *Pacific Philosophical Quarterly* 93: 417–37.

Castaneda, Hector-Neri. 1968. "A Problem for Utilitarianism." *Analysis* 28: 141–42.

Chisholm, Roderick. 1963. "Supererogation and Offence: A Conceptual Scheme for Ethics." *Ratio* 5: 1–14.

Clarke, Randolph. 2000. "Modest Libertarianism." *Philosophical Perspectives* 14: 21–45.

Clarke, Randolph. 2003. *Libertarian Accounts of Free Will*. New York: Oxford University Press.

Clarke, Randolph. 2011. "Alternatives for Libertarians." In Robert Kane, ed., *The Oxford Handbook of Free Will Second Edition*. New York: Oxford University Press, 329–48.

Clarke, Randolph. 2014. *Omissions*. New York: Oxford University Press.

Clarke, Randolph. 2014. "Agency and Incompatibilism." *Res Philosophica* 91: 519–25.

Copp, David. 1997. "Defending the Principle of Alternate Possibilities: Blameworthiness and Moral Responsibility." *Nous* 31: 441–56.

Copp, David. 2003. " 'Ought' Implies 'Can', Blameworthiness, and the Principle of Alternative Possibilities." In David Widerker and Michael McKenna eds., *Moral Responsibility and Alternative Possibilities: Essays on the Importance of Alternative Possibilities*. Aldershot, UK: Ashgate Press, 265–99.

Davidson, David. 1963. "Action, Reasons, and Causes." *Journal of Philosophy* 60: 685–700.

Dennett, Daniel. 1978. "On Giving Libertarians What They Say They Want." In D. Dennett, *Brainstorms*. Montgomery, VT: Bradford Books, 286–99.

Driver, Julia. 1992. "The Suberogatory." *Australasian Journal of Philosophy* 70: 286–95.

Ekstrom, Laura Waddell. 2000. *Free Will: A Philosophical Study*. Boulder, CO: Westview Press.

Ekstrom, Laura W. 2011. "Free Will is not a Mystery." In Robert Kane, ed., *The Oxford Handbook of Free Will Second Edition*. New York: Oxford University Press, 366–80.

Fara, M. 2008. "Masked Abilities and Compatibilism." *Mind* 117: 843–65.

Feldman, Fred. 1978. *Introductory Ethics*. Englewood Cliffs, NJ: Prentice Hall.

Feldman, Fred. 1986. *Doing the Best We Can*. Dordrecht: D. Reidel Publishing Company.

Feldman, Fred. 1990. "A Simpler Solution to the Paradoxes of Deontic Logic." *Philosophical Perspectives* 4: 309–41.

Feldman, Fred. 1992. *Confrontations with the Reaper: A Philosophical Study of the Nature and Value of Death*. New York: Oxford University Press.

Feldman, Fred. 1997. *Utilitarianism, Hedonism, and Desert*. Cambridge: Cambridge University Press.

Fields, Lloyd. 1994. "Moral Beliefs and Blameworthiness." *Philosophy* 69: 397–415.

Fischer, John M. 1995. "Libertarianism and Avoidability: A Reply to Widerker." *Faith and Philosophy* 12: 11–25.

Fischer, John M. 2006. *My Way: Essays on Moral Responsibility*. New York: Oxford University Press.

Fischer, John M. 2010. "The Frankfurt Cases: The Moral of the Stories." *The Philosophical Review* 119: 315–36.

Fischer, John M. 2011a. "Frankfurt-Type Examples and Semi-Compatibilism." In Robert Kane, ed., *The Oxford Handbook of Free Will, Second Edition.* New York: Oxford University Press, 243–65.

Fischer, John M. 2011b. "Indeterminism and Control: An Approach to the Problem of Luck." In Michael Freeman, ed., *Law and Neuroscience.* Oxford: Oxford University Press, 41–60.

Fischer, John M. 2013. "The Frankfurt-Style Cases: Philosophical Lightening Rods." In I. Haji and J. Caouette, eds. *Free Will and Moral Responsibility.* Newcastle upon Tyne: Cambridge Scholars Publishing, 43–57.

Fischer, John M. 2014. "Toward a Solution to the Luck Problem." In David Palmer, ed., *Libertarian Free Will.* New York: Oxford University Press, 52–68.

Fischer, John M., and M. Ravizza. 1992a. "Responsibility, Freedom, and Reason. Critical Review of *Freedom Within Reason* by Susan Wolf." *Ethics* 102: 368–89.

Fischer, John M., and Ravizza, Mark. 1992b. "When the Will is Free." *Philosophical Perspectives* 6: 423–51.

Fischer, John M., and M. Ravizza. 1998. *Responsibility and Control: A Theory of Moral Responsibility.* Cambridge: Cambridge University Press.

Foot, Philippa. 1978. "Are Moral Considerations Overriding?" In Philippa Foot, *Virtues and Vices.* Oxford: Blackwell.

Frankfurt, Harry. 1969. "Alternate Possibilities and Moral Responsibility." *The Journal of Philosophy* 66: 829–39.

Frankfurt, Harry. 1971. "Freedom of the Will and the Concept of a Person." *Journal of Philosophy* 68: 5–20.

Frankfurt, Harry. 1994. "Autonomy, Necessity, and Love." In Hans Friedrich Fulda and Rolf-Peter Horstmann, eds., *Vernunftbegriffe in der Moderne.* Stuttgat: Klett-Cotta, 433–47. Reprinted in cited from Frankfurt 1999, 129–41.

Frankfurt, Harry. 1999. *Necessity, Volition, and Love.* Cambridge: Cambridge University Press.

Franklin, Chris. 2011. "Farewell to the Luck (and Mind) Argument." *Philosophical Studies* 156: 199–230.

Franklin, Chris. 2014. "Event-causal Libertarianism, Functional Reduction, and the Disappearing Agent Argument." *Philosophical Studies* 170: 413–32.

Ginet, Carl. 1966. "Might We Have No Choice?" In Keith Lehrer, ed., *Freedom and Determinism.* New York: Random House, 87–104.

Ginet, Carl. 1990. *On Action.* Cambridge: Cambridge University Press.

Ginet, Carl. 1996. "In Defense of the Principle of Alternative Possibilities: Why I Don't Find Frankfurt's Argument Convincing." *Philosophical Perspectives* 10: 403–17.

Ginet, Carl. 2003. "Libertarianism." In M. J. Loux and D. W. Zimmerman, eds., *The Oxford Handbook of Metaphysics.* New York: Oxford University Press, 587–612.

Goetz, Stewart. 1998. "A Noncausal Theory of Agency." *Philosophy and Phenomenological Research* 49: 303–16.

Graham, Peter. 2011. "'Ought' and Ability." *Philosophical Review* 120: 337–82.

Griffith, Meghan. 2010. "Why Agent-Caused Actions are Not Lucky." *American Philosophical Quarterly* 47: 43–56.

Haji, Ishtiyaque. 1993. "Alternative Possibilities, Moral Obligation, and Moral Responsibility." *Philosophical Papers* 22: 41–50.

Haji, Ishtiyaque. 1998. *Moral Appraisability: Puzzles, Proposals, and Perplexities.* New York: Oxford University Press.

Haji, Ishtiyaque. 2000a. "Control Requirements for Moral Appraisals: An Asymmetry." *Journal of Ethics* 4: 351–56.

Haji, Ishtiyaque. 2000b. "Indeterminism, Explanation, and Luck." *Journal of Ethics* 4: 211–35.

Haji, Ishtiyaque. 2002. *Deontic Morality and Control.* Cambridge: Cambridge University Press.

Haji, Ishtiyaque. 2009a. *Incompatibilism's Allure: Principal Arguments for Incompatibilism.* Peterbrough, ONT: Broadview Press.

Haji, Ishtiyaque. 2009b. "A Conundrum Concerning Creation." *Sophia* 48: 1–14.

Haji, Ishtiyaque. 2012a. *Reason's Debt to Freedom.* New York: Oxford University Press.

Haji, Ishtiyaque. 2012b. "Modest Libertarianism and Practical Reason." *Philosophical Issues* 22: 201–16.

Haji, Ishtiyaque. 2012c. "Reason, Responsibility, and Free Will: Reply to My Critics." *Journal of Ethics* 16: 175–209.

Haji, Ishtiyaque. n.d. "Luck's Extended Reach." *Journal of Ethics.*

Haji, Ishtiyaque and Stefaan Cuypers. 2008. *Moral Responsibility, Authenticity, and Education.* New York: Routledge.

Haji, Ishtiyaque and Stefaan Cuypers. 2011. "Ultimate Educational Aims, "Overridingness, and Personal Well-Being." *Studies in Philosophy and Education* 30: 543–56.

Harman, G. 1977. *The Nature of Morality.* Princeton, NJ: Princeton University Press.

Hebert, Ryan. n.d. *Teleologism Full Stop: A General Theory of Ability, Agency, Know How, Obligation, and Justification.* PhD diss.: University of Calgary.

Heyd, David. 1982. *Supererogation.* Cambridge: Cambridge University Press.

Hobart, R. E. 1934. "Free Will as Involving Indeterminism and Inconceivable Without It." *Mind* 43: 1–27.

Hodgson, David. 2005. "Responsibility and Good Reasons." *Ohio State Journal of Criminal Law* 2.2: 471–83.

Humberstone, L. 1971. "Two Sorts of 'Oughts." *Analysis* 32: 8–11.

Hume, David. [1739] 2000. *A Treatise of Human Nature.* Edited by D. F. Norton & M. J. Norton, New York: Oxford University Press.

Hunt, David. 1999. "On Augustine's Way Out." *Faith and Philosophy* 16: 3–26.

Hunt, David. 2000. "Moral Responsibility and Unavoidable Action." *Philosophical Studies* 97: 195–227.

Hunt, David. 2005. "Moral Responsibility and Buffered Alternatives." *Midwest Studies in Philosophy* 29: 126–45.

Jackson, Frank. 1991. "Decision-Theoretic Consequentialism and the Nearest and Dearest Objection." *Ethics* 101: 461–82.

Kane, Robert. 1985. *Free Will and Values*. Albany: State University of New York Press.

Kane, Robert. 1996. *The Significance of Free Will*. New York: Oxford University Press.

Kane, Robert. 1999a. "On Free Will, Responsibility, and Indeterminism: Responses to Clarke, Haji, and Mele." *Philosophical Explorations* 2: 105–21.

Kane, Robert. 1999b. "Responsibility, Luck, and Chance: Reflections on Free will and Indeterminism." *Journal of Philosophy* 96: 217–40.

Kane, Robert. 2005. *A Contemporary Introduction to Free Will*. New York: Oxford University Press.

Kane, Robert. 2011. "Rethinking Free Will: New Perspectives on an Ancient Problem." In Robert Kane, ed., *The Oxford Handbook of Free Will Second Edition*. New York: Oxford University Press, 381–404.

Kane, Robert. 2013. "Frankfurt-Style Examples and Self-forming Actions." In I. Haji and J. Caouette, eds. *Free Will and Moral Responsibility*. Newcastle upon Tyne: Cambridge Scholars Publishing, 58–73.

Kane, Robert. 2014. "New Arguments in Debates on Libertarian Free Will: Responses to Contributors." In D. Palmer, ed. *Libertarian Free Will*. New York: Oxford University Press, 179–214.

Lehrer, Keith. 1968. "'Cans' Without 'If's.'" *Analysis* 29: 29–32.

Levy, Neil. 2011. *Hard Luck*. Oxford: Oxford University Press.

Locke, John. 1975 [1690]. *An Essay Concerning Human Understanding*. Ed., Peter H. Nidditch. Oxford: Oxford University Press.

Manne, K. 2011. *Not by Reasons Alone*. PhD diss., MIT.

Marples, Roger, ed. 1999. *The Aims of Education*. London: Routledge.

McCann, Hugh J. 1998. *The Works of Agency: On Human Action, Will, and Freedom*. Ithaca, NY: Cornell University Press.

McKenna, Michael. 2012. *Conversation and Responsibility*. New York: Oxford University Press.

McNamara, Paul. 1996a. "Making Room for Going Beyond the Call." *Mind* 105: 415–50

McNamara, Paul. 1996b. "Must I do What I Ought? (or Will the Least I Can Do Do?)." In M. Brown and J. Carmo, eds., *Deontic Logic, Agency, and Normative Systems*. New York: Springer, 154–73.

McNamara, Paul. 2008. "Praise, Blame, Obligation, and Beyond: Toward a Framework for the Classical Conception of Supererogation and Kin." In Ron van der Meyden and Leendert van der Torre, eds., *Deontic Logic in Computer Science*. Berlin: Springer Verlag, 233–47.

McNamara, Paul. 2011a. "Supererogation, Inside and Out: Toward an Adequate Scheme for Common-sense Morality." In Mark Timmons, ed., *Oxford Studies in Normative Ethics, Volume 1*. New York: Oxford University Press, 202–35.

McNamara, Paul. 2011b. "Praise, Blame, Obligation, and DWE: Toward a Comprehensive Framework for the Classical Conception of Supererogation and Kin." *Journal of Applied Logic* 9: 153–70.

Melden, A. 1961. *Free Action*. London: Routledge & Kegan Paul.

Mele, Alfred. 1992. *Springs of Action*. New York: Oxford University Press.

Mele, Alfred. 1995. *Autonomous Agents: From Self-Control to Autonomy*. New York: Oxford University Press.

Mele, Alfred. 1996. "Soft Libertarianism and Frankfurt-Style Scenarios." *Philosophical Topics* 24: 123–41.

Mele, Alfred. 1999a. "Ultimate Responsibility and Dumb Luck." *Social Philosophy and Policy* 16: 274–93.

Mele, Alfred. 1999b. "Kane, Luck, and the Significance of Free Will." *Philosophical Explorations* 2: 96–104.

Mele, Alfred. 2003a. *Motivation and Agency*. New York: Oxford University Press.

Mele, Alfred. 2003b. "Agents' Abilities." *Nous* 37: 447–70.

Mele, Alfred. 2006. *Free Will and Luck*. New York: Oxford University Press.

Mele, Alfred. 2007. "*Free Will and Luck*: Reply to Critics." *Philosophical Explorations* 10: 195–210.

Mele, Alfred. 2008. "A Libertarian View of Akratic Action." In T. Hoffman, ed., *Weakness of Will from Plato to the Present*. Washington, DC: Catholic University of America Press, 252–75.

Mele, Alfred. 2013a. "Is What You Decide Ever up to You?" In I. Haji and J. Caouette eds. *Free Will and Moral Responsibility*. Newcastle upon Tyne: Cambridge Scholars Publishing, 74–97.

Mele, Alfred. 2013b. "Moral Responsibility and the Continuation Problem." *Philosophical Studies* 162: 237–55.

Mele, Alfred and Robb, David. 1998. "Rescuing Frankfurt-Style Cases." *Philosophical Review* 107: 97–112.

Mele, Alfred and Robb, David. 2003. "Bbs, Magnets and Seesaws: The Metaphysics of Frankfurt-Style Cases." In Michael McKenna and David Widerker, eds., *Freedom, Responsibility, and Agency: Essays on the Importance of Alternative Possibilities*. Aldershot, UK: Ashgate Press, 127–38.

Mellema, Gregory. 1991. *Beyond the Call of Duty: Supererogation, Obligation, and Offence*. Albany: State University of New York Press.

Mill, John Stuart. (1863) 1989. *Utilitarianism*. New York: Macmillan.

Moore, G. E. 1912. *Ethics*. Edited by William H. Shaw. Oxford: Oxford University Press.

Nagel, Thomas. 1976. "Moral Luck." *Proceedings of the Aristotelian Society* Supplementary Volume 50: 137–51.

Nagel, Thomas. 1986. *The View from Nowhere*. New York: Oxford University Press.

Nelkin, Dana. 2007. "Good Luck to Libertarians: Reflections on Al Mele's *Free Will and Luck*." *Philosophical Explorations* 10: 173–84.

Nelkin, Dana K. 2008. "Responsibility and Rational Abilities: Defending An Asymmetrical View." *Pacific Philosophical Quarterly* 89: 497–515.

Nelkin, Dana K. 2011. *Making Sense of Freedom and Responsibility*. New York: Oxford University Press.

Noddings, Nel and Slote, Michael. 2003. "Changing Notions of the Moral and of Moral Education." In N. Blake, P. Smeyers, R. Smith and P. Standish, eds., *The Blackwell Guide to the Philosophy of Education*. Oxford: Blackwell, 341–55.

Norcross, Alastair. 2006. "Reasons without Demands: Rethinking Rightness." In J. Drier, ed., *Blackwell Contemporary Debates in Moral Theory*. Oxford: Blackwell, 6–38.

O'Connor, Timothy. 2000. *Persons and Causes*. New York: Oxford University Press.

O'Connor, Timothy. 2007. "Is it all Just a Matter of Luck?" *Philosophical Explorations* 10: 157–61.

O'Connor, Timothy. 2011. "Agent-Causal Theories of Freedom." In Robert Kane, ed., *The Oxford Handbook of Free Will Second Edition*. New York: Oxford University Press, 309–28.

Palmer, David. n.d. "Frankfurt Cases and the Dilemma Defense: Haji's New Counterexample."

Palmer, David. 2013. "Capes on the W-Defense." *Philosophia* 41: 555–66.

Parfit, Derek. 1984. *Reasons and Persons*. Oxford: Clarendon Press.

Pereboom, Derk. 1995. "*Determinism* al Dente." *Nous* 29: 21–45.

Pereboom, Derk. 2001. *Living Without Free Will*. Cambridge: Cambridge University Press.

Pereboom, Derk. 2003. "Source Incompatibilism and Alternative Possibilities." In Michael McKenna and David Widerker, eds., *Freedom, Responsibility, and Agency: Essays on the Importance of Alternative Possibilities*. Aldershot, UK: Ashgate Press, 185–99.

Pereboom, Derk. 2013. "Book Review of *Reason's Debt to Freedom*." http://ndpr.nd.edu/news/38268-reason-s-debt-to-freedom-normative-appraisals-reasons-and-free-will/.

Pereboom, Derk. 2014. *Free Will, Agency, and Meaning in Life*. New York: Oxford University Press.

Perez de Calleja, Mirja. 2014. "Cross-World Luck at the Time of Decision is a Problem for Compatibilists as Well." *Philosophical Explorations* 17: 112–25.

Persson, Ingmar. 2008. "A Consequentialist Distinction between What We Ought to Do and Ought to Try." *Utilitas* 20: 348–55.

Persson, Ingmar. 2013. *From Morality to the End of Reason: An Essay on Rights, Reasons, and Responsibility*. Oxford: Oxford University Press.

Rosen, Gideon. 2003. "Culpability and Ignorance." *Proceedings of the Aristotelian Society* 103: 61–84.

Rosen, Gideon. 2004. "Skepticism about Moral Responsibility." *Philosophical Perspectives* 18: 295–313.

Ross, William David. 1930. *The Right and the Good*. New York: Oxford University Press.

Sartre, Jean-Paul. 1953. *Being and Nothingness*. Translated by Hazel E. Barnes. New York: Washington Square Press.

Scanlon, Thomas M. 2008. *Moral Dimensions*. Princeton, NJ: Princeton University Press.

Schlick, Moritz. 1939. "When is a Man Responsible?" In *Problems of Ethics*. Translated by D. Rynin. New York: Prentice Hall, 143–56.

Schroeder, M. 2007. "Reasons and Agent-Neutrality." *Philosophical Studies* 135: 279–306.

Schroeder, M. 2011. "Ought, Agents, and Actions." *Philosophical Review* 120: 1–41.

Schueler, G. F. 2003. *Reasons and Purposes: Human Rationality and the Teleological Explanation of Action*. Oxford: Clarendon Press.

Sehon, Scott. 1994. "Teleology and the Nature of Mental States." *American Philosophical Quarterly* 31: 63–72.

Sehon, Scott, 1997. "Deviant Causal Chains and the Irreducibility of Teleological Explanation." *Pacific Philosophical Quarterly* 78: 195–213.

Sehon, Scott, 2005. *Teleological Realism: Mind, Agency, and Explanation*. Cambridge, MA: MIT Press.

Sehon, Scott. n.d. *Free Will and Action Explanation: A Non-causal, Compatibilist Account*. Oxford: Oxford University Press.

Sher, George. 2006. *In Praise of Blame*. Oxford: Oxford University Press.

Siegel, Harvey. 1988. *Educating Reason. Rationality, Critical Thinking, and Education*. New York: Routledge.

Siegel, H. 1997. *Rationality Redeemed? Further Dialogues on an Educational Ideal*. New York: Routledge.

Slote, Michael. 1983. "Admirable Immorality." In Michael Slote, ed., *Goods and Virtues*. Oxford: Clarendon Press, 77–107.

Smith, Angela. 2007. "On Being Responsible and Holding Responsible." *Journal of Ethics* 11: 465–84.

Smith, Angela M. 2008. "Control, Responsibility, and Moral Assessment." *Philosophical Studies* 138: 367–92.

Smith, Holly. 1991. "Varieties of Moral Worth and Moral Credit." *Ethics* 101: 279–303.

Standish, Paul. 1999. "Education Without Aims?" In R. Marples, ed., *The Aims of Education*. London: Routledge, 35–49.

Steward, Helen. 2012. *A Metaphysics for Freedom*. Oxford: Oxford University Press.

Stocker, Michael. 1990. *Plural and Conflicting Values*. Oxford: Clarendon Press.

Strawson, Galen. 1986. *Freedom and Belief*. Oxford: Oxford University Press.

Strawson, Galen. 1994. "The Impossibility of Moral Responsibility." *Philosophical Studies* 75: 5–24.

Strawson, Peter. 1962. "Freedom and Resentment." *Proceedings of the British Academy* 48: 1–25. Reprinted in and cited from Watson 1982, 59–80.

Streumer, Bart. 2007. "Reasons and Impossibility." *Philosophical Studies* 136: 351–84.

Streumer, Bart. 2010. "Reasons, Impossibility, and Efficient Steps: Reply to Heuer." *Philosophical Studies* 151: 78–86.

Thomson, J. J. 1991. "Self-Defense." *Philosophy and Public Affairs* 20: 283–310.

Tognazzini, Neal. 2011. "Owning Up to Luck." *Social Theory and Practice* 37: 95–112.

Urmson, J. O. 1958. "Saints and Heroes." In A. I. Meldin, ed., *Essays in Moral Philosophy*. Seattle: University of Washington Press, 198–216.

Van Inwagen, Peter. 1983. *An Essay on Free Will*. Oxford: Clarendon Press.

Van Inwagen, Peter. 1989. "When Is the Will Free?" *Philosophical Perspectives* 3: 399–422.

Van Inwagen, Peter. 2000. "Free Will Remains a Mystery." *Philosophical Perspectives* 14: 1–19.

Van Inwagen, Peter. 2008. "How to Think about the Problem of Free Will." *Journal of Ethics* 12: 327–41.

Van Inwagen, Peter. 2011. "A Promising Argument." In Robert Kane, ed., *The Oxford Handbook of Free Will Second Edition*. New York: Oxford University Press, 475–83.

Vargas, Manuel. 2013. *Building Better Beings*. New York: Oxford University Press.

Velleman, J. D. 1992. "What Happens When Someone Acts?" *Mind* 101: 461–81.

Vihvelin, Kadri. 2004. "Free Will Demystified: A Dispositional Account." *Philosophical Topics* 32: 427–50.

Vihvelin, Kadri. 2013. *Causes, Laws, and Free Will*. New York: Oxford University Press.

Vranas, Peter B. M. 2007. "I Ought, Therefore I Can." *Philosophical Studies* 136: 167–216.

Waller, Bruce. 1988. "Free Will Gone Out of Control." *Behaviorism* 16: 149–67.

Waller, Bruce. 2011. *Against Moral Responsibility*. Cambridge, MA: MIT Press.

Watson, Gary. 1975. "Free Agency." *Journal of Philosophy* 72: 205–20.

White, J. 1982. *The Aims of Education Restated*. London: Routledge and Kegan Paul.

White, J. 1990. *Education and the Good Life. Beyond the National Curriculum.* London: Kogan Page.

White, J. 1999. "In Defence of Liberal Aims in Education." In R. Marples, ed., *The Aims of Education.* London: Routledge, 185–200.

Widerker, David. 1991. "Frankfurt on 'Ought Implies Can' and Alternative Possibilities." *Analysis* 51: 222–24.

Widerker, David. 1995. "Libertarianism and Frankfurt's Attack on the Principle of Alternative Possibilities." *Philosophical Review* 104: 247–61.

Widerker, David. 2000. "Frankfurt's Attack on the Principle of Alternative Possibilities: A Further Look." *Philosophical Perspectives* 14: 181–201.

Widerker, David. 2003. "Blameworthiness and Frankfurt's Argument against the Principle of Alternative Possibilities." In David Widerker and Michael McKenna eds., *Freedom, Responsibility, and Agency: Essays on the Importance of Alternative Possibilities.* Aldershot, UK: Ashgate Press, 53–73.

Widerker, David. 2005. "Blameworthiness, Non-Robust Alternatives and the Principle of Alternative Expectations." *Midwest Studies in Philosophy* 29: 292–306.

Widerker, David. 2006. "Libertarianism and the Philosophical Significance of Frankfurt Scenarios." *Journal of Philosophy* 103: 163–87.

Widerker, David. 2009. "A Defense of Frankfurt-Friendly Libertarianism." *Philosophical Explorations* 12: 87–108.

Wiggins, David. 1973. "Towards a Reasonable Libertarianism." In T. Honderich, ed., *Essays on Freedom of Action.* Boston: Routledge & Kegan Paul.

Williams, Bernard. 1973. *Problems of the Self.* Cambridge: Cambridge University Press.

Williams, Bernard. 1976. "Persons, Character and Morality." In A. Oksenberg Rorty, ed., *The Identities of Persons.* Berkeley: University of California Press, 197–215.

Williams, Bernard. 1981. "Moral Luck." In *Moral Luck.* Cambridge: Cambridge University Press, 20–39.

Wilson, George. 1989. *The Intentionality of Human Action.* Redwood City, CA: Stanford University Press.

Winch Christopher. 1999. "Autonomy as an Educational Aim." In R. Marples, ed., *The Aims of Education.* London: Routledge, 74–84.

Winch, Christopher. 2002. "Strong Autonomy and Education." *Educational Theory* 52: 27–41.

Wolf, Susan. 1980. "Asymmetrical Freedom." *Journal of Philosophy* 77: 151–66.

Wolf, Susan. 1982. "Moral Saints." *Journal of Philosophy* 19: 419–39.

Wolf, Susan. 1990. *Freedom Within Reason.* New York: Oxford University Press.

Zimmerman, Michael J. 1987. "Luck and Moral Responsibility." *Ethics* 97: 374–86.

Zimmerman, Michael J. 1988. *An Essay on Moral Responsibility.* Totowa, NJ: Rowman & Littlefield.

Zimmerman, Michael J. 1990. "The Range of Options." *American Philosophical Quarterly* 27: 345–55.

Zimmerman, Michael J. 1993. "A Plea For Ambivalence." *Metaphilosophy* 24: 382–89.

Zimmerman, Michael J. 1996. *The Concept of Moral Obligation.* Cambridge: Cambridge University Press.

Zimmerman, Michael J. 1997. "A Plea for Accuses." *American Philosophical Quarterly* 34: 229–43.

Zimmerman, Michael J. 2002. "Taking Luck Seriously." *Journal of Philosophy* 99: 553–76.

Zimmerman, Michael J. 2006. "Moral Luck: A Partial Map." *Canadian Journal of Philosophy* 36: 585–608.

Zimmerman, Michael J. 2008. *Living With Uncertainty.* Cambridge: Cambridge University Press.

Zimmerman, Michael J. 2011. *The Immorality of Punishment.* Peterborough, ONT: Broadview Press.

Zimmerman, Michael J. 2014. *Ignorance and Moral Obligation.* Oxford: Oxford University Press.

INDEX

Ability
Intentional (*I-ability*), 278
Simple (*S-ability*), 278
Act-focused appraisals, 90, 104, 165, 202,
  257, 304
Acting from duty, 196–98
Agent-focused appraisals, 90, 91, 165, 177,
  257, 318
Akratic action
  and present luck, 285–86
Almeida, M., 236n15
Alternative possibilities
  requirement for impermissibility, 26–27
  requirement for obligatoriness, 27
  requirement for permissibility, 27–28
  strong, 34, 218, 321, 324
  weak, 34, 321, 322, 323, 324
Amoral, normative status, 27–28, 32,
  33, 61, 91, 97, 104, 109, 165, 193,
  201, 236n11
Ann/Beth scenario, 304, 331–32, 335,
  336, 337
Anscombe, G.E.M., 240
Arational, normative status, 32, 109, 113,
  229, 230
Argument From Limitation, 96
Aristotle, 93, 242, 260n6
Arpaly, N., 156
Asymmetry thesis, 46, 48, 49, 52–55
Audi, R., 127n9

Autonomy, 242, 248, 249, 250, 251, 252,
  260n7, 261n8
Axiological impermissibility, 121
  principle of, 125

Bernstein, M., 236n15
Berofsky, B., 236n14
Bishop, J., 127n9
Blameworthiness, 1
  and belief in impermissibility, 9, 156–64
  complex subjective view, 158–164, 183,
    280, 339n3
  and impermissibility, 9, 82–92, 130–31, 181
  ledger view, 86–87, 171
  nonmoral varieties, 231–34
  objective view, 156–57, 166–67,
    182–83, 219, 221, 236n1, 236n7, 338
  for permissible options, 82–86
  Scanlon's account, 172–73
  simple subjective view, 157–58
  Strawsonian view, 86, 161, 170
Blameworthiness/Impermissibility, 50, 54,
  67, 68, 85, 156, 166, 205–206, 230
  Capes's objection to, 166–70
  considerations against, 82–91,
    205–207, 183
  and *Kant's Law*, 50–51, 54–57
  and scope of responsibility, 8–9, 191–92
Brand, M., 127n9
Brandt, R., 162, 163

and suberogation, 91
and Vihvelin's rejection of, 273–79
Franklin, C., 4, 236n15, 339n11
Free will
    defined, 2
    as a requirement for responsibility, 2

Ginet, C., 2, 3, 15n2, 37, 226
Goetz, S., 226
Going beyond the call, 84, 85, 90, 91,
    120, 161
Graham, P., 101–107
Griffith, M., 306–11

Harman, G., 110,
Hebert, R., 28, 62
Heyd, D., 128n13
Hobart, R. E., 4
Hodgson, D., 3
Humberstone, L., 110
Hume, D., 4, 236n16
Hunt, D., 38, 41

Impermissibility
    and alternative possibilities, 26–27
    as implying "can," 23, 25–26
Impermissible/Can, 28, 47
Impermissible/Obligation Possibility, 25, 26
Impermissible/Permissible Possibility, 25, 26
Impermissibility/Control, 70
Incompatibilism
    regarding free will, 2
    regarding moral obligation, 5–6, 279–80
    regarding moral responsibility, 1, 3, 280
Indeterminism, 1
    and obligation, 5–6, 320, 322–24
    and randomness, 4

Jackson, F., 179

Kane, R., 3, 35, 37, 104, 135, 154n7, 226,
    236n15, 258, 276, 278, 283, 286, 297,
    339n4, 339n5
Kant's Law, 5, 20
    Graham's objection to, 101–07
    and tracing, 148–150
    Waller's objection to, 92–101

Lehrer, K., 154n5
Levy, N., 325, 328
Locke, J., 41
Luck
    characterization, 6, 16
    circumstantial, 17
    constitutive, 17
    and probability, 17
    resultant, 16
    situational, 16
    and Zimmerman's sequence
        of cases, 18–19
Luck Inducing Extraneous Factor
    (Lief), 329–36
Luck Principle, 201
    and *Blameworthiness/
        Impermissibility*, 205
    and the changeability of obligations
        with time, 205–06

Manne, K., 111
Marples, R., 260n3
McCann, H. J., 226
McKenna, M., 86, 161, 171, 236n3,
    261n9, 263
McNamara, P., 62, 83, 84, 89, 128n14,
    128n17, 158, 189
Melden, A., 127n10
Mele, A., 4, 29, 35, 38, 39, 44n14, 127n9,
    153, 154n2, 154n3, 154n4, 176,
    224, 226, 227, 235, 236n14, 236n15,
    261n8, 263, 278, 283, 285, 289, 290,
    300, 301, 304, 325, 329, 331, 333,
    339n2, 339n4, 339n7, 339n9, 339n10
Mellema, G., 128n13, 128n16, 156
Mill, J. S., 196
MO, 22–23
MO-1, 25, 60
MO-2, 34, 61, 106
Modest libertarianism
    characterization, 281–82
    and Davidsonian reasons, 320
    liberal, 299
    one-way, 299
    and pro-tanto reasons,
        305–06, 318–19
Moore, G., 5, 181, 183, 236n1

Winch C., 260n7
Wolf, S., 54, 127n3, 236n8

Zimmerman, M. J., 2, 17, 21, 22, 23, 43n1,
44n4, 44n5, 44n12, 62, 64, 69, 87,
127n1, 127n7, 146, 157, 171, 236n1,
236n2, 236n4, 236n5, 264

on a Jackson-like case, 181–82
on limited options, 139–41
on luck, 18–19, 200
and the prospective view of
obligation, 181